THE WAY WE WORK

THE WAY WE WORK:
ON THE JOB IN HOLLYWOOD

Edited by Bruce Ferber

A VIREO BOOK | RARE BIRD BOOKS
LOS ANGELES, CALIF.

A Genuine Vireo Book

A Barnacle Book | Rare Bird Books
453 South Spring Street, Suite 302
Los Angeles, CA 90013
rarebirdbooks.com

Set in Minion
Printed in the United States

10 9 8 7 6 5 4 3 2 1

Publisher's Cataloging-in-Publication Data
Names: Ferber, Bruce, editor.
Title: The Way We Work: On the Job in Hollywood / edited by Bruce Ferber.
Description: First Trade Paperback Original Edition | A Genuine Vireo Book |
New York, NY: Los Angeles, CA: Rare Bird Books, 2019.
Identifiers: ISBN 9781644280140
Subjects: LCSH Motion picture industry—United States. | Motion pictures—
United States. | Motion pictures—United States—History. | Motion pictures—
Production and direction. | Motion picture authorship. | Television broadcasting.
| Television industry—United States. | Television—Production and direction. |
Television authorship. | BISAC PERFORMING ARTS / Film /
General | PERFORMING ARTS / Television / General
Classification: LCC PN1993.5.U6 .W393 2019 | DDC 384/.80973—dc23

CONTENTS

INTRODUCTION

M OST YOUNG PEOPLE ARE encouraged to choose a profession with a clear path, where education and training
yield a reasonable chance of finding a job that leads to long-term
employment. Some, however, are determined to reject all that
makes sense in favor of amorphous rules, erratic pay, and zero job
security. These are the wages of chasing the Hollywood Dream.
The true believers go on to amass a long list of diverse and often
desperate stabs at earning a living before hitting their stride—
if they're lucky. The less fortunate ultimately throw in the towel to
pursue a more pragmatic dream.

As I looked back on the arc of my own career, the common
thread seemed to be that nothing in Hollywood operated quite
like anything in the "real world." From the way in which I got
paid, to the lack of any kind of dress code, to the unorthodox
behavior that was not only tolerated but celebrated in the name of
creativity, this was a fly-by-the-seat-of-one's-pants life choice that
I would have been hard-pressed to find performing surgery or
working for an insurance company. There wasn't even a consensus
on what constituted good work. While a majority of cardiologists
can agree on what defines a successful bypass, according to
esteemed screenwriter Robert Towne, "no one can really say what
makes an effective screenplay because no one really knows what
makes a screenplay effective." Unfortunately, by the time the rest

of us figure that out, it is either too late to apply to medical school or we are already hooked.

While the notion of different rules (or the lack of any) certainly wasn't a sudden revelation to me, what did seem remarkable, all these years later, was the sheer number of Hollywood stories my compatriots and I had managed to accrue. Whether born of artistic frustration, quasi-abusive stars, or nonsensical premises handed down by the networks, they never failed to provide entertainment value and insight. I concluded that while most people in the entertainment business probably don't have an entire memoir in them, everyone has a mini-memoir because each of us has a story to tell.

I started to wonder how I might go about assembling and archiving some of these gems. I also thought about the two hundred or so people who worked for me when I executive-produced television shows: the cameramen, the editors, the hair and makeup people, the boom guy—the entire crew. These "below the line" craftspeople had their own Hollywood tales but rarely got to share them because attention was always focused on the glitz: the superstar actors, writers, producers, and directors.

This concept of unheard voices took me back to Studs Terkel's storied portrait of American life, *Working: People Talk About What They Do All Day and How They Feel About What They Do.* A journalistic masterpiece, white- and blue-collar workers from every calling speak freely about the nuts and bolts of their jobs and how they feel about what they do. From the doctor to the coal miner to the mailman, Terkel deduced:

"It is about a search....For daily meaning as well as daily bread, for recognition as well as cash, for astonishment rather than torpor; in short, for a sort of life, rather than a Monday to Friday sort of dying."

I landed on the idea of an inclusive anthology, setting out to find a balanced cross section from both above and below the line. Some contributors would craft essays recounting a specific story, insight, or multiple episodes from their colorful careers. The rest would be interviewed, using the opportunity to delineate their specific responsibilities through the prism of personal experience.

The collection is grouped into nine sections, each exploring a different aspect of the working life. Some of the contributors you will instantly recognize (Chris Rock, J. J. Abrams, Robert Towne, Gabrielle Union). The others you already know through their work, which has been integral to the success of countless award-winning movies and television shows. You'll hear from the NYU film student/future Hollywood success story who faced trial by fire on Martin Scorsese's breakthrough feature *Mean Streets.* You'll be taken to the set of *Tootsie,* where the clash between star and director nearly shut down the production. You'll see Lucille Ball get stalked, meet Orson Welles's dog, Flora, and discover how Gene Wilder learned to curse a bunch of chickens in fluent Yiddish. You'll also get better acquainted with one of the directors of *The Simpsons,* the cinematographer for *Entourage,* the editor of *Bosch,* the casting director of *Arrested Development,* the makeup artist for *Black-ish,* and many, many others…

In assembling these wonderful pieces, I marveled at how the act of storytelling gave the participants permission to celebrate the breadth and depth of the invaluable roles they play. It is my hope that the fun, the absurdity, and the unbridled commitment to excellence are conveyed within these pages because, to me, this rich mix is what defines the Hollywood experience.

—Bruce Ferber

ONE

THE STORY

WHETHER STRIVING TO CREATE suspense, laughter, or tears, there is no film or television without a narrative that successfully engages an audience. But how does one go about unearthing and crafting a story that resonates?

Academy Award–Winner **Robert Towne** explores the challenges inherent in making that crucial connection. Emmy–Winner **Seth Freeman** breaks down his process, showing us how the myriad elements come together. Mega-hyphenate **J. J. Abrams** recounts his journey from geeky kid doing magic tricks to serious storyteller. Screenwriter **David Kukoff** writes of a time when film studios dictated a bizarre formula for what constituted a marketable script.

Putting together a compelling story is hard enough. Doing it in Hollywood? Read on.

THE PLIGHT OF SCREENWRITERS

THE DIFFICULTY OF MAINTAINING THE CINEMATIC ILLUSION

By Robert Towne

"Until the screenwriter does his job, nobody else can do theirs. In other words, this is the asshole who keeps everybody else from going to work."

N O ONE CAN REALLY say what makes an effective screenplay because no one really knows what makes a screenplay effective. Certainly part of the problem stems from the fact that screenplays can't be judged by reading them. They may read well or badly, but that often says more about the reader than the screenplay.

The only way a screenplay can be evaluated, almost by definition, is not on the page, but by viewing the movie it caused to be made. It certainly can be read and even enjoyed, but you're stuck with the inescapable fact that it was written to be seen.

"Causing the movie to be made," incidentally, is no small thing. From it stems the historic hatred Hollywood has always displayed for the screenwriter. No matter what is said about how a movie gets made, one fact is inescapable: until the screenwriter does his job, nobody else, like actors, can do theirs. In other words, this is the asshole who keeps everybody else from going to work.

The hatred on Hollywood's part usually takes the form of contempt because the writer's not good enough to put them to work—and fear of the writer because they need that finished script to go to work. Meanwhile, their wrath at being kept waiting is likely to assume various forms. In a sort of mini-Dante-esque exercise, we might say studio execs and agents rage at being kept in limbo, ambitious actors and producers fulminate about doing time in purgatory, and aging movie stars and all directors swear you've damned them to hell.

Another reason for their anger is the pervasive tendency to underestimate the true difficulty of the screenplay form. It started with contempt for the form itself, born and bred in those decades when novelists and playwrights would come out to a California bungalow and condescend to knock out a script in a couple of weeks for big bucks so they could go back to their daytime job and do some really serious writing. It's rare, however, that anyone has an understanding of how disciplined a good script must be, and how much work goes into achieving that discipline.

Then, too, the usual readers of the screenwriter's script—studio execs, producers, director, cast, and crew—could not exactly be said to approach their task with enlightened disinterest. There is hardly anything more threatening to them than this 120-odd-page document. Generally, the writer's professional colleagues, particularly actor, director, and producer, ask three questions as they read his work, none of which anyone is in a position to answer: 1) Will this script be any good as a movie?, 2) Will it make me look good?, and 3) Will I work again if I do it?

Most screenwriters have never been an ongoing part of a motion-picture production, and most production personnel know it. They therefore know that a screenplay is a peculiar act of prophecy by someone who's no more licensed to work with a crystal ball than he is experienced in working on a film. That he would presume to write something that's going to cost $50 million, be cast with actors he doesn't know and has never met, made with a director and crew he doesn't know and has never met, on locations that may or may not exist, in weather conditions that may make it impossible to shoot, can only confirm their suspicions about him. The mere fact of writing the screenplay is an act of astonishing arrogance and proves the writer should never have written it in the first place.

However, I think it is true that narrative skill in screenwriting may be at an all-time low. There was an undeniably greater story sense evidenced by the preceding generation of filmmakers. It may have been due in part to the fact that directors like George Stevens and producers like Darryl Zanuck (who also wrote)— and, for that matter, everyone from Ernst Lubitsch to William Wellman—began their careers in silent pictures. Without sound, they were obliged to think very carefully about making the story and motivation clear. This obsession with story and with clarity never abandoned them when they abandoned silent film.

Why are the director, the producer, the writer less skillful at filming a story now? Some of it lies in the disadvantages of present training. A large part of directing talent today comes from the world of music videos and commercials. Directors generally work in thirty- to sixty-second "bytes," and therefore narrative skill takes a distinct back seat to visual impact. It's also regrettably true that the effect of their sixty-second visual/ aural barrages is to limit their attention span even as they limit the television audience's attention span. They don't allow the actor or the audience to do any "work"—visually, they do it for them with shock cuts and long lenses and wild juxtaposition of imagery—so very often, an actor working in motion pictures for a director honed and toned in commercials is shot more like a perfume bottle than a person.

But there are other reasons for the dearth of affecting dramatic screenplays. To look at what I believe is the most critical one, it helps me to go back to the time when I first started looking at movies.

◆◆◆

SAN PEDRO, CALIFORNIA, IN the early forties, was a big seaport and a small town. It was full of fishermen, merchant marines, cannery workers, dock workers, shipyard workers, soldiers at Fort MacArthur, sailors from everywhere, first-generation Slavs, Italians, Portuguese, Germans, Filipinos, Mexicans, and even a sprinkling of blacks and Jews. Only if you were five years old could you count on English not being the second language of your peers.

It was with just such a crowd of my peers that one Saturday morning in 1941 I took my half-dozen DiCarlo bread wrappers, my dime, and myself to the Warner's Theater on Sixth Street in San Pedro to see a bunch of Saturday serials and Sergeant York. Alvin York was a religious pacifist from a rural Kentucky community so shut off from the outside world in 1917 that it didn't have electricity, phones, or movies—and for whom New York, let alone Europe, was as far away as Mars.

Still, kids in small-town San Pedro found that they shared common values with a rural Kentuckian like York. Like him, our folks, like most Americans then, didn't believe in sticking their noses into other people's business. They were God-fearing, wanting mainly a chance at a decent job, $5,000 in the bank, and the opportunity for their children to have an education and a better life than they had had. These were York's values, and they were ours. They were the truths we held to be as self-evident as the right to life, liberty, and the pursuit of happiness.

If all this is redolent of a Norman Rockwell portrait, a Rush Limbaugh wet dream, its validity didn't lie in the likelihood that it was or would come true. Like most dreams, its greatest significance was our belief in it. We took heart and example from Sergeant York: his beliefs mattered and his actions counted. And even when our society changed dramatically in the sixties and seventies, many films—*The Godfather*, *Taxi Driver*, and *Chinatown* among them—found receptive audiences. They did so by dramatizing the disparity between the establishment's view of the country and what many Americans were beginning to take to be the awful truth: Vietnam, Watergate, perceptions of hideous racial inequality. Again, a series of shared beliefs, in this case focusing on what was wrong with the country, created a sense of communion between filmmakers and filmgoers.

We share no such beliefs today. That, in fact, is pretty much at the heart of the screenwriter's difficulty now: it's tough to write effectively without common ground between you and your audience. Shared beliefs, like shared experience and shared myths, provide that ground. They give us substance and structure, allow us to interpret and make sense of experience, tell us how we should and shouldn't behave, help us find significance in our lives. It is belief that makes the real world real and not a surrealistic nightmare. It is belief that makes us think there is such a thing as truth. It is belief that makes drama—"make-believe"—possible.

For me, this is the problem the contemporary screenwriter faces: How can one tell a compelling story when there's nothing the audience believes to be self-evident? How can one create an illusion without a contrasting reality against which to gauge the effectiveness of the illusion? It's difficult to lie credibly without belief in the truth.

Robert Towne *is best known for his Academy Award-winning original screenplay for Roman Polanski's* Chinatown, *which is widely considered one of the greatest screenplays ever written. He also wrote the sequel,* The Two Jakes, The Last Detail, *and* Shampoo, *and the first two* Mission: Impossible *films. Towne directed the sports dramas* Personal Best *and* Without Limits, *the crime thriller* Tequila Sunrise, *and the romantic crime drama* Ask the Dust.

FINDING THE STORY

By Seth Freeman

"Once, in search of the right story for an episode of a television series,
I found myself spending the better part of a night in a brothel..."

A GOOD STORY, ONE that engages us and draws our interest
in a movie, a play, or a novel, is more than just a series of
connected events. A story, in the sense that professional writers
think about these things, is not simply: "This happened, then
this happened, then this happened." A good story has a shape,
a forward motion, which pulls us along as viewers or readers
because we want to find out where it is going. It tells us something
new, unexpected, and intriguing about the world in which we
live. A good story changes people, both the characters *in* the story
and the readers or viewers who are exposed to it. The challenge—
where a worthy story lies in any particular subject is not always
obvious, so sometimes a writer will have to dig deep to find it.

The search for a story can be a purely cerebral exercise,
but just as often it involves research in the real world, in places
far removed from the writer's desk. For me, getting out in the
field and experiencing up close and personal how other people
do their jobs and spend their days has been one of the most
interesting, enjoyable, and often surprising aspects of plying my
trade. I am always deeply honored and grateful when people are
willing to allow me into their lives and places of work, taking the

time to explain the complexities of their professions, entrusting me to make a good faith effort to get it right when depicting their private worlds in a work of art.

I have ridden through inner cities in the backs of police cars, tagged along on wilderness rescue missions, visited crime scenes and crime labs, hung out with dolphin and sea lion trainers, toured NASA bases, spent hours in hospital emergency departments and inside locked psychiatric wards, ventured deep into urban war zones with gang workers, prowled through dozens of print and TV newsrooms, followed vice cops on investigations, interviewed FBI forensics experts, talked to the mayors of big cities and little cities and to members of congress and other politicians, and once, in search of the right story for an episode of a television series, I found myself spending the better part of a night in a brothel.

Some context:

After graduating college, I worked as a carpenter's assistant and gardener, taught in elementary and high schools, took a job as a shipping clerk in a children's sandal factory in Downtown Los Angeles, and spent long, exhausting days as a "gofer" on numerous commercials and short films. Eventually I landed a few low-paying assignments on an early-morning television show for small kids. I had to wake up while it was still dark outside in order to be able to see my credit for the first time on a television screen, after which I immediately went back to sleep.

Then, after several years of trying, I suddenly learned that I had broken into primetime. In the space of a couple of days, I had three simultaneous series television writing assignments, on the comedy series *Rhoda* and *Phyllis* and on the family drama *The Waltons*. Shortly thereafter, I had the unusually good fortune to become the junior member of a team with four of the most talented people ever to work in television. Allan Burns and James

L. Brooks had created *The Mary Tyler Moore Show, Rhoda,* and later *Lou Grant,* the series on which I joined them. A third creator of *Lou Grant* was Gene Reynolds, an excellent director as well as producer who had developed, along with Larry Gelbart, the iconic series *M*A*S*H.* In the first year of *Lou Grant,* the creators had also brought on an executive story editor, the fine writer Leon Tokatyan, whose credits included such highly regarded TV series as *The Defenders* and *The Senator.*

Lou Grant was an especially rewarding series on which to work because the fact that our protagonists were journalists enabled us to explore a wide range of topics that interested us. Yet, as we learned time and again, finding a topic interesting doesn't mean that you have a story to tell about it.

Gene felt that series television often came across as false and artificial because the busy writers, cranking out multiple episodes on a tight deadline, tended to stay in their air-conditioned Hollywood offices and make stuff up, or even lift ideas from recent popular films. It was not uncommon in a writers' room to hear someone propose as their original idea, "Hey, we could do *Serpico*!" Or: "Let's use that setup from *In the Line of Fire.*" Gene's alternative was to do research in preparation for writing, an approach that had served him well on *M*A*S*H* (he and Larry had traveled to South Korea) and earlier on the high school series *Room 222* (based on interviews and observations at a Los Angeles inner-city school).

Thus, when the proliferation of massage parlors became a frequent topic of local news stories, it became my task to try to investigate this subject. Fortunately, before I was forced to troll Hollywood Boulevard in search of massage parlor girls to interview, our enterprising staff researcher made a creative deal with the legal supervisors of a group of hookers who had been busted, convicted, and sentenced to do community service. She persuaded the authorities to count the time spent talking to me as part of the hookers' hours of community service.

There are many legitimate places to get an actual massage in Los Angeles and other cities, but for some reason the term "massage parlor," at least locally, always seems to mean a place where sex is traded for money, despite parlor being a word for the sitting room in your grandmother's house. The hookers assigned to spend time talking to me as their punishment, all worked in massage parlors. In fact, they continued to work in massage parlors at the same time they were doing their community service as a sentence for the crime of working in massage parlors.

I went to my first appointment at the Beverly Hills office of an organization dedicated to helping sex workers, having no idea what story I wanted to tell. I met two young women, whom I will call Cheryl and Debbie. Whatever I was expecting, Cheryl and Debbie turned out to be pretty, friendly, funny, and extremely bright. I liked them both immediately. The cliché but also inevitable question, especially for two people with as much going for them as Cheryl and Debbie, was "why?" Why did bright, attractive young women feel their best option for making a way in the world was to sell their bodies? For whatever reason, neither had much formal education, and they were undoubtedly correct when they argued that, with their limited skill sets, they could make a lot more money doing what they were doing than in other jobs for which they *might* be qualified. Both had had difficult upbringings. In Debbie's case, her father was a successful physician and distinguished professor of medicine at a prestigious Southern university. He was also a cross-dresser, hiding this fact from his professional community but not from his family. Debbie had childhood memories of his coming home after being out on the town in, as she put it, "full regalia."

I didn't show or feel any moral judgment about the way they were making a living, but I think they sensed that at some level I did because I sincerely believed they had so much to offer. I secretly hoped they could find more rewarding careers.

When I returned to the studio and briefed my colleagues, one of the first things I shared was how much I liked Cheryl and Debbie. They were, I told the group, terrific people. The reaction of all the men—every male on our writing staff, crew, as well as company executives (although none of the women), was universal. "Think about what you're saying," they responded with some heat. "These are prostitutes. You didn't really like them." It was somehow impossible for the guys to believe that Cheryl and Debbie were as nice and intelligent as I described.

Now I had a story. The intriguing and unexpected twist was less about what happened in the prostitutes' profession and more about the deeply held beliefs and prejudices others harbored toward them. In the episode I ended up writing, called "Hooker" and starring Dee Wallace (who soon became familiar to movie-goers as the mom in *E.T.*), a reporter meets a young woman about her own age while covering a police beat story of a massage parlor bust. The young woman who works at the massage parlor has aspirations to do more with her life. She is bright, personable, funny, and attractive. When the reporter, Billie Newman, returns to the newsroom and tells Lou how much she likes the hooker she met, Lou reacts with disbelief and disdain. "Think about what you're saying," he tells her. "She's a prostitute."

In a later scene, Lou finds Billie having lunch with a friend in the nearby reporters' hangout. He joins the two young women for a time and tells Billie later what a lovely person her friend is. "A pal from college?" he asks her. The friend was, of course, the hooker Billie had met earlier.

Cheryl and Debbie continued to use their community service obligation as an opportunity to educate me about their profession. They insisted that I couldn't get a real feel for what it was all about without spending a shift in the actual massage parlor where they worked. So one cool fall evening, I walked up the steps to the porch of the pale blue clapboard bungalow in Santa Monica where Cheryl and Debbie made a living. There were two other young women working there that night as well. Their names were Brandy and Amber. Of course. Prostitutes never use their real names. Work names are employed for safety reasons, but I also think it enables the women to mentally separate what they are doing to make a living from who they feel they truly are.

Cheryl and Debbie parked me in the kitchen of what was once somebody's home. Almost immediately, I overheard a kerfuffle between the women and the owner of the massage parlor. I could also have listened in on some of the verbal exchanges in the front room between the women and potential clients, but I wasn't comfortable eavesdropping, so I just hung out and waited for them to come in and chat if they felt like it. They did. Their punishment, talking to me, was apparently more fun than the actual work. Some of that night's customers might have gotten a little less time than they paid for.

By no means were all the prostitutes I met while doing research for this episode as bright and appealing as the two I'd happened to come across in that first meeting. Cheryl and Debbie were special. If my research hadn't led me to them, I might not have found my way into the story: the cognitive dissonance in people's views of women who work in the world's oldest profession. The episode turned out to be one of the series most highly regarded.

This story has a coda, a dismal turn of events, which I never could have seen coming. I had continued to hang out with both

Cheryl and Debbie, but eventually we lost touch. Then I happened to bump into Debbie, who was working at a florists shop in Santa Monica. She told me that Cheryl had found some success as a porn movie actress and also that she had had a baby. Some years after that, I received one of those mass-distribution postcards in the mail, the kind that contain the sort of messages which we used to see on milk cartons, flyers for lost or abducted children. Under the heading "Have you seen me?" was the picture of a little girl with more than a passing resemblance to Cheryl. There was also a photograph of Cheryl.

The text said that the adult shown on the card was believed to have kidnapped the child. There was a reward for information leading to her apprehension.

◆◆◆

I HAD BEEN LUCKY enough to learn how to hunt for and recognize a good story by working in the trenches alongside some of the sharpest minds in the business. Occasionally I would wonder if such writing skills could be taught, and my conclusion was always one of skepticism. So it was with a certain ungracious wariness, much later in my career, that I allowed myself to be drafted by my friend from *Lou Grant*, Allan Burns, into participating as a mentor in a weekend workshop on writing for former and current members of our armed forces.

Yes, I had taught for a bit in the past before I'd locked into writing as a full-time profession, but it had been years since I had been put in charge of a classroom, and how was I supposed to teach people how to tell a story? I had reservations that any real learning could come out of this exercise.

The good news was that they assigned me to an interesting group. The five aspiring writers were from all branches of service, and they managed to comprise, within that tiny random sample, a quintessentially American cross section of ethnicity, gender, and age. Eddie was twenty-three, in his last weeks in the service. Michael was seventy-four, a former Korean War paratrooper. His son had served in the military, and a granddaughter was on her way to Afghanistan. What quickly became obvious was that the quality of men and women who serve in our armed forces these days is exceptionally high.

The participants came with stories (or at least what they thought were stories) that they wanted to tell. In most cases the subject matter was unrelated to their military experience. We thought it would be helpful to the entire group to create, for the two days of the workshop, our own "writers' room." This is a uniquely Hollywood phenomenon, most often a part of the process in developing scripts for television series, where writers collaborate and help each other with their scripts.

Within ten minutes, our group felt like a team. The military training probably contributed to the ability of a handful of strangers to blend into a cohesive unit, but it is also true, I believe, that when we are at our best, this knack of being able to come together with a unity of purpose is a distinctly American talent.

The short stories, novels, and movie scripts the participants were working on are proprietary, including the screenplay and TV series pitch that former Army Staff Sgt. Thom Tran was developing. But I want to share some of Thom's own story because in it he was able to find the real story he wanted, and needed, to tell.

In the first few days of his posting to Iraq, Thom's best friend was killed. Within the first week, Thom was shot through the head. *Through the head.* Thom had a camera with him on patrol the day he was wounded in Iraq. The video has footage of the vehicle in front, which halts as it starts to take fire. You hear the sound of gunfire, then the shouts when Thom gets hit. Then the camera is turned, and you see the moment when Thom discovers that the back of his head is covered in blood.

For a year he didn't smile. He wanted to return to the front, but the doctors wouldn't okay it. Before he left for Iraq, Thom had been an upbeat person, with ambitions to write, act, and do stand-up comedy. But now he was going through a very black time. In the miserable year that followed Thom's injury, he searched less for a story to tell and more for a way out of deep depression. He discovered both together, more by chance than design. His mother and his sister had refused to watch the video of their loved one being grievously injured, but Thom's father, a former soldier, felt compelled to show that he could handle it with a warrior's stiff upper lip and straight spine. Thom and his dad watched the entire sequence in tense silence, with Thom very unsure how the older man would react. When the video clip ended and Thom shut off the TV, his father quietly told him, "You are going to get so laid."

Thom knew a good comedy punch line when he heard one. In that instant he recognized the story he had to tell and that in telling it with humor, he would also begin his long, difficult climb out of the darkness.

On Memorial Day weekend (appropriately enough), my family and I went to the Improv on Melrose Avenue in Hollywood where Thom was doing his new stand-up routine. He used a clip of the Iraq shooting video in his sketch. The audience was riveted, then, as Thom sprung on them the surprise of his dad's unexpected comment, they gave him the biggest laugh of the night. In the comic, not military, sense of the term—he killed.

Service in the armed forces can involve taking risks. Writing, at its most interesting, is also about taking risks, and those I mentored had the courage to face both kinds of risks.

Thom, in discovering the story within a sequence of events, had transformed a wrenching military experience into, of all things, stand-up comedy.

When I was approached to share some Hollywood experiences for this book, I knew that my career had been an interesting adventure: sometimes enjoyable, sometimes disheartening, ultimately full and satisfying. However, I didn't know if I had a story worth telling until it occurred to me that perhaps the story itself was the one most central to my craft—how writers search for their stories.

Seth Freeman *is a writer/producer of television, a playwright, and a journalist. He produced the long-running drama* Lou Grant *and created the series* Lincoln Heights. *He has received three Emmys (eight nominations), Golden Globes, Writers Guild Awards, Peabody, PEN, First Amendment, Christopher, Humanitas, Image, Cine Golden Eagle, and numerous other honors. His play* Legacy *received First Place in the 2016 New Works of Merit Playwriting Contest, and there have been over 170 presentations of his plays worldwide. He also writes for print (*The New York Times, Southern Theatre Magazine, The Wall Street Journal, Los Angeles Times, Stars and Stripes, California Magazine, Los Angeles Magazine, the Huffington Post, The Hill*). He contributes non-writing time to community and international organizations dealing with health care, education, the empowerment of women, and human rights.*

BEGINNINGS

By J. J. Abrams

"I was just hoping to get to a place where maybe I could write something, and they'd ask, 'Well, who should direct this?' And I could say, 'Well, I want to.' Luckily, that's what happened."

I WAS BORN IN New York and moved to Los Angeles when I was five. My father worked for CBS selling commercial time, so he was really on the business side of things at the network. When I was about eight, I went to Universal Studios and I realized that movies and TV shows were things you could actually make. We had a camera at home, and I got the bug. Around the same time, my father started getting interested in production as opposed to commercial sales; he became an assistant to a producer of TV movies and soon became an associate producer, coproducer and, eventually, an executive producer. But the interest that I had in this thing was born out of what I saw behind the scenes at Universal. Before it was an amusement park, it was really just a tour. Lucille Ball's dressing room was a big deal. I remember being in that little tram and going past Quinn Martin's office. With my father getting involved with this business, I was incredibly lucky that he was actually doing the thing I was turned on by. I remember my father taking me to productions and going to the sets of various things he was working on. And it was the luckiest thing in the history of time. It was this portal—a kind of tangible, experiential vantage point....It let the interest I had become real and physical and material, and that was an amazing thing. I remember watching things and wondering: "Why is the director putting the camera there?" I'd observe what the extras were doing, and how the director would talk to the people in the background. It was this bizarre, intimate point of view into a world of which most everyone saw only the final product.

The bug started when I was making Super 8 movies. That was something I loved to do. But whether it was making movies, putting on plays, drawing comics, or doing magic tricks, there was always something appealing about creating some kind of illusion and getting a response from an audience. It was a weird feeling, as a complete and utter geek, doing magic as a kid—that feeling of knowing, ultimately, that it's an illusion. It's not real, yet you're doing something that's aware of someone's specific point of view, the eyeline to the place a coin or a card may be hidden. You're doing something very technical, but at the same time, creating an effortless, magical event. I was intrigued by that idea, whatever form it took—the use of some sort of technical sleight of hand to effect an emotional response. So the form it took was stupid magic tricks, and equally stupid Super 8 movies.

Later came plays, and short plays that were no better. All through college, I was writing and constantly working on different ideas, whether for animation or, when computers became available, visual effects: How could I use computers to create an illusion? Even something as basic as writing an incredibly simple program to see if you could put together words and sentences and have a computer respond as if it were talking back to you. But whether I was coming up with primitive visual effects, making movies, doing plays...whatever it was, I loved the process of creating things. How I would ever do that as a profession remained a mystery to me.

I ran into a friend, Jill Mazursky, and it turned out she had sold a few screenplays. I immediately begged her to write something with me; I wanted to take advantage of the first friend I knew who was doing this professionally. In a typically charitable moment, she agreed to work with me, and we wrote and sold a treatment to Disney when I was a senior in college. That was the first opportunity that felt concrete, as an engagement with the business. I wasn't exactly strategizing, thinking that I would use writing as an entry point, but it certainly made the most sense. I knew I wasn't going to be an actor. I knew that while I wanted to direct, no one would let me. Writing felt like the most promising and most tangible path. I was just hoping to get to a place where maybe I could write something, and they'd ask, "Well, who should direct this?" And I could say, "Well, I want to." Luckily, that's what happened.

I had written a number of movies and had done a bunch of script doctoring, and I was sort of lost in terms of what I was working on. I felt like I had gotten to a place where I was doing the work, the job, but I wasn't feeling inspired. And then I met a woman, Katie McGrath, who became my wife. Very early on, she reminded me to write the thing I love. It was sort of the most obvious reminder, but it was a good one and I needed to hear it. A little while later, I was having dinner one night with my good friend Matt Reeves. I said, "Listen, I have this idea for this story about this girl who graduates from high school and follows this boy." It was a rough idea, and we decided at dinner that it would be better for a TV series than a movie. We sketched out what the pilot could be, and in a couple of weeks, I wrote the first draft of the script. Matt had notes that made it better, so I did another pass, and we had a script. Again, it wasn't a strategic thing. It just came from the inspiration of what this thing could be. I knew nothing about television series. So we sent it to our agent, who gave it to Imagine Television, which was just forming at the time. Tony Krantz was the new head of TV at Imagine, and he had never produced anything before; he had been an agent about ten minutes earlier. So we went and met with the WB. It was a brand-new network. It had *Buffy* and *Dawson's Creek* just starting.

We had a meeting; we left the script on the table. A couple hours later, we got a call saying, "We want to make it." We were suddenly producers of a television pilot. We didn't really know how to approach it. We had made some movies before, and Matt had directed. That was always the agreement: Matt would direct, and I would write it. So we ended up doing this pilot, *Felicity*.

Being a feature screenwriter, you truly are a cog in a massive machine. I know what it's like to be fired. I know what it's like to be rewritten. I know what it's like to be asked to rewrite. I know what it's like to be used as a pawn in a much bigger game. But to have written this show and suddenly have my name and the director's name as big as anything was an incredible moment. I had never seen myself as a producer before. What the WB did was make us seem legitimate. Not just to the public, but also to ourselves.

Lost literally came to us when ABC executive Lloyd Braun called and told us he wanted to do a show about survivors of a plane crash. We had no time to develop it, just time to write it. I agreed to make an attempt just as a Hail Mary. I met Damon Lindelof on a Monday, and by that Friday, we had turned in an outline. On that Friday, I told Lloyd that I had an idea, and that it wasn't going to be *Cast Away*. A lot of survival stuff, but the island itself was a character. There was a hatch in the island. It was a place that had a history and mysterious elements, which would be discovered over time. There was something terrifying in the jungle. It was an incredibly vague pitch, but it had feeling and tone.

Lloyd said, "I love it," which, I admit, surprised me. We turned it in to ABC. Got the green light. But it was still just an outline.

We had to write the script, cast it, location scout, film it, and post and deliver it all in under twelve weeks. So it was a very rushed, intense, but also special and sort of weird experience. It felt like there was no time to second-guess any of it. A huge amount of money—$13 million—was being spent on the two-hour pilot. The pilot got the show off the ground, but ultimately, Damon and Carlton Cuse ran the series. Their writing, over the six years the show was on, is ultimately what galvanized the thing. The pilot aside, the show didn't grow roots with one or two episodes; it was the years of work they put in. But I could tell while we were shooting it that it was a stepping-stone. I knew, while we were doing it, that it didn't feel like a normal pilot, job, or show. It was epic in scale: a big cast, visual effects, huge locations. It really didn't feel like any show I had seen before.

When you begin a story, you may think you know everything. Think about Dickens turning in one chapter at a time to get published in the paper. But you're building upon mythology you just created. People will argue about how much any given author knows at the start. Some details are planned and planted, and some are not. I'm friends with certain filmmakers and certain authors who have jumped into famous movies or novels without a fucking clue how it would resolve. And yet when you read or see the thing, there's an inevitability to it. You feel like, come on, you must have known. But on a number of occasions—and this is the only consistency I can see with this—when I've been lucky enough to get to talk to them about it, they've said, "I did not know how that story was going to end, or how that movie would end." And in a weird way, that's the power. Because if you don't know, and you're writing it, then that's what the audience is feeling. If it's clear to you, it's clearer to the audience than you want it to be. The power in great storytelling is going, "Ooh, I'm so intrigued by how this will turn out." The piece, through osmosis, takes on a kind of electricity and uncertainty in not knowing what's going to happen.

J. J. Abrams *is a director, producer, screenwriter, actor, and composer. He wrote or produced such films as* Regarding Henry, Forever Young, Armageddon, Cloverfield, Star Trek, Star Wars: The Force Awakens, *and the upcoming* Star Wars: Episode IX. *Abrams's directorial work includes* Mission: Impossible III, Star Trek *and its sequel* Star Trek Into Darkness, Super 8, *and* Star Wars: The Force Awakens, *the first film in the* Star Wars sequel trilogy *and the third highest-grossing film of all time. A multiple Emmy Award-winner, Abrams has created and cocreated numerous television series, including* Felicity, Alias, Lost, *and* Fringe.

HIGH TIMES IN THE WORLD OF HIGH CONCEPT

By David Kukoff

"Sometimes I'll get a glimpse of my former self in the faces of the younger writers who don't know that this industry wants to keep you from growing."

I REMEMBER THE MOMENT the pilot light went on.

I was twenty-eight years old and about to become a father. My then wife and I had a four-digit bank account, and our professional prospects weren't much more robust. After devoting most of film school to studying sitcoms, I'd come achingly, narrowly close to nailing down a gig first on *The Simpsons*, then on *Murphy Brown*, before flaming out entirely. With the baby's due date getting closer and closer, I figured it was high time to steer my muse down from the lofty climes of make-believe and into the realm of the real.

Well, I came close.

Not close to making any actual money, mind you. No, I'd come dangerously, fecklessly, what-the-fuck-could-I-possibly-have-been-thinking close to losing my mind. I was convinced that my recently penned novel of four friends who travel to Las Vegas to save a buddy from getting married was my generation's *Bright Lights, Big City*. So much so that I cried tears of rage when an editor at St. Martin's Press told me that, despite a morning of lobbying on my behalf, he hadn't been able to shepherd my book all the way through to publication.

I'd always heard it said that when one door closes, another one opens, although that afternoon, I wasn't drawing on that phrase for inspiration so much as I was wishing it applied to every actual high-floor New York City window I passed. And yet, while I semi-fantasized about heaving myself onto the sidewalk alongside my equally splattered aspirations, forces beyond my control were at play that would radically alter the fabric of both my literary dreams and my writing reality. Little did I know that in three short years I would be earning very real money as a writer...albeit at the service of some pretty unreal subject matter.

◆◆◆

I MET MY WORK spouse through my actual spouse. Matt was working at a publishing house where my wife had taken a business meeting. He subsequently read my book and told me that he thought my talents would be better suited to writing screenplays, which he'd been toiling on at night. I was intrigued, not only because it was the only writing medium in which I hadn't yet failed. No, it was because Matt seemed to have a handle on the all-important elixir that had eluded me my entire life: commerciality. Which, in the mid-nineties, could be summed up in two words: high concept.

A high-concept movie was one whose entire premise could be boiled down to one sentence. Premises like "Arnold Schwarzenegger and Danny DeVito are twins" or "a woman's husband comes back as a spirit to help her find his murderer." Not only does it grab your attention, it tells you everything you need to know about the movie's plot, characters, tone, and themes. And the more I watched these movies, the more I began to detect another common denominator that defined the high-concept film: its premise was invariably one that couldn't happen in real life.

Talking babies were high-concept. Ghosts were high-concept. Time travel was high-concept (but strangely, on-time air travel wasn't). And it seemed as though the high-concept rule also applied to concepts that, even if technically possible, were too outrageous for real life. So *Pretty Woman*, while not technically breaking any rules of physics, still hinged on just-south-of-plausibility assumptions like a) Julia Roberts works as a prostitute on Hollywood Boulevard, b) billionaire Richard Gere forgoes a high-end escort service and instead cruises Hollywood Boulevard, and c) a movie that ends happily, and not in the mugging of German tourists, can be set on Hollywood Boulevard.

Two days after my son was born, Matt visited us in the hospital and pitched me an idea about an over-competitive youth basketball coach who trades his non-athletic son to a different team for a better player. We called it *Swapping Sam* and went off to work. A year later, we had an agent and a contract with the nascent Wonderful World of Disney. Our first studio rewrite assignment was *Kindred Spirits,* the story of a paranoid 1950s family that had fled to their bomb shelter, died of a gas leak, and awakened as ghosts in the present day, ready to haunt a dysfunctional nineties family. We made the story as coherent as we could, punched up the comedy a bit, and turned it in. Two weeks later, we were given *Blue Angels,* about a squadron of the famed aviators who, true to their name, are actual angels.

Our upward trajectory continued. We got an office on the Disney lot, which felt like a cross between being old-time studio writers and college freshmen. The people-watching in the dining commissary alone was worth the extra zero the studio invariably kept out of our paychecks. Everyone from Lowell Ganz and Baba-loo Mandel, who'd written pretty much anything you'd ever seen from Ron Howard at that point (and who lunched in the wordless manner of an old Jewish couple who'd been married for half a century), to the affable *Pretty Woman* director, Garry Marshall, to a TV writer we called "The Big Fat Hack" because he'd just signed a huge studio deal and took this as license to storm around the lot like…well, a Disney character, spewing hot air to anyone who had the temerity and misfortune to wander into his orbit.

Outside the commissary, we were onto a project called *Model Behavior*, a "Prince and the Pauper"-esque tale of a high school girl and a model who switch places. Kathie Lee Gifford, who was then hosting an ABC morning talk show, was interested in playing the mother character, which was the network's condition for green-lighting the movie. Yet to sign Kathie Lee, we needed to agree to *her* condition: that we write a part for her son, Cody. So for anyone who saw the movie and wondered why the model has a little brother with no real function in the movie and isn't funny to boot, there you go. I'll never forget the day our producer called us into his office and showed us a clip of Kathie Lee talking breathlessly about how her son was "so talented, he just landed a big part in this wonderful new Disney movie. And guess what? There's a role in it for me too!"

The compromises didn't end there. One day, after turning in the first act for *Switching Goals* (*Swapping Sam* had been retitled and somewhat re-premised after getting the Olsen twins attached), we were summoned by our boss.

"Close the door," he said when we arrived.

He took out the pages we'd sent over and thrust them out, all of three feet from our faces.

"See this?" he asked. "What do you see here?"

"Our…script?" I offered meekly.

"Good. No glasses for you. Now look closer."

We squinted and stared at a page in which one of the twins gives a long speech about the rejection she feels every time their dad lights up when her sister scores a goal.

"Some dialogue?" Matt said.

"Some? SOME??! Looks like a page's worth to me. Would you agree?"

He tossed the script aside and sat down across from us.

"Let me spell it out for you. These are the Olsen twins, not Meryl Streep. They can't say all this dialogue. Hell, I'm not even sure they can *read* all this dialogue. So your assignment today is to go back to your office, take out a red pen, and remove the words."

"Any words in particular?"

"No. No words in particular. Make big, slashing motions. Be indiscriminate, I don't care. Just lose the words."

Here I was, a professional writer working on a major project for a top studio, and the main note was "lose the words."

Right as the Wonderful World of Disney signaled its shift to fewer, more high-profile movies per year, we sold an original script to MGM and became a hot writing team at all the studios, the subjects of our very own front-page article in *Variety* and a nice mention in *Entertainment Weekly*. We scored rewrite gigs, had fans all over town, and even got invited to the occasional premiere, one of which was a Paramount venture called *Snake Eyes*.

As forgettable as the movie was, I remember two things from that night. Right before it started, I wound up at the refreshments table, where two older comedy writers were talking about one of their projects. These writers had started in their late twenties, then had pretty much stayed at the same level for their entire careers. And I realized, that was the thing about high-concept—its lack of reality had a way of keeping you from making the one thing we all make when we live in the real world: progress. Even though this team had been incredibly successful, I found myself wondering if they'd never failed because, at the very core of it all, just like one of Disney's greatest high-concept characters, Peter Pan, they'd never tried to grow up.

The second thing I remember from that night was my wife's water breaking, signaling the imminent arrival of our second child.

And then, somehow, it was all over.

I had two children—one born the same day as my high-concept writing career, another right on the heels of the script sale that would be my high-water mark. Two movies made—two other screen credits denied. Two marriages—one personal, one professional. The parallels in my life and writing career were unavoidable right down to the new writing on the wall, as high-concept script sales started slowing. Babies and ideas had forged their way out of consciousness and onto terra firma, both needing very real nourishment…with only one, as I would start to realize, nourishing me in return.

Sometimes I'll get a glimpse of my former self in the faces of the younger writers who don't know that this industry wants to keep you from growing. Whether through the countless applications of high concept in my day, or by making you a safe, trusted "brand" as is more the case today, what it all entails is remaining flat. And while it might be a dramatic stretch to call that "flatlining," you're still just biding your time until your career dies.

These days, my reality works both on and off the page. I sold a script about the battle between Gloria Steinem and Phyllis Schlafly over the Equal Rights Amendment. I wrote a novel based on my experiences growing up and edited a non-fiction anthology about Los Angeles in the 1970s. I've embraced the at-times harsher realities of truth and fact where once I played in the sandbox of make-believe. And I've never been happier. Not without hardship, mind you. The paydays aren't what they once were, and both my personal and professional marriages are things of the past. But somewhere in the wake of it all, in a piece of personal Phoenician mythology, something else happened—something seemingly so unreal that it bordered on high concept.

I was born.

David Kukoff *is the author of the novel* Children of the Canyon *and the editor of the bestselling anthology* Los Angeles in the 1970s. *Kukoff's contribution to that book, "It Was Fun While it Lasted," was excerpted in* Los Angeles Magazine *in November, 2016. His script,* An Uncivil War, *was bought by FilmNation and is slated to go into production with Oscar nominees Dee Rees directing and Carey Mulligan starring as Gloria Steinem. Another recent screenplay,* Borough of Churches, *is being produced by* Rocky, Goodfellas *and* Wolf of Wall Street *producer Irwin Winkler.*

TWO

THE ICON

THE SMARTEST HOLLYWOOD ASPIRANTS *know they stand on the shoulders of giants: the innovators, the game-changers, and the visionaries who, by thinking outside the box, managed to turn industry into art.*

Occasionally, through perseverance and a little bit of luck, a newbie can find himself working alongside a Hollywood icon. One day you're a student watching Citizen Kane; *the next, Orson Welles is riding shotgun in your '72 Ford Gran Torino. You worshipped* I Love Lucy *as a kid, and suddenly Lucille Ball is complimenting you on your comedic timing. Martin Scorsese was your film school's most celebrated alumnus; now he's dissecting classic cinema for you between takes.*

These were the extraordinary experiences of future literary agent, **Nancy Nigrosh,** *future writer-producer,* **Billy Van Zandt,** *and future assistant director,* **Stu Goldman.**

MASTER CLASS ON MULBERRY STREET

By Nancy Nigrosh

"Marty effortlessly cited a shot-by-shot list of the forensic cinematic strategy John Ford had used to create the immortal impact of The Searchers. *I was having this conversation on a working film set, and not in one of my classrooms."*

WHILE STILL A STUDENT at NYU, I landed my first (paid!) job in the film business as the New York location script supervisor for Martin Scorsese's seminal classic, *Mean Streets*. Little did I suspect this small independent film would be selected years later for preservation by the National Film Registry for the Library of Congress, or that the experience would ultimately take me to Hollywood where, unlikely as it seemed at the time, I would find my calling as a literary agent.

As a graduate of Girls' Latin School in Boston, I'd received an education based on a curriculum that hadn't changed since 1635. Ivory-tower mentality is hard to shake, so when I arrived at NYU intending to study linguistic anthropology, my not-so-modest ambition was to one day unlock the universal language key.

"Don't waste your time!" said one of my Manhattan-raised roommates. "The universal language is music. Or, maybe it's body language…or, maybe film." Putting my New England roots aside, I ditched anthropology and enrolled at the School of the Arts film department.

The department turned out to be a single story of a non-descript structure simply known as the East Building. As the elevator door opened onto the eighth floor, I knew a threshold of some kind was definitely being crossed when I noticed that both genders used the one lavatory. There were only eight women in the entire department.

The film student "look" ran the gamut from fantastically hip seventies chic to nerdy urbanite. There were also a few vets still wearing their army jackets. They all seemed obsessed to the point of frenzy on the past, present, and future of world cinema. As newbies, my cohort soon learned that a recent graduate, who'd gotten his master's in filmmaking from NYU, had become a popular directing instructor. I remember looking at his last name on my schedule, wondering how to pronounce it. Then I was told on the first week of school that "Marty" had left teaching. Yet somehow he still cast a presence on the eighth floor. Our TA screened Marty's smart and funny student short film *It's Not Just You, Murray*, plus his eerily cool shoestring feature, *Who's That Knocking At My Door?* and *Street Scenes*, a documentary of Vietnam War protests that a number of Marty's students had worked on. It wasn't unusual to overhear Marty's name being mentioned in the hallways or in class, especially the fact that he'd moved to Los Angeles. Though most of us had never met him, we vicariously followed his effort to become established.

We were learning every aspect of filmmaking, testing our skills out on each other's projects. One night, while editing a documentary championing the cause of tenants protesting their poor housing conditions on the Lower East Side, I noticed it was ten o'clock at night, and I'd been working for about eleven hours straight.

"Who wants to work on a movie?" a voice from somewhere pitched over the din of our old-time Moviolas—the same seriously durable film sewing machine model used by all the studios since their heyday. (It now occurs to me that these are what inspired George Lucas's *Star Wars Episode V*'s AT-AT Walkers.)

Editing film at that time was a simple cut and paste. We used a special form of scotch tape to make temp edits and then carefully scraped the tape with razor blades to carve the film's sprocket holes—a frustrating and messy business. Hours easily melted away.

"I need two camera assistants…two gaffers and a script girl," announced a voice I recognized as belonging to Mitchell Block, our teaching assistant—who would eventually go on to become an award-winning documentary filmmaker.

Groans were heard.

"Okay, there's coffee in it, on me," the voice piped up even louder.

Heads poked out. The now five guys plus me, the only "girl" around, threw on our coats and shuffled past the school's purple walls trimmed with glossy yellow-orange paint, yawning and stretching.

We piled into a new station wagon parked in a red zone. I asked, "Is this your car?"

"No," Mitchell answered. "It belongs to the bank. It's a lease car."

"What's a lease car?" I wondered.

We pulled in front of Gramercy Park Hotel, a seedy place in those days. The lobby couldn't have been creepier. But the elevator, an old-fashioned cage, was. It occurred to me, as we were being yanked up a few flights, that maybe I'd made a mistake.

The cage opened onto a fairly well-lit hallway. But that wasn't a good thing. The run-down place reeked of desperation.

A door opened and light spilled out like the sun had just come up. Our little flock poured into the room where guys were pacing around as far as the phone cords would take them. They barely noticed us.

Things settled down, however, when the eye of this storm, a dynamo with shoulder-length black hair and a dark but smiling countenance, entered the scene, instantly becoming the center of attention.

"Mitchell!" he beamed and grinned. "So, are these the kids?"

"Yeah, Marty," Mitchell said, pointing out the required two camera assistants, two gaffers, and me, whom he called "the script girl."

Marty just stared at me. "This girl? I mean look at her. Look at me...look at her." Just as he directed, the entire silent room took a good, long look at my height. Finally, Marty threw up his hands, shaking his head. Then, he left the room.

I felt my feet move to follow Marty to another part of the suite, where someone was still on the phone to "the coast." Then it hit me that all these people were here from California, a place I'd never been. I also became very aware of the dozens of sketches of scenes from the film they were making, posted on every wall. This was a very serious business.

Marty sat down at a nearby desk that was also piled high with sketches and notes.

Instinctively I sat down and said, "I don't *have* to be tall."

He grinned that grin again, only this time he said, "That's good."

He showed me some of his sketches. I noticed that though they were basic drawings, they were also very detailed and in careful sequence. He leaned in and explained how carefully I would need to record the continuity of action and character notes he would be giving me, since he'd be referring to them weeks and months later in the editing room in California. I worried about my generally illegible handwriting, and hesitated. Maybe he was right—maybe I was the wrong "girl." His studied my expression, and I could see he was getting impatient.

"So, you think you can do this?" he asked.

"Yes, I can," I nodded, even though I wasn't at all sure I could.

Then we both stood up. "Okay," he said, sounding as if inspiration had just struck. He threw his shoulders forward as if to model a dance move, or do a James Cagney imitation.

I followed his lead and gently hunched forward at his direction, notching down my height. He beamed, "Yeah, that's good."

◆◆◆

THE PLAN WAS TO film on the actual streets of Manhattan's Little Italy where Marty grew up.

That first night I held tight to my shooting script. I'd read it the night before and was impressed by how tight the cultural noose was around the main character, and I realized how lucky I'd been to make that break from my own past by moving to New York and going to film school. Maybe I'd even move to Los Angeles someday. This overwhelming thought was interrupted by Mitchell, who handed me a stopwatch so I could time scene rehearsals and actual takes.

"Put it around your neck. Always wear it. Never take it off," Mitchell instructed.

Then he checked in on the rest of the student crew. Though we'd been well schooled in how to behave on set, our production toys could hardly compare to the scale of the dozens of steel boxes the California camera crew was unloading and inspecting.

Most of the students in my classes were young men who believed they were destined to direct or shoot or produce films. To them, the constant cycle of packing and unpacking from one location to the next, fitting all the camera and lighting equipment parts together again to form a state-of-the-art production engine, was an exciting game. The students on the camera and lighting crew were happy to be doing what they already knew they loved. They were far better prepared for their jobs than I was for mine, and in my case, the director had already expressed his doubts.

Looking around, I became aware that there were a lot more people, including two women, with jobs in and around the production—and I wasn't completely sure about what they did. I later learned one of the women was a publicist and the other a liaison to the company financing the film. They were a decade older than me, dressed nicely, and seemed at ease. I tried to approach them, without much success. They could see exactly who I was: a girl who hunched over a script almost to teetering, all the while clutching her stopwatch.

"Listen up, everybody! Our time here is limited!" announced the assistant director. I later learned he'd also worked with Marty on editing *Woodstock*.

"You need to not only be vigilant about the work you do, but also keep in mind that we're a non-union production, so we have to stay one step ahead of the local teamsters. Got it?" There were cocky nods all around, except from me since I wasn't sure what "nonunion" meant.

Luckily, I soon learned that there were Little Italy cops watching out for our nascent film director and his crew. Marty's ties to the neighborhood were its own kind of union, and you could tell that everyone we met was proud of him. He had already directed two independent low-budget features, but this one was a serious look at the neighborhood itself.

I tried to keep my insecurity to myself, but I definitely couldn't hide anything from Marty. Though he moved at a physical and verbal pace I'd never seen anyone equal, he could also simultaneously read the people around him. I discovered that getting his attention could be fun.

He had encyclopedic knowledge of classic films. "You know that scene at the end of *The Searchers*?" Marty asked, excitedly beaming. I could nod to this question with confidence. He'd guessed correctly that like every kid on the eighth floor, I was deadly serious about the art and craft of filmmaking. Of course I knew that scene.

"They finally find Natalie Wood…but then…she runs away, runs for her life from the obsessive, even barbaric racism in her Uncle Ethan's eyes that made him look more barbaric than her "people," the Indians who kidnapped her…" Ever the teacher, Marty effortlessly cited a shot-by-shot list of the forensic cinematic strategy John Ford had used to create the immortal impact of *The Searchers*. I was having this conversation on a working film set, and not in one my classrooms. Marty was directing me, very generously, to be at ease.

◆◆◆

THE FIRST SCENES WERE documentary-style pickup shots of the neighborhood's annual San Gennaro Festival. Marty had to place the actors on unmistakably New York streets, since most of the film had already been shot in California. The local Italian-American population marched devoutly forward, a world apart, fanatical and medieval, like in *The Godfather*.

We strategically focused on getting the footage Marty needed as if our lives depended on it. We worked eighteen-hour days. Sleep was something the rest of the world did. One night, Marty's mom, Catherine, acted in a scene while many other Scorsese family friends (Joe Cupcake, Frankie Bananas, and Larry the Box) either gave additional support to the crew or acted as extras. A restaurant in Marty's old neighborhood opened its doors at three in the morning and treated us to the meal of our lives. For years afterward, Joe Cupcake sent me Christmas cards.

Standing for hours hunched next to Marty, I was finally keeping pace with the speed of his notes. During the breaks, I was neatening and polishing them as fast as I could.

Only once did I totally fuck up.

In one scene, "Bobby" aka Robert De Niro was holding a gun. In the middle of shooting a take, he switched hands.

I shouted in a panic, "The gun needs to be in your other hand!"

Needless to say, I had broken a cardinal rule and I made the man angry. De Niro stepped out of the scene. He walked up to me.

"Please don't do that," he said in that soft voice that made you feel like you had his complete attention and maybe that wasn't a good thing. Then he walked back into the scene as though nothing had happened.

Later, De Niro and the rest of the cast were very sweet, understanding, and friendly. After such dizzying intensity in the filmmaking real world, it was hard to imagine going back to school.

The last scene took place in an old cemetery. The camera crew surprised me with flowers because it happened to be my birthday. Finally I got to stretch out on the cold ground; lean against a thin granite tombstone. Clutching my shooting script, now fat with notes to Marty, I held tight to the flowers.

I gripped the stopwatch around my neck. I hated the idea of giving it back. Then I looked up at the moon and thought, "So this is the film business. Wonder if anyone will ever see this little movie."

Nancy Nigrosh *heads the Motion Picture and Television department at The Partos Company, a Santa Monica-based agency which represents directors of photography, production designers, and costume designers. A top Hollywood agent for over twenty-three years, Nigrosh headed the Literary Department at both the Gersh Agency and Innovative Artists, where she also served as a team member of the Talent Department. A partial list of the world-class writers, directors and authors she's represented includes Kathryn Bigelow* (Zero Dark Thirty)*, John Cameron Mitchell* (Hedwig and the Angry Inch)*, Amanda Brown* (Legally Blonde)*, and Stuart Beattie* (Pirates of the Caribbean, Collateral)*. She earned her BFA in Film and Television from New York University's Tisch School of the Arts and is an MFA alumna of UCLA's School of Theater, Film & Television. She also holds an MA in Education and two Clear California Teaching Credentials from Antioch University.*

I STALK LUCY

By Billy Van Zandt

"Between scenes, she tells me about Room Service with the Marx Brothers and how they spent an entire day without pants when a busload of nuns came to visit the set."

1000 N. Roxbury Drive: A white Modern Colonial. Black shutters. Set on prime Beverly Hills real estate between Mr. and Mrs. Jack Benny, Mr. and Mrs. Jimmy Stewart, and across the street from Ira Gershwin, Rosemary Clooney, and José Ferrer.

It's the same house I've seen in magazines and on the episode of *I Love Lucy* when the show goes on location to film Lucy and Ethel sneaking across Richard Widmark's front lawn.

It's Lucille Ball's home.

It's 1977. I've just flown to Hollywood to film scenes for *Jaws 2,* my first movie as an actor (yet to realize that the glamour of Hollywood filmmaking will involve swimming in polluted waters outside a cat food cannery in Long Beach).

It's my first time here. I don't go to Grauman's Chinese Theater, Dodger Stadium, or the Hollywood Bowl. I go to Lucy's house—straight from the airport.

I pull up in front of #1000 in my rented Toyota and fling open the car door. Jane, my girlfriend at the time, freaks out.

"What do you think you're doing?!"

"I'm going to meet Lucy!" I say as I jump out.

Jane won't get out of the car. She buries her blonde head under the dashboard as I stride up the brick walkway to ring the bell.

Lucy is the reason I'm in show business. She taught me comic timing. Her writers taught me how to write. Desi Arnaz showed us all how to produce. And Lucy is the one who still makes me laugh more than anyone else.

The Lucy character and I more than connect. Most of the time I feel like I'm living an *I Love Lucy* episode, fearlessly jumping into one situation after another, then figuring out how things will work out after the fact.

The front door opens and a little Japanese houseboy pops his head out.

"Yes?"

I announce myself: "Billy Van Zandt is here to see Lucille Ball."

"She's not home," he says, slamming the door in my face.

I walk back to the car, get in, grab my camera, and start snapping as Jane peels out.

◆◆◆

Ten years later.

Sitting inside Lucy's house after watching the premiere of *Life with Lucy* with Lucy, her husband Gary Morton, Gale Gordon, John Ritter, and members of the show's cast, including my friend Ann Dusenberry. The topic turns to Buster Keaton.

Lucy tells us that Mr. Keaton taught her how to use props—to set and rehearse with them until they're as much a part of you as your arms and legs. How to time a gag, listen, react, and then act.

I ask Lucy if she ever met Charlie Chaplin, since it's obvious he has influenced her. I've never seen a photo of them or heard they'd met.

She says, "No. But in 1976, Gary and I were in Switzerland. I found out where he lived, so Gary and I drove over. When we pulled up in front of Chaplin's house, I jumped out, but Gary hid his head under the dashboard and refused to leave the car. I left him sitting there, walked up to the front door, and rang the bell. A housekeeper opened the door and asked what I wanted. I said, 'Lucille Ball's here to see Charlie Chaplin.' She said, 'He's not home' and slammed the door in my face."

◆◆◆

THREE WEEKS EARLIER I was in New Jersey preparing to open a new theater with Jane. Plus, we were opening our show *Drop Dead!* off-Broadway at the same time.

I got a phone call that put it all on hold.

My *Jaws 2* buddy, Ann Dusenberry, had landed the role of Lucy's daughter on her new TV series, *Life with Lucy*. Ann told me, "After my mother, you were the first one I called."

I, of course, realized there was only one reason Lucy was coming back to TV—so I could meet her, learn from her, and ultimately work with her.

With no notice, and Ann's permission, I leave the theater duties to Jane and jump on a plane to LA to watch Lucy rehearse the second episode.

When I arrive, Ann tells me she's sorry, but she's just been told it's a "closed set." No one can enter the soundstage during rehearsals, let alone watch. I tell her I understand. Then I sneak up to the bleachers.

I look down. There she is. A mop of orange hair. Big sunglasses.

◆◆◆

I HAD SEEN LUCY in person once before, in New York City filming the TV-movie *Stone Pillow*. I was on the West Side in a meeting with Sean Penn and Director James Foley for *At Close Range,* a project I helped put together. In the middle of my meeting, I heard Lucy's voice booming through the heating vents. "Where's that coming from?" I asked. The casting lady explained that Lucille Ball was rehearsing in the next room.

Sean, with whom I'd acted in the movie *Taps,* knew of my Lucy obsession and started laughing. He motioned, "Go ahead."

Ten minutes later, in a pair of overalls supplied by the casting lady, I enter the *Stone Pillow* rehearsal room pretending to be an air conditioner repairman and stand next to the air conditioner unit (which was working perfectly fine) and mime pushing buttons. My very own *Lucy Meets Billy* episode, but I don't accidentally set the star on fire or knock down a wall. I watch for five minutes, then leave before I get the casting lady fired.

◆◆◆

THAT WAS TWO YEARS earlier.

Now, I see Lucy spotting me in the bleachers. She leans over to say something to Ann, who whispers back.

Lucy rises, walking to the edge of the bleachers, and looks up. I think: "I just got Ann fired."

And: "I'm going to get thrown out. By Lucy."

Instead, she stares at me. And in her best "It's a moo-moo" Martian-voice, she says, "Hello, Billy. I heard you were coming."

For the rest of the week, it's still a closed set. With one exception: Lucy plays to an audience of one. Me.

◆◆◆

WATCHING HER WORK IS surreal. Lucy holds back in rehearsal, walking through, "marking" where her laughs will come. Then she runs scenes over and over. As she gets more comfortable,

59

her confidence builds and she gets funnier and funnier until it looks effortless.

From the bleachers, I watch her figure out physical bits in a mechanical way, then rehearse them until they seem spontaneous. I realize that I rehearse the same way—probably a result of me watching her for twenty years, imitating her timing. It's also my belief that every comedian is born hearing a certain rhythm. I think I connect with Lucy because we both have the same ear, only she's a master and I'm still learning.

In a scene with the kid playing her grandson, Lucy—in character—keeps saying, "What?"—forcing him to talk louder. I'm told she did the same thing with Richard Burton and Elizabeth Taylor when they guest-starred on *Here's Lucy.*

"Who the hell does she think she is, doing that to me?" Sir Richard Burton demanded.

To which Elizabeth Taylor answered, "The Queen of Comedy, dear."

◆◆◆

LUCY STARTS ONE SCENE and, still in character, tells the gaffer which light is incorrectly focused behind her. Without missing a line, she changes an actor's blocking by dragging him by his arm while they play the scene out—silently pointing out where he should stand for a better camera angle—against the director's silent objection.

An actor starts to deliver a line while walking, apparently sacrilege to Lucy.

She yells, "What the hell's the matter with you? Talk! *Then* walk!"

He doesn't do it again.

◆◆◆

From the first day, Lucy is "on." Seeing her in person as the only audience member, I feel like I'm ten years old, lying on the floor in front of the TV in my parents' living room.

During a break, Gale Gordon tells me that Lucy must like me because she's apparently performing for me personally.

"Normally she doesn't work this hard."

◆◆◆

Between scenes, she tells me about *Room Service* with the Marx Brothers and how they spent an entire day without pants when a busload of nuns came to visit the set. She talks about Desi Arnaz. How underappreciated he was in Hollywood, despite the fact that he virtually invented the sitcom.

We share a Snickers bar and talk about plays I've written, which I confess are thinly disguised *I Love Lucy* episodes with me in the male Lucy role.

Lucy listens, pauses, then asks if I could do anything with "this"—indicating the script. I'm too terrified to say an unkind word about the original *Lucy* writers who are producing *Life with Lucy*, so I assure her I think it's funnier than she does, probably passing up my first TV writing job in the process.

"Is it?" she answers. "I haven't known what's funny for thirty years. When everybody laughs at everything you do, how can you know?"

◆◆◆

A few days into the week, Director Marc Daniels takes me aside.

"Knock it off."

"What did I do?"

"She's telling you too many stories. It's making the day longer."

I go back up into the stands.

Where I see next week's script.

At first I think the white light in it is from heaven but quickly realize it's just a work light.

I open the script and see two words written especially for me, right there in the cast list: "Delivery Guy."

In one scene, Lucy has messed up the hardware store's computer system so that Gale Gordon's character somehow ends up listed dead in the newspaper, and the Chamber of Commerce sends flowers to his funeral. Does it make sense? No. But who cares? The flowers have to be delivered by a delivery guy! In a scene with Lucy *and* Gale Gordon!

I run across the lot into the casting director's office—a man who has no idea who I am or why I'm standing in his office—and demand to read for the role. He's snippy, telling me, "We don't hold auditions for *Lucy*. We only watch actors' videotapes."

"I don't have any tape with me—I'm on vacation."

"Then you're out of luck. No videotape—no audition."

With the help of Lucy's video archivist, I go to the local video store and rent my only two movies of note: *Jaws 2* and *Taps*.

We splice together an acting reel of videotape.

Two hours later I walk into the casting director's office, flinging my tape on his desk. The casting director is either amazed at my spunk or terrified that I will kill him if I don't get this audition.

He grants me an audition with Madelyn Davis and Bob Carroll Jr.

◆◆◆

THE NEXT MORNING IN the waiting room I look at the sign-in sheet. There is one other name up for the same role. A comedian named Arsenio Hall.

I'm called in to read first. I ask Bob and Madelyn if I can share something before I read the scene. They say yes.

And so I speak from the heart for about ten minutes: How they've influenced me as a writer and shaped my entire life with their work. How every television writer owes them everything—for creating the rules and showing how it's supposed to be done. I don't care if I get the role or not. Nothing can stop me from thanking them.

When I'm done rambling, I read the scene for them—all four lines. They laugh. I thank them again and, thinking I've blown the audition by brownnosing, I go back to the bleachers to watch the rest of the rehearsal.

Madelyn finds Ann and informs her that she can be the one to tell me—I got the job.

That night I call Jane back in New Jersey. I tell her I'll be staying an extra week.

I'm going to act with Lucy!

◆◆◆

THE FOLLOWING MONDAY, I walk onto the soundstage. Gale Gordon comes up to me, sticks out his hand, and says, "Welcome to the family."

The hairs on the back of my neck stand up.

◆◆◆

WE READ. WE REHEARSE. And here I am—acting with Lucy and Gale, directed by the great Marc Daniels who has directed some of my favorite *Lucy* episodes—in a show produced by Bob and Madelyn—with a script written by Arthur Marx, the son of my male comic idol, Groucho.

I'm terrified. Especially when, after the first day's rehearsal, they start cutting down the script because it's too long. I panic, certain that my meeting with destiny will be written out of the show. Instead, they move the scene intact from the hardware store set to the house set.

Phew!

The week is a blur, except for loving every second of it.

◆◆◆

THE BEST IS WHEN Marc Daniels tries to change something I'm doing and Lucy booms, "Leave him alone. He knows what he's doing. He's a very talented comedian."

I call Jane that night to tell her that if the plane goes down on my flight home, it's okay with me. Lucy said I was talented.

◆◆◆

FRIDAY IS OPENING NIGHT. We shoot the show.

It feels like a theater opening night. Everybody has butterflies. The actors and the sets are hidden from the audience with big screens. We're told we will only do each scene once—just like a live play.

As we sit backstage waiting to start, Lucy, in a silly mood, goes around to each one of us and mimes that she's feeling each one of us up. I have no idea why. But that's what she does. She's just one of the gang.

I say, "I'd feel you up, too, but I'd feel funny feeling up an institution."

She laughs that big, deep, hearty laugh of hers. And the show begins.

◆◆◆

IT IS AN ETERNITY waiting to get on stage, but once my cue comes, out I walk. Gale Gordon feeds me my cue, I get my quick laughs and I exit.

As the door shuts behind me, I too loudly tell actor Donovan Scott, waiting for his own entrance, "I want to do it again!"

He shushes me. The show is still going on.

I've waited my whole life for this moment and now it's over.

I have instant images of being the Sid Gould of the show—Gary Morton's brother-in-law who appeared on every *Here's Lucy* episode as the delivery guy, the mailman, the UPS guy, whatever they needed. Not much of a goal, I admit—and one I guarantee absolutely no one on earth has ever had before or since—including Sid Gould.

After the show, Lucy thanks me for a great job. And poses for a photo with me. A hundred flashbulbs go off as the fans who stayed behind snap photos of The Queen of Comedy.

◆◆◆

I NEVER KNEW WHO took those photos of Lucy and me that night, but I sure would like a copy—my auto focus camera focused only on the set behind Lucy and me. On the bright side, Lucy probably would have preferred knowing we shot a soft-focus still.

◆◆◆

AS THEY CALL THE show a wrap, I ready myself for the flight back to the real world and the unfinished work I've left to Jane.

Until Lucy says, "What are you doing next Monday?"

"Nothing."

"Come over the house. I'm having a few people over to watch the first episode."

I call Jane. "One more week."

I hope the big pause before she says, "Oh, that's great," means she's thrilled for me.

◆◆◆

ANN AND I ARRIVE at Lucy's house.

Just like ten years earlier, I walk up the brick driveway. Only this time no houseboy opens the door.

It's Lucille Ball herself—with a big stem glass in her hand filled with what looks like either tequila or Mountain Dew.

The reviews are out and they haven't been nice. In fact, they've been cruel.

In her best Lucy-Carmichael-with-way-too-much-to-drink voice, she pretends to stagger and slur her words as she announces herself to us at the front door: "Hello. I used to be in television!"

◆◆◆

WE EAT SPAGHETTI AND meatballs. And Duncan Hines chocolate cake for dessert.

I compliment Lucy on the food. She bows her head graciously, then, pointing to the Japanese couple in the corner, announces, "Yeah, they can cook anything."

After dinner, I sit on the floor in front of the TV and watch the first network airing of *Life with Lucy*.

Halfway through the show, I realize that Lucy, who is sitting in the back of the room, isn't watching the TV. She's watching me watch the show. A surreal moment made more surreal.

Later that night as we leave, a small group of fans has gathered on the sidewalk. The starstruck new owner of Jack Benny's house leans out her window to say hello to Lucy. It's unsettling, thinking Lucy has to endure these fans every single day—and that I'm one of them.

Lucy thanks me for my good work on the show and wishes me luck with the New Jersey theater and the New York play. I thank her for teaching me so much and showing me what I wanted to do with my life. She gives me a hug, which I don't expect, and I walk out into the night.

◆◆◆

MY BIO FOR OUR show's Playbill that year reads, "He worked with Lucy once."

Billy Van Zandt *has built a long and successful career in both television and theater. His TV credits include* Martin, Newhart, Suddenly Susan, Anything But Love, *and the Emmy-nominated* I Love Lucy: The Very First Show. *Billy's work has received multiple People's Choice, Image, and NAACP Image Awards. His twenty-five plays are produced worldwide, including the summer stock perennial* Love, Sex, and the IRS, *and Off-Broadway comedies* Drop Dead!, You've Got Hate Mail, *and* The Boomer Boys. *"I Stalk Lucy" is from Billy's television memoir* Get in the Car, Jane. *Visit vanzandtmilmore.com.*

RECOLLECTIONS FROM THE OTHER SIDE

By Stu Goldman

*"Hollywood Eye-Opener Number One—the auteur behind one of
the most lauded motion pictures of all time,* Citizen Kane,
now had to scrape to meet his shoestring budget."

MAY 17, 1974. WE were in Santa Monica, a small progressive
city cradled between Los Angeles and the Pacific Ocean, in
a room on the second floor of a well-kept motel. I sat with another
kid about my age and a heavy, older man, transfixed by the real-life
drama being played out on television. Hundreds of LAPD officers,
the FBI, the California Highway Patrol, and the Fire Department
had laid siege to a small house in the city of Compton, roughly
twenty-five miles away. Members of a terrorist group called the
Symbionese Liberation Army, which had famously kidnapped
Patty Hearst (of the Hearst publishing empire), robbed banks,
and murdered people, were holed up inside. Over a thousand
rounds of bullets and multiple tear gas canisters would be fired by
the time the siege ended, with the house burnt to the ground. Six
terrorists were killed. Patty Hearst was not among them.

Even during that relatively primitive era of live news
coverage, the unfolding spectacle was gripping. We watched
intently as the older man provided occasional commentary, most
of it unremarkable. That is, until the part about Nixon. He began
to rail against the president (who was in up to his neck in the

Watergate scandal) and boldly claimed that he was on Nixon's reputed "Enemies List." I had no reason to disbelieve him.

Because he was Orson Welles.

Yes, *that* Orson Welles.

I was a pup, a punk, an insecure stripling, little more than a year and a half out of college. What was I doing sitting in a motel room, following the Patty Hearst drama with the legend whose cinematic masterpiece had been based on the life of William Randolph Hearst?

Well, like so much in Hollywood (and in real life, too), it had to do with who you know.

When I was in the seventh grade, around the time The Beatles were just taking off, I became friends with a kid named Rick Waltzer, with whom I would remain close for years. As we got to high school, we both realized that we had an interest in film and television. Rick and I wound up sharing a dorm room as freshmen at Penn State, but only for the first semester. He was serious about moviemaking and eventually enrolled in USC's film school. We stayed in contact though, and once I graduated with a degree in communications and speech, he beckoned me to join him in Los Angeles.

Rick had made some inroads in Hollywood, having worked as a production assistant on Peter Bogdanovich's *Paper Moon*. When I arrived in LA, he was housesitting for Verna Fields, the celebrated, soon-to-be Academy Award-winning film editor. Ms. Fields had worked for directors Peter Bogdanovich, George Lucas, and Steven Spielberg (she won an Oscar for *Jaws*). I remember looking at the editing equipment she kept in the backyard room behind her swimming pool and wondering which well-known films she had used it for. Interestingly, I also learned that her swimming pool had been used by Spielberg to do a quick underwater reshoot of a *Jaws* scene featuring a fisherman's disembodied head.

I started out doing odd jobs: working as a gofer on a local commercial shoot, cataloguing film for a television editor, spending the Christmas holiday pushing electric shavers at a long-gone department store. Jobs in the entertainment industry were not that easy to find.

Then in early March of 1974, I got a call from Rick. Through his connection with Peter Bogdanovich, he had found work as some sort of assistant on a film Orson Welles was shooting in Scottsdale, Arizona, called *The Other Side of the Wind*. Welles had been filming bits and pieces of the movie since 1971, whenever he could raise the money to pay for it. (Hollywood Eye-Opener Number One—the auteur behind one of the most lauded motion pictures of all time, *Citizen Kane*, now had to scrape to meet his shoestring budget.) Rick asked if I'd like to fly down and help out as a production assistant. I packed some clothes and caught the first flight to Phoenix.

Arriving at Sky Harbor Airport, I was picked up and brought to the motel where the production crew was lodging. I'd been under the impression that movie crews consisted of dozens and dozens of grips, gaffers, set dressers, and many other production personnel, but that was not the case with this project. I don't recall more than six or so people working on the physical production the entire time I was part of it. And we all, I believe, shared the same motel room, which meant that some of us slept on the floor. Being young, that wasn't really a problem.

Gary Graver, the film's cinematographer, was one of my roommates. In 1970, Gary had called Orson out of the blue and announced that he wanted to work for him. (Up until that point, the bulk of Gary's output had been B movies.) Orson took him on, and the two were tied together professionally for the rest of their lives. Gary was supremely dedicated to his director and would go on to write a book about their experiences together (*Making Movies with Orson Welles*).

◆◆◆

THE CENTER OF *THE Other Side of the Wind*'s narrative is an extended party thrown to honor the seventieth birthday of a movie director, Jake Hannaford (played by John Huston), who is struggling to stay relevant in Hollywood. Orson had rented a stage at Southwestern Studios in Carefree, Arizona, adjacent to Scottsdale. The stage had been home to *The New Dick Van Dyke Show* for part of its run, and the living room set, still furnished, remained standing. I remember using a bathroom in one of the dressing rooms and wondering if Dick Van Dyke had peed there. (Years later I would work with him. Our bathroom history never came up.)

The large cast of the movie features several famous directors (John Huston, Peter Bogdanovich, Paul Mazursky, Henry Jaglom, Norman Foster) and well-known actors (Susan Strasberg, Lilli Palmer, Mercedes McCambridge, Dennis Hopper, and Edmond O'Brien, among others). Over the long course of production, some of the parts were shot and then reshot with different performers as people became unavailable, dropped out, or passed away.

◆◆◆

MY JOB WAS TO help Gary on set, assist with the few props, run errands; do anything that didn't require much technical experience. I remember being on stage one day when John Huston and Peter Bogdanovich were there. Filming appeared to move quickly, and I seem to recall both Gary and Orson operating the camera. At lunchtime, the six or so of us on the crew retreated to the bleachers (used for a live audience on sitcoms) and some of the cast sat down at a large table in the stage left portion of the set. While we munched on sandwiches, Orson, Huston, and Bogdanovich regaled each other with inside stories of old-time Hollywood, smoking cigars and having a jovial time. We listened and watched with fascination. Pictures were taken of that midday break. (Google "Welles, Huston, Bogdanovich.")

◆◆◆

ORSON HAD RENTED A private mansion set in the boulders of Carefree, which he used as a residence for himself, his partner (and mistress) Croatian actress Oja Kodar, who was also in the film, and other important members of the company. Ms. Kodar helped take care of Orson and managed his affairs. The mansion was also used as a shooting location. I remember delivering groceries and food a few times. Orson ate a lot of cottage cheese and drank a lot of Fresca, perhaps because he was mindful of his weight, which was a problem. Sometimes Orson and Oja requested steak tartare, which they would feed to their dog, a boxer named Flora. Whether they also partook of the raw meat, I can't be sure.

Once, when Rick and I were at the mansion, Orson picked up a movie camera and asked us to climb up and over the small boulders that lined a patio area. As he sat on a patio chair in his purplish robe, he looked through the viewfinder and gave us direction. He followed our movements for a little while and then told us we could stop. I don't know if he was actually shooting us or staging a shot to film later, but being directed by Orson Welles is something you never forget. (Rick actually appears in some of the film's party scene footage.)

◆◆◆

I RECALL AN EVENING when Orson, Oja, Rick, and I went to a restaurant for dinner. We were quickly seated in a booth, and suddenly everyone was staring at us. Obviously, they recognized Orson, but that didn't prevent me from momentarily basking in the glow of celebrity. If memory serves, upon finishing the meal, we simply got up and left. I never saw anybody pay.

◆◆◆

NEAR THE END OF production in Arizona, Oja's younger sister Nina appeared on the set. She was from Zagreb, a city now in Croatia (formerly Yugoslavia), had been a dancer, and dabbled in acting. At the time, I was a pretty decent-looking guy, although I didn't really believe it. Nina seemed to take an interest in me…

Eventually production wound down, probably in late March. Around this time, Orson learned that one of his producers had embezzled a huge chunk of the film's budget, which may have contributed to the fact that the shoot had to end. We made plans to pack up and head home.

Once back in Los Angeles, I planned to lay low for a day or two, but suddenly Nina reappeared. Somehow I learned, perhaps through Rick, that she had accompanied Orson and Oja back to LA and wanted to see me. So we got together, with Rick letting us use his apartment for our first "date," since it was nicer than mine. It made for a very pleasant evening, and we began a quick romance. Nina didn't speak English all that well, but we didn't have much trouble communicating.

We spent a few more nice days together before she flew back to Europe. I managed to pick up a couple of tickets for a taping of *The Tonight Show*, and as we watched Johnny Carson do his monologue, a very large naked man ran across the stage, "streaking" right in front of him. The audience erupted in hysterics.

Streaking was a fad that had taken the country by storm that year, highlighted by a streaker crashing the Academy Awards telecast. I remember Nina turning to me with an incredulous look, as if to say, "This is American television?"

She returned home, and we sent some letters back and forth but inevitably lost touch…

◆◆◆

ORSON AND OJA HAD now established themselves at the Santa Monica motel mentioned earlier, and asked me to continue working for them. I would drive to Santa Monica each day from my little studio apartment near the Atwater Village area of Los Angeles, and Orson would have me run errands. When he realized I drove a good-sized sedan, a 1972 Ford Gran Torino, and that it would be comfortable for him, I became his driver. Orson was very heavy, and he used a cane to help himself walk. He had a problem with one of his legs and couldn't move quickly. More than once, I watched him struggle climbing the stairs to the motel's second floor.

I drove him all over town. I remember taking him to an office on the Twentieth Century Fox lot (I think it was Bogdanovich's) and making an ill-advised quick turn in front of oncoming traffic to get off of Pico Boulevard and up to the security gate. He rocked to his right on the bench seat and was pushed up against the door, shooting me a not-so-friendly look. I apologized.

◆◆◆

ONE DAY, I DROVE him to a restaurant in Century City, on LA's West Side, where he was to be interviewed by Charles Champlin, then principal film critic for *The Los Angeles Times*. When I dropped Orson at the door, he told me to wait in the car and enter the restaurant forty-five minutes later with a couple of his cigars, in case he wanted another. I dutifully did as told, walking up to him and Mr. Champlin, offering the smokes. He certainly could have brought more cigars in with him, but I think he wanted the show of attention. For me, it was an honor to be part of the ploy.

I made Orson Welles laugh once. I had picked him up from a restaurant, along with the director Norman Foster and another gentleman, and was taking everyone home. When we got to Mr. Foster's street, likely in Beverly Hills, Mr. Foster said it was fine to drop him at the beginning of the block, even though his home was in the middle. I slowed to a crawl and Orson lightheartedly objected, saying that I should pull right up to his door. Mr. Foster, then in his seventies, said he didn't want to be a bother; he was fine getting out where we were. I piped up. "It's really no bother. All I have to do is push this little pedal. Watch." Orson burst out laughing (it must have been in the delivery) as I gave the car some gas. Mr. Foster's protests were pushed aside, and we dropped him at his house.

♦♦♦

OJA AND ORSON OFTEN had me drive from my apartment to Santa Monica and then back into the Hollywood area to complete an errand, which was a waste of effort, since I could more easily stop in Hollywood on my way to Santa Monica and avoid doubling back. After a while, I worked up the nerve to ask him to call me at home on the mornings he needed things done in Hollywood. To my surprise, he often did. I remember answering my phone and hearing that big voice, "Stu, I need you to..." and he would give me an assignment picking up photographs, or film, or whatever. After one of his calls, I remember opening my college dictionary and looking for his name, and there it was. Now *that* was cool. A man who had his name in the dictionary had just called *me*.

◆◆◆

I SPENT A NUMBER of hours alone with Orson in my car, but we never talked about anything substantive. In fact, we didn't converse much at all. It's not that he was difficult; in fact, I don't remember him ever getting angry with me. It was more a case of me being intimidated. That booming baritone combined with his size—and his pithiness—made for a daunting presence. I suppose if I had tried to push the conversation and the topic interested him, he might have engaged more. But he was generally quiet and I was too green of a kid to take advantage of the opportunity.

Jumbles of other memories still stick in my head: taking one of Orson's suits to be dry-cleaned and how heavy it was, since he was so big; being in the editing room and hearing the comment that footage from the shoot was too dark to use; watching the huge fire at Goldwyn Studios on May 7, 1974 that destroyed three soundstages; having to race from Santa Monica to Westwood to get a pizza for Orson and Oja; Oja slipping me a hundred dollar bill every ten days or so to keep me working for them; Flora the dog playing on the beach by the motel... They all add flavor to my perception of that time.

◆◆◆

IT WAS IN JUNE, I think, when Orson and Oja left Southern California for Europe. Filming of *The Other Side of the Wind* would continue, in fits and starts, through January of 1976, when principal photography was completed. Sometime later in 1976, I saw Orson being interviewed on a talk show. He was loquacious and ebullient, charming both the show's host and the audience. I remember being awed by his performance. Of all the time I was around him, even when he was with his director peers, I had never seen him so smooth and cheery. That, I thought, is what being an actor is all about.

I would have nothing to do with Orson or Oja again. As for *The Other Side of the Wind*? Due to complex legal problems, the film would remain unfinished at the time of Orson's death in 1985. Remarkably, thirty-two years later, producers would launch a crowdfunding campaign, raising more than $400,000 to complete the movie. The great Orson Welles's intended comeback, but ultimate swan song, would finally be released by Netflix in 2018, twelve years after the death of cinematographer Gary Graver, the film's most ardent champion.

I would go on to establish a long career in network television production. Having Orson's name on my résumé was instrumental in landing a job as a page at the old Metromedia Studios, where Norman Lear had just moved his hit shows from CBS. In 1975, I was hired by Lear's company, Tandem/TAT Productions, and my work in the entertainment business began in earnest.

When I look back on those months in 1974, a time of wide-eyed, youthful energy, I do so with gratitude. Having spent some time in the presence of Orson Welles was a fortunate treat. None of my other Hollywood experiences would come anywhere close to having the same lasting impact.

Stu Goldman *spent twenty-eight years as a stage manager, associate director, and assistant director on hundreds of episodes of network situation comedy series and pilots. He also dabbled in writing, selling a sitcom episode. Stu lives in the San Fernando Valley with his grown son Jack and wife Cara, to whom he has been married for twenty-one years, though it seems longer.*

THREE

THE SUIT

OVER THE COURSE OF *a Hollywood career, it is not uncommon for the "creative" (eg: writer, director, actor) to develop a distinct distrust of the "suit" (aka executive), who wields the power to make, break, or bastardize projects. Years later, after the suit has long left the job, the creative will invariably run into this person and be mystified by how nice and reasonable the executive now seems. Former William Morris agent Len Rosenberg accounted for the suit's previously feared incarnation thusly: "It's not the person, it's the chair."*

Here, we are treated to a human and humorous glimpse of life in that chair from former network and studio honcho **David Neuman**, *movie-of-the-week executive* **Charles Freericks**, *and studio VP* **Steve Gordon**.

DAVID NEUMAN

Film and TV Executive/Producer

*"A smart friend of mine once reminded me that every job has
'dishes and laundry.' The trick is finding a job where
you don't mind the dishes and laundry."*

I WAS A KID from the Midwest who grew up obsessed with the
film and TV industry and was fascinated by Hollywood. I moved
to Los Angeles to attend UCLA, but my real agenda was to break
into Hollywood and become a movie producer. While at UCLA,
I had the good fortune of being exposed to dozens of successful
actors, directors, writers, and producers in film and television, via
guest-speaking engagements, special classes, etc., so I could learn
a lot about the industry before my career formally started. I also
did internships at several different companies. Each internship
taught me new things and added to my contacts and "network."
After college, I applied to dozens of companies seeking a creative
job, ideally in the movie business. Most places I couldn't get
arrested. Finally, one of the dozens of leads I was pursuing led to
an interview for the management training program at NBC, where
they groomed new programming executives. It wasn't in the movie
business, but it was a fantastic opportunity, a dream way to enter, as
opposed to a long slog as an assistant or PA. So I was eager to ace it.

The interview, conducted by Brandon Tartikoff and his
deputy in the series area, Jeff Sagansky, seemed to be going

pretty well. Then Brandon asked me about my favorite TV shows growing up. I told him that *The Mary Tyler Moore Show* was my favorite show of all time, but then I also volunteered that if you asked me what show I watched more than any other growing up, it was *Gilligan's Island*, because they played it in syndication in the afternoons after I got home from school. The minute *Gilligan's Island* came out of my mouth, I knew it had been a mistake and I so wished I could have retracted it. Brandon received my answer with a cold stare, then turned to Sagansky and cracked a very small smirk. Then looked back at me with the cold stare again. I didn't have a good feeling about it. I'd just gone into the head of NBC, the network dominating the Emmys with shows like *Cheers* and *Hill Street Blues*, and referenced a dumb 1960s sitcom.

When the interview was over, I called the only other person I knew at NBC, a young woman who was also in the Associates Program, and she asked me how it went. "I blew it," I confessed. I explained, and then she started shrieking on the phone. "Oh my God! It's like an inside joke at NBC! *Gilligan's Island* is like Brandon's favorite show of all time!"

I was hired three weeks later, over several internal candidates who had been previously favored. In a little over a year, I was promoted to Manager of Current Comedy Programs, where I worked on shows like *Cosby, Family Ties, Cheers, Golden Girls, Night Court, Alf, Facts of Life, Silver Spoons, Diff'rent Strokes, A Different World, Gimme a Break!, Molly Dodd,* and many others. Eventually I was promoted to VP of Current Comedy Programs and VP of Comedy Development, before I left to become a producer at Fox. While there, my first project was *Drexell's Class,* a sitcom I conceived and developed that starred Dabney Coleman, Brittany Murphy, and Jason Biggs.

To create things, you really have to hold onto the sense of wonder, fun, and possibility of your own inner child. And you notice that the most talented people you come across in the industry do that very well. Great actors, writers, directors, and other creators often have a childlike sense of wonder and excitement; they "play" at work, they suggest things spontaneously and intuitively. In short, they act like children—in a good way. Of course, this can and is taken to excess in other, less productive ways: tantrums, spoiled behavior, narcissism, touchiness, and immaturity. But to me, the tradeoff is worth it!

◆◆◆

I'M AWARE OF MANY other industries—Wall Street, or the auto industry, or Silicon Valley—where there is a strong sense of community and an agenda and cast of characters that everyone knows. But because we have celebrities, perhaps more people are aware of ours. I think the sense of "community" is lessening as the industry gets bigger and more diverse. When I started as a full-time employee in TV, there were three networks doing original scripted and unscripted programming. Today there are literally hundreds. It felt much more "clubby" when there was a lot less production because there weren't many people involved. In the days of limited inventory, you could actually know everyone who was a significant contributor. Once you were in the club, you kind of had lifetime tenure unless you were a total jerk or incompetent. You were also likely to make a great deal of money just for being in the game. Now the world is much bigger, jobs are less protected, there's less of a safety net, and it's much harder to get very, very rich if, for instance, you're a TV writer or producer, than it was in the eighties and nineties. In those days, you could get away with being mediocre at your job and modest in your contribution, but still be employed and paid well. Not anymore. It's more competitive, there's less tolerance for mediocrity, and if you don't change and evolve with the new industry landscape, you'll be left behind unmercifully.

◆◆◆

FOR ME, GOING FROM job to job is rough every single time. I've never had a great first day of work, anywhere. I often feel out of place, getting my bearings, and maybe feeling a bit of buyer's remorse. I've just come to accept it as part of the process and part of what you have to deal with to be in our industry.

If I had to pick a "best job," it would be my time as head of programming for Channel One, a satellite-delivered news service that was presented as part of the school day for over eight million teenagers, a larger daily teenage audience than watched the Super Bowl. As the executive producer of the daily newscast, seen by eight million teenage middle and high school students, I had complete creative freedom. I went to work every day with such a sense of purpose: to inform and enlighten the next generation about the important things going on in the world. We covered compelling subjects like HIV/AIDS, the War in Bosnia, famine in Somalia, the rise of Islamic extremism and terrorism, China's economic rise, the 1992 US election, etc. We also covered teenage issues like abusive relationships, depression, drug and alcohol use, bullying, etc. It was a fun, receptive audience, open to innovation and new storytelling techniques. We took full advantage of that and got to a level of consistent creative excellence, in my view. In the process, we gave starts to some of the major news and documentary stars of today, like Anderson Cooper and Lisa Ling.

The worst job, for me, was being head of a major TV studio. The company was great, the position paid well and had lots of perks, but the essential nature of the job wasn't creative. In those days, studios sold shows to networks and the network buyers determined creative choices. A studio head was a third wheel in that creative process. The job was pure management: budgets, process, keeping the train on the tracks. A smart friend of mine once reminded me that every job has "dishes and laundry." The trick is finding a job where you don't mind the dishes and laundry. That studio job was *all* dishes and laundry. For me, it was an important epiphany: No matter what the money is or what the perks are or what the title is, I have to actually like what I'm doing.

◆◆◆

I LOVE THIS BUSINESS and the stories that come out of it. When I was at NBC, I found out that a writer on one of my shows was among the six credited screenwriters on *Blazing Saddles*, one of my favorite films as a kid. So, I peppered the writer with questions about it. He said the script was written in a conference room of the Gulf and Western building in New York and that Mel Brooks, who supervised the whole thing, really wanted Richard Pryor to join the writing team. Pryor told Mel that he would do it on the condition that every day, Mel had to have a fifth of Jack Daniels and a gram of coke in front of Pryor's seat at the conference table, and that Mel agreed to it. This writer was incredulous. "Mel, how could you possibly agree to that?!" He said that Mel shrugged his shoulders and said, "Look, some people need a bagel. Some people need a cup of coffee." (I have no idea if that's true, but I don't know why this writer—a modest man who didn't need to impress anyone—would have told me if it weren't.)

Also from my tenure at NBC—we were thinking of casting Bea Arthur in a pilot called *The Golden Girls*. Everyone knew she could hit a joke like no other, but one of my bosses at NBC had heard that she could be difficult to work with. So I was sent on a clandestine scouting mission to dig up some more intel about this, before we cast her. I was aware that the director and producing partner on one of my shows, Hal Cooper, had directed Bea in *Maude*, so I thought that would be a good place to start. I reached Hal in the control room at the Metromedia lot, where *Gimme a Break* had just finished taping.

"Hey, Hal, I need to talk to you in confidence."

"Sure, what's up?"

"Well, we have a pilot script, and it's very good, and we're thinking of casting Bea Arthur in it, but we're a little nervous about that. We've heard she's difficult. Is she?"

There was no hesitation in his answer: "Let me tell you something about working with Bea Arthur, David. You could tell her to take a dump on the stage. And she'd say, 'where, and how much?'"

That seemed to end any concerns.

◆◆◆

MY MOST MEANINGFUL EXPERIENCE was shepherding the "coming out" episode of *Ellen* for the Walt Disney Company in 1997. There had never been a major star of a primetime television show, or a lead character in a primetime TV show, openly identified as gay. The company was nervous, Ellen and her representatives were nervous, the network was nervous, and the show's production staff felt the stress and burden of all of the players. We all had a sense that what we were doing was historic and everyone wanted to do it right. When it finally reached the air, it was a cultural earthquake, which, I hope, really advanced the cause of the full acceptance and love of gay people in our society. Ellen was brave, the company was brave, and the reaction was sensational. The

Time Magazine cover ("Yep, I'm gay"), the Emmys, the Peabody, the Golden Globes, everything. It's always fun to do well by doing good, and that's something I look back on with pride and humility. We got to do society a service. It was our moment, and we rose to it.

There isn't a career like mine available anymore because the formats, the companies, the genres, the skill sets, and the players are continuously evolving. The "TV Industry" in 1965 was not that different in 1990. Today that industry is unrecognizable in every way. But there are hundreds of avenues for people who want to tell stories to do so, and every format variation, length, combination of genre, etc., that you could imagine. It's just whether the content will be on your phone, say, in short-form, and in the Snapchat vocabulary, or long-form on premium cable, or the OTT platforms, or maybe even on the big screen in retro glory like *La La Land*.

The sine qua non, I think, is desire. You have to desire it very badly and you have to know what it is you desire, so you can get after it. And nowadays, you simply must stay mentally sharp and adapt with the times. The saddest people are the ones who can't think outside the box, because the box is gone now. It's the Wild West.

David A. Neuman *is a television, film, and digital media producer and executive. He began his career as an executive trainee at NBC Entertainment and was eventually promoted to vice president. As president of Walt Disney Television and Touchstone Television, David oversaw* Home Improvement, Ellen, Boy Meets World, The Wonderful World of Disney, *and the development of* Felicity, *J. J. Abrams's first television series. David was president of Programming for Channel One. He served as chief programming officer at CNN, where he received a special commendation from the Academy of Television Arts and Sciences for his participation in the network's coverage of the events of September 11, 2001. Beginning in 2004, David joined partners Al Gore and Joel Hyatt to create Current TV, the pioneering network for millennials. Since that time, he has been an independent producer and writer, developing scripted TV and film projects as well as news and information projects for TV and digital media.*

A TALE OF TWO BOBS

By Charles Freericks

*"'Movies-of-the-Week'? He shook his head. 'Bad demo.
When the MOWs are on I hear the sound of walkers scraping
toward the TV. You need to stop making those.'"*

IN THE LATE 1990s and early 2000s, I worked as an executive for two companies, both of which happened to have a CEO named Bob. There was Bob Wright at NBC and Bob Shaye at New Line Cinema.

Coincidentally, my most prominent memory of both men is of them walking toward me at a party: one, an NBC gathering and the other, a New Line soirée.

With Bob Wright, this happened at the 1996 NBC Affiliates Conference in Scottsdale. At the time, I had never met him and wouldn't have recognized my ultimate boss had we passed on the street. There were two to three hundred people on the bouncy lawn of the Arizona Biltmore. Dinner-jacketed waitstaff serpentined through the crowd with trays of Absolut appletinis and chicken satay skewers. Much of the throng was made up of local television station general managers, the men in Hawaiian shirts and ironed jeans, their wives wearing "Rachel" haircuts and pastel tops. The lawn was littered with banners and buntings that read "Must See TV" and held pictures of the casts of *Frasier, Friends, Mad About You*, and *Seinfeld*.

As a man who stands six feet three inches tall, I looked a bit like one of those sliver skyscrapers that get built among the brownstones in Manhattan. I was attempting to schmooze any affiliate who happened to land near my own personal orbit. But I wasn't actually introducing myself to anyone, let alone starting conversations. This was due to my acute "communiphobia," or, as defined by the *Diagnostic and Statistical Manual of Mental Disorders*, "fear of schmoozing."

Conversations with powerful people involve a risk of misstatements, with the potential to mushroom into an ill-conceived "wow-them-with-what-you-know" strategy that is prone to backfire as a result of not knowing enough. In other words, at some point in my trying to participate in a TV-expert-to-TV-expert conversation, a lie (unintentional) would fly from my lips, requiring much misinformation bracing and scaffolding to prop up. Soon I would be barreling down a road of deceit that I had never intended, forced to fill gaps by beginning sentences with no idea where I was going. Then I'd be obliged to pull back the curtain of self and reveal that I was, in fact, an utter fraud, with none of the necessary mental tools or knowledge of television essential to being a successful executive.

Thus, I was in the mutually exclusive mindset of trying to schmooze while trying not to schmooze at the same time. Picture a small giant hiding among the masses while scarfing down stuffed mushroom caps from a cocktail napkin.

The lawn shimmered in the late Arizona sun and the affiliates milled about as my fellow network execs approached, right hands extended and smiles etched into expressions usually reserved for agents, talent, or higher-ranking executives. I scanned the crowd and spotted a phosphorescent couple about a hundred yards in front of me. They looked like Tinkerbells, glowing magically and turning from person to person to sprinkle each with fairy dust (like in the opening sequence of *The Wonderful World of Disney*). As the enthralling man and woman stopped to introduce themselves, everyone they spoke to broke into a goofy, I'm-not-worthy-to-talk-to-you, ear-to-ear grin. Others rushed to them to shake their hands and gush effusively. In the pair's wake, people nodded their heads in awe, beaming at the receding royalty.

A voice broke my reverie.

"Hey, are you one of the guys behind *Frasier*?" a station general manager asked while noticing my peacock pin. I tore my eyes from the anointed ones.

"No, I'm in long-form."

He went on obliviously, "Why is *Frasier* so much better than everything else?"

I stopped for just a second before responding, "They don't take network notes." This was one the most closely held secrets at NBC. The showrunners on *Frasier* were left alone and were producing one of the best series we had. The GM smiled at me conspiratorially.

"Better keep that to yourself," he advised. "You'll be out of a job."

"I'm in long-form," I restated.

"What's that?"

"MOWs and miniseries," I answered.

"Movies-of-the-Week?" He shook his head. "Bad demo. When the MOWs are on, I hear the sound of walkers scraping toward the TV. You need to stop making those."

The GM nodded, pleased to have provided me with the key to my and the Peacock's future success, probably not realizing it would mean the end of my career.

When I looked up again, the glowing couple, the godlike Tinkerbells from the other side of the lawn, were waiting to shake our hands. The man shook the station GM's hand while his wife took mine.

"I'm Susie Wright," she said.

Her fine linen pantsuit, Rolex Oyster, and diamond tennis bracelet were dazzling. We spoke for just a minute or so about who I was when Susie picked up that I had a newborn. I found myself in the most pleasant conversation with this charming woman about smelling newborns' heads and how it was the most wonderful thing to do. Without missing a beat, she told me it had been great to meet me and moved on to the next person while her husband swung around to talk to me.

He had the most perfect hand I had ever held…I mean shook. This was a handshake like no other. It was exactly as firm as it could be without introducing pain. His man paw was a womb. The downthrust and upthrust of the shake were symmetrical from the center, creating both an elliptical and parabola. His hand was slightly cooled by the desert breeze and had just a hint of summer perfume on it. Throw in his gleaming white smile and sparkling blue eyes and I found myself falling in love.

"I'm Bob Wright," he crooned.

"Bob Wright, Bob Wright, Bob Wright," I sang in my head like Barbra Streisand singing Nicky Arnstein. Bob Wright was a Kennedy, a Monroe, and a Vanderbilt rolled into a toned and fat-free exec, wearing a business casual outfit that probably cost more than my monthly salary.

"What do you do?" he asked.

"I'm in long-form, movies and minis," I told him.

"Really?" he responded. "Come talk to me."

The two of us turned our backs to the party. Two NBC executives of varying ranks colluding on a major corporate decision. My heart raced.

"You're my movie expert," he stated rather than asking.

I didn't answer. Silence and nodding were my friends.

"This conversation goes no further."

I nodded "of course" gently, the way top execs nod to each other when others may be looking.

"We're looking at buying Castle Rock or New Line. Which one would you buy?"

Holy crap. I was about to decide what mini-major studio would become a part of NBC.

"Castle Rock," I spit out. "They're smart. They tell grown-up stories. New Line's a schlock outfit. Do you want to be producing *Shawshank Redemption* and *A Few Good Men* or *A Nightmare on Elm Street 96*?"

Bob nodded. "That's a good point," he said. He blinked a couple of times, clearly using the time to file my thoughts in a place where he could recall them later.

I felt like I did when I was five and brought my toys from the bedroom to the living room to show them to a pretty babysitter. Tingles exploded at the back of my neck. Bob Wright had asked me my opinion and I had swiftly and confidently given him one that would shape NBC's tomorrows for years to come.

Bob Wright and I spoke for what I thought was a strikingly long time considering how little he had been giving to others. He even mentioned that MGM was available too, but without the library, and both of us said, in unison, "MGM makes no sense without the library." Finally, he thanked me for my insight and said goodbye, leaving me feeling as if I had just earned my keep, using my keen prescience and understanding of business to steer our ship into blue seas and golden sunrises.

From that point on, Bob Wright and I were polite to each other, and I even got him to crack up loudly at a joke once in the middle of a huge scheduling meeting, but I'm not certain he ever realized I was the guy who told him to buy Castle Rock and not New Line.

A decade and a half later, Castle Rock hadn't had a major hit since my grand pronouncement, while at the time, New Line was developing *The Lord of the Rings*. NBC didn't buy New Line, but they did kind of trade me to them.

A couple of years later, a New Line TV exec came over to join us at NBC just before I left NBC and took a job at New Line. Sadly, my contact with Bob Wright ended forever.

As I started my new career with Hollywood's last mini-major, I still thought of Bob Wright as the perfect CEO: handsome, charismatic, athletic, inspirational, and brilliant at business. I also feared that I had left a soaring rocket at NBC to climb aboard a sputtering Vespa at New Line. NBC had "Must See Tuesday," and "Must See Thursday," a pair of money-growing trees. New Line was still two years from releasing *The Lord of the Rings*. What seemed even worse was that I had gone from having a godlike CEO to a CEO with shag-carpet sideburns and an infamously short fuse. This was Bob Shaye. I was first introduced to him by the elevators when someone told him I was the new TV guy. Bob was wearing a velour jacket with elbow patches from the seventies. His face was ragged with saggy stubble, his sideburns gray skeins of frayed yarn that buried his ears with the enthusiasm of kudzu. He wore a sardonic sneer. I said hello and he grunted. Literally. He grunted.

I worked for New Line for seven years and in that time got to know Bob Shaye well. If there was one thing that colored my relationship with him over the full seven years, it was that he scared the living shit out of me. He yelled a bit and even when he wasn't yelling, he was a hair's breadth away from yelling.

Still, within two years of my having left NBC, they were stumbling, with *Survivor* pushing CBS higher in the ratings. New Line, meanwhile, had released the first of the *Lord of the Rings* movies to great fanfare and acclaim. We'd literally pass each other saying, "We're making a lot of money," the way USC students pass each other and say, "Fight on."

It was a good time to be at New Line. I had lunch one day with another former long-form exec, and she said to me, "You know, you got the last good job in Hollywood."

Bob Shaye felt vindicated and, frankly, relieved that the gamble he'd taken, risking the entire company on a single series of films, had paid off. But even a happy Bob was an unhappy Bob. One day, Bob's assistant handed me a script that had been in development at New Line for at least ten years. "Bob wants you to sell this to TNT with him attached to direct," I was told.

It wasn't very good, but it was Bob's pet project and TNT, being a sister company, put it into development. We had a nice meeting with them (I drove Bob Shaye, a billionaire with his own Gulfstream, to TNT in my Honda Accord). Then TNT tried to sit on the project, which was fine by me because I well understood this project was the ultimate poisoned chalice and I wasn't anxious to drink.

A couple of months later, I was riding up in the freight elevator with thirty other people (it was a big elevator). Bob was in the very back corner. I tried to hide in the front corner, but being six foot three, of course my head stuck above the throng. "I'm not happy," Bob spit out. I turned toward him, hoping he was speaking to someone else, but his eyes were boring in on me. "What the fuck is going on at TNT?" he asked. The other elevator riders all looked down as if they'd communally discovered their shoes were untied. I was alone…with Bob…in a freight elevator with thirty cowards.

While I believe the ride only lasted a minute or so, my memory is that he yelled at me for half an hour, spewing an invective-filled word storm that questioned my career, my right to breathe, and my species.

I thought to say, "It's TNT, not me." Unfortunately I was mid-panic attack and all I managed to do was squeak like a castrato chipmunk, "I'll call them."

The network had some sympathy when I told them what had happened, and they agreed to a meeting to give notes, but they had no intention of ever making it and it never did get made. My saving grace was that Bob hired the writers for other work and ended up back-burning the whole thing himself.

I still picture Bob at the New Line 2003 Summer Party in the Pacific Palisades. This was after all three *Lord of the Rings* movies had been released and the company was cash-bloated. Bob stood on the beach with a plate of barbecued chicken in his age-spotted right hand—which, unlike Bob Wright's, always gave you a boney and uncomfortable feeling when you shook it.

Around us, hundreds of New Liners lined the taupe curtains of sand that made up Will Rogers State Beach. As opposed to the dinner-jacketed waitstaff of the NBC party, this crew wore Polynesian costumes and traversed the crowd with trays of mojitos and pulled pork sliders. The partygoers were in gray New Line polo shirts, most with the collars turned up to protect their necks from the sun. The men were in cargo shorts, the women in denim skirts. The mingled scents of Neutrogena SPF 100 sunscreen, barbecue, and beer hung in the air.

I hung off to the side, talking to a fellow vice president. I liked this guy. He was a few years older than me, had been with the company a bit longer, and, most impressively, was both tall and skilled at hiding in public. I sensed a kindred level of schmoozing fear that made him easy to talk to. I didn't have to worry about steering lies to conclusion. I could simply say, "You know what, I misspoke," and save myself from the exhaustion of weaving a tangled web.

In front of us, waves roared against the sand while New Line assistants chattered about their boss's projects. Out of the corner of my eye, I saw Bob Shaye look over from his conversation with senior VPs and exec VPs to the two of us, the plain VPs. Bob got up and made a beeline toward us—well, as much of a beeline as one could make while tipsy and slogging through sand. He looked like one of those plastic running backs on an electric football game from the sixties buzzing his way forward. He was on a mission, either to yell at me or to get to the bar, which was behind me.

"Geez, he's walking right toward us," the other VP said. In hindsight, I think he was more scared than me. Still, the two of us stood there like trembling poodles who had just peed on the rug.

What was more unsettling was how Bob didn't stop when he reached my comfort zone. He slogged into my personal space as if we'd both suddenly become Italian. He was angry, ready to scream. Our faces were a foot apart. He squinted away the sun. There were missed hairs on the tops of his cheeks where the razor hadn't reached. He sucked air through his mouth, made a barely perceptual nod at something behind us, and growled at me.

"Let's do shots."

Then he kept walking.

I turned to the other VP, not certain what I had heard, and asked, "What did he say?"

"I think he said, let's do shots."

"Then we probably should."

Bob ordered shots of Gran Patrón for all of us (the bottle had been hidden under the bar). It was smooth and the drunk came fast as the agave hit my stomach.

Bob smiled. His eyes sparkled in a way that said, "We did it."

New Line was at the top of its game and so was Bob…crusty, mean Bob with his wild hair, leering stare, and reputation for verbally kneecapping lesser men. I took a second shot of Patrón and felt it warm me. I looked over and smiled at the unkempt and besotted man standing next to me, Bob Shaye, the smartest and finest Hollywood CEO I have ever known in my life.

Charles Freericks *is a former television executive originally from Paramus, NJ. He received a BA from George Washington University and a master's from the University of Southern California. While at the latter he took a one-day temp job filing at CBS that turned into a twenty-year-long career. He likes to tell folks he "had a good run while it lasted." He held executive positions at CBS Entertainment, Wilshire Court Productions (Paramount TV), Water Street Pictures, and NBC Entertainment, and he spent his last seven years as a VP at New Line Cinema. When he inevitably aged out of the TV development world, he moved into corporate training, first writing eLearning courses, and then developing overall training programs for companies like Princess Cruises and Viacom. He is presently an Engagement Executive with LRN.*

STEVE GORDON

Television Executive

"As I was trying to keep track of four or five different camera crews all speaking Chinese, I became aware that it was going out of control."

WORKING IN HOLLYWOOD IS not the real world. Everything is about "the business." You are surrounded by opulence and ego. When you start out, you have to be willing to do anything and everything (that is legal). It is a job of twenty-four-hour dedication, always carrying with it the risk of "falling from grace" and having the next person ready to step in and over you. It is also the greatest job in the world. To adopt and live the creative process, to be able to work with amazing people and, once in a while, to come up with something television viewers actually like, is a real charge. And you get paid well. You should, because work can easily dominate your life. You never get a real rest. There are always scripts to read, notes to give, shows to watch, and many, many meetings. It was hard for family and friends to understand what I actually did. I used to tell my mother, "I talk on the phone and take people to lunch." And that really was a big part of the job—communicating with the business and creative "engines" that could help my company and me achieve success. Meanwhile, my father and father-in-law were always pitching me shows.

My journey began with a degree in hotel administration and a Volkswagen van. I had worked my way up to being the youngest department head in a large resort/casino corporation in Nevada when I asked myself, "Is this all there is?" So, I quit, bought the wheels, drove around the United States for a few months, and then struck out for Hollywood. Like most, I used a connection. I was lucky enough to land a production assistant job (called a "runner") at Company Three Productions. They worked in a variety of genres—adventure, music, and sketch comedy. Soon after I started, the location manager of the company's comedy show quit, and because I owned a Sony Betacam (the consumer version), I was put in that position and drove all over LA finding and photographing potential locations. It was very stressful. We shot five days a week and I could barely stay ahead of the locations we needed. Also, I didn't know LA very well and we didn't have GPS then. Despite that, I learned much about production, and the cast and crew became a close family. It was Howie Mandel's first series, and he always kept us laughing.

I moved up through the production ranks and finally made associate producer on a pilot for a new network—The Travel Channel. Still, I wondered what it would be like on the "other side"—the creative side of producing. When I was invariably laid off from one of my production jobs, I became a freelance script reader. I sometimes read five scripts a day at about thirty-five dollars apiece, trying to earn enough to live in LA. Reading and giving notes on scripts was a great learning experience, but the painful part was that this was prior to word processing and I was a terrible typist. It was such a pain in the ass for me to correct all my stupid typos on my Smith-Corona—it took me longer to correct the coverage than it took me to write it.

Finally my dream came true. My old boss, Toby Martin, who was a partner of Carolyn Raskin (from Company Three) on several series projects, had been hired by Viacom and there was a position opening as Director of Development for the studio. I was in heaven—in a big company, reading scripts, coming up with ideas, being creative. I did not know what I was doing at first but learned enough to stay with the company for the next twenty (mostly great) years.

The first show I sold (*we* sold, but I was in charge) was called *Key West* for Fox. The showrunner, David Beaird, wrote a truly remarkable pilot. The only problem was that Beaird was not really a showrunner—he was a playwright. Two other executive producers, renowned TV movie producers Dick Berg and Allan Marcil, were also ill equipped to handle such an unorthodox personality as Beaird. The show received rave reviews, but internally, it was an agonizing battle to produce.

We shot on location in Key West, and news came that a hurricane was approaching and we would have to evacuate. Beaird, Fisher Stevens, the star, and several other key personnel refused to leave. They reasoned (along with locals on the crew) that Key West had survived several hurricanes and they weren't going to run off to Orlando, where the rest of the cast and crew would be sequestered to wait out the storm. I was torn but decided I had better stay with the star. Soon after the plane with the evacuees left, I felt as though I had made a huge mistake. As the police, fire trucks, and ambulances lined up in a staging area near the home in which we were going to hunker down, I felt tremendous guilt. I was putting my safety on the line. I had a wife and young kids at home.

I joined the others in wait and it turned out to be an amazing bonding experience. We stayed with the local crew in a house that was over a hundred years old and had survived two hurricanes, dined, drank wine, and swam before retiring late at night to watch the Weather Channel report of the impending storm. There was palpable fear as the winds started to whip up and shake the rafters. The hurricane largely passed around us, but not before making a big mess and taking out all the power. We had no way of informing the evacuees or our families that we were safe. I sent a runner north up the Keys until he could find a working line (no cell phones then), and he put out the word that we had survived!

◆◆◆

MY BEST JOB EVER only lasted an hour and a half. I was hired as a production coordinator for a Rod Stewart concert for HBO. I rode down to the San Diego Sports Arena for the 2:00 p.m. call time, and I was a little surprised to see a large group of fans already assembling for the 8:00 p.m. concert. Then I realized that Rod Stewart's fans were mostly (90 percent?) women. As a twenty-nine-year-old single male, a whole new attitude about the job emerged. I did my "production coordinator thing"—basically listening to the UPM and ordering production assistants around. I had my walkie-talkie and "All-Area" pass. Just before 6:00 p.m., I was called on the talkie to go see the producer. He told me that Mr. Stewart wanted 150 attractive women in the "front center" section and showed me a huge stack of tickets. "Can you do it?" he asked. I was confident. "Yes, I'll get it done." He gave me the tickets, and I took a production assistant with me. He had a stack of release forms for the "attractive" women to sign, as they would very likely be in the shots.

In the heat of the moment, I did not even think of the sexist connotations of this assignment. I talked to one girl, word got out, and for the next hour or so, while Rod hunkered down in his dressing room, I was the biggest star in that arena, and possibly all of San Diego. Phone numbers, smiles, even kisses were flung at me. The production assistant was delighted to soak in the aura of my exquisite production coordinating. When the last ticket was given out and I got my last appreciative eyeful of gratitude, I realized that I would never have another job like this one.

◆◆◆

MY WORST JOB WAS on a pilot called *The Disciples* for the old UPN Network. Our director, Che-Kirk Wong, had come off a successful action feature, and the pilot was a somewhat complicated *Matrix*-type show. I sat with Mr. Wong at lunch and told him of my concerns about his ability to hold budget. He convinced me he could do it and we hired him. Later, as I was trying to keep track of four or five different camera crews all speaking Chinese, I became aware that it was going out of control. The director and showrunner developed a hatred that became physical at one point, the budget was soaring, and neither I, nor our production executive, Paul Mason (a legend in his own right), could get it under control.

In the middle of this mayhem, I got a call from the showrunner asking if I knew what Che-Kirk had planned for a scene where the four disciples jump off of a building, one of the big action scenes. I said, "They're going to jump and the parachutes are going to open." He said, "You'd better go to wardrobe now." So I did, and the parachutes they showed me were elaborate and expensive "butterfly wings." *Why butterflies?* I freaked, the production executive freaked, everybody was incredulous. It wasn't in the script!

Mr. Wong was so convincing in his argument about the cinematic benefits of his plan that I succumbed, and the next day, the disciples put on their wings and jumped off the building. When the pilot was finally finished, I watched it being tested in a focus group. Guess what took the audience out of the story, caused noticeable chuckles, and earned us a poor review for our work? You guessed it—the butterflies.

◆◆◆

WHEN YOU BELIEVE STRONGLY in something and someone disagrees, there is going to be conflict. One instance I remember was particularly painful. I was VP of Drama at Viacom and we had been working on a script at NBC for a year. It was a life-rights story, about a family that conceived a child in the hope that the bone marrow would be a match for their daughter, dying of cancer. The transplant was her only option. I was close with the writer and the family. Suddenly, we got word that the network was green-lighting another movie—about a girl who needed bone marrow to live. I flipped out, called our NBC executive, Ruth Slawson (who was a good executive and I liked her), and unloaded: "Why did this get green-lit and not ours?!" It ended badly, and I thought our movie was dead.

Later I was called into the "principal's office" and my boss, Gus Lucas (who was also an extremely nice guy), took me to task for treating the network the way I did. The next day, with hat in hand, I trekked with Mr. Lucas to NBC and groveled at the feet of Ms. Slawson. I knew I was wrong. I was deeply humbled and it was difficult for me. Lesson learned.

A short time later, our movie was ordered and became one of the highest-rated movies of the year for the network.

◆◆◆

I DO THINK THAT Hollywood is more difficult today. A lot of it has to do with money. When the business contracted in the nineties, there were cuts made to middle management that still have not recovered. Also, financially pinched companies started using lower-level (and lower-paid) positions to accomplish middle management tasks. It's become harder to move up. I tell my students: you have to use any connection you can find, work very hard, be the first to arrive and the last to leave, and be amiable because you need people to like you. Volunteer for things, stay off your phone, be an interested observer who can learn from any part of the process, have ideas but don't volunteer them until asked, be thankful for your opportunity (and look at it as an opportunity), believe in yourself, and stick with it. Eventually, you will rise up, like I did.

Currently an associate professor teaching television production, development, and digital distribution at Ithaca College, **Steve Gordon** *remains an active producer. He spent twenty years in the television industry as executive vice president of Creative Affairs for Viacom Productions. There he was in charge of prime-time programming, where over two thousand hours of series episodes and films were produced including the series:* Sabrina The Teenage Witch *for ABC,* The Chris Isaak Show *for Showtime,* Ed *for NBC, and the Emmy nominated* 4400 *for the USA Network. His recent creating/producing work includes a television pilot for MEG productions,* Date My Dog, *a public service film on assault prevention for the New York State Police, and a documentary short film,* Remembering Robert. *Recently, he coproduced a film for Lifetime Television,* Santa Con, *reuniting with* Sabrina *Executive Producer Paula Hart and Star/Director Melissa Joan Hart. He also finished the second in a three-part series,* Conjuring Creativity, *for the Academy of Television Arts and Sciences Foundation.*

FOUR

THE SANDBOX

ONE RARELY HEARS AN accountant describe a typical workday as "playing in the sandbox." Yet this is exactly the phrase actors voice to sum up what they do for a living. It is an apt metaphor for the way in which they, in concert with the director, experiment with action, inflection, and nuance to extract the most honest realization of the characters in a script.

A reasonable question might be: If the sandbox is your desired destination, how do you gain admission to the playground? For one thing, you need to be chosen for the part. Casting director extraordinaire **Deb Barylski** takes us through the selection process, while actors **Bernie Kopell, James Morrison,** and **Rena Strober** discuss the hurdles of being on the other side.

Perhaps the most extreme hurdle in Hollywood is overcoming a legacy of exclusion. Addressing this inequity, writer-actor-director **Chris Rock** and actor-author **Gabrielle Union** offer biting exposés on the importance of unlocking the gates.

DEBORAH BARYLSKI

Casting Director

*"I try my best to hold, support, and honor each actor
who comes in to audition."*

MY JOB, IN A nutshell, is to find, audition, and hire actors for TV and film. I consider myself the first "filter"—meaning that I am usually the first person an actor must meet and/or audition for before auditioning for producers/directors. I hire the actors once choices are made, compiling cast lists and contracts. If it's a pilot, I coordinate with business affairs in preparing a proper offer and guiding negotiations. Once we are in production, any aspect of dealing with the actor is filtered through the casting office.

After earning a BA in theater and a master's in Directing and Theatre Management, I was teaching at the university level when I was twenty-five. Getting hired by the Cal State Long Beach Theatre Department brought me to California. I taught acting, directing, and theatre management, as well as serving as the business/publicity/front-of-house manager for the department for three years. I left CSULB because I became disillusioned with life on campus (especially by some of the tenured professors I met who were just "phoning it in"), and I felt I was too young for tenure. I was offered the job of Publicity and Front-of-House Manager for the Performing Arts Center on the University of

Alaska, Anchorage campus, and lived in Alaska for two years. I was also publicity director for South Coast Rep until I decided that I never wanted to write another press release, so I gave my notice and quit.

I was back in LA, the entertainment capital of the world, and decided to see if I could create some kind of career in film/TV. I knew no one in the industry but was confident that I could find an entry-level job, having worked my way through undergrad and grad school with office skills. I signed up at a few employment agencies that served the biz and within a couple of weeks I had landed a position as assistant to the producers of *Lou Grant*. My primary job was to type and edit scripts in rewrites, which was no small feat as we used Selectric typewriters—no computers yet. I used that position to investigate careers in the biz and narrowed it down to taking the test for the Assistant Directors Program or Casting. Casting won. I asked Gene if he would help me get into the Casting Department at MTM and he placed a call to Grant Tinker while I watched. I was working as a casting coordinator for *Lou Grant* the next season.

Most people don't understand what I do. All they know is what they see, and what they see is the finished product and maybe the actors in public, winning awards. It seems very exciting and flashy. And it can be. But the life of a casting director is sometimes just plain drudgery and so stressful that I want to quit. But then there are those days that are magic: when a pilot falls in place, or when an actor I've been championing books the role.

The process of auditioning actors is very intimate and, for me, an honor. I have always considered the audition room a sacred space. I became familiar with this term through my own meditation work and from the reading I had done and classes I had taken. Because the act of creating requires openness and intimacy, it is what actors must submit themselves to, day in and day out. And they have to do it in a room with bad lighting, with people who sometimes don't respect them or don't listen to them. Often they're going on tape for a producer who is not in the room. Even when the audition goes well, they're told "no" 90 percent of the time.

The *only* way an actor can be successful is to be vulnerable. And I feel that's where one of my jobs starts. I usually try to get to the casting room before anyone else so I can say a quick prayer or, if that's not possible, just breathe and "hold space" for them. I like it when someone else reads with the person auditioning, so I can really *watch* and help provide a safe space for that vulnerable actor. For me, "holding space" is when I try, with my energy, to create a bubble of safety. I try my best to hold, support, and honor each actor who comes in to audition.

Energy is real. When I was casting the pilot for *Frank's Place*, we had one role that we hadn't cast. (Isn't there always that *one* role?) And I knew the person who could nail it, but he was on tour with his choir and we were running out of time. I got (Exec Producer) Hugh Wilson to wait for him before deciding which actors to show to the network. This actor came in, and after all the build-up I had given him, he didn't give a good audition. *But I knew he could do it.* So as Hugh gave him notes, I just held him up—energetically. Slowed my breathing. I was trying to will him into giving the audition I knew he could. And then he did it. He knocked it out of the park and Hugh not only took him to the network, he got booked for the role. After the first table read, the actor asked if he could talk to me. He told me I was the reason he booked the role. He said he was sitting there, listening to Hugh's notes, and then suddenly my third eye opened right up and he saw it. He said, "When your third eye opened up, I sat up and said to myself, 'I better pay attention here.'" I wasn't trying to open my third eye—I was just doing what I usually did, creating a safe and sacred space. I believe that most actors "feel" this energy and just perceive it as my being kind and respectful in the room.

◆◆◆

GOING FROM JOB TO job can get tiring—moving your stuff, setting up new offices, loading equipment, developing working relationships each time you start a new project. It's a gift when one gets a long-term gig like *Home Improvement*. For eight years I did not have to move all my books, photos, tapes, and equipment home for hiatuses. With long-term gigs, you get to know a studio's system and the people who run it, so tasks are streamlined. Also, with the creative team, there is a kind of shorthand and *trust* that develops. With some short-term gigs, I felt that every casting session was *my* audition; that if I blew one session I might lose my job. I hated that.

I'd have to say my best job was *Arrested Development*, because I won the Emmy for casting the pilot and the first season, and I developed a great relationship with Mitch Hurwitz, who had written such a good script with such interesting characters. But it was also one of my worst because I only had a little under three weeks to cast the pilot. I loved casting *Doctor, Doctor* with Norman Steinberg. He read with the actors in our sessions and he was wonderful and playful. He spent so much time with each actor that most felt they had booked the role when they left and were *so* disappointed that they hadn't. Tape nights were fun, too, because we hired people who were truly great improvisers (as was Norman). So we'd get one solid scene in the can as written, then he'd tell the cast that they had one "for them." They were allowed to say anything they wanted as long as the gist of the scene was honored. So much fun. I could never figure out how the editing department fused those versions, but they did. I was also partnered with Cami Patton at the time, and we worked very well together. I'd have to also mention casting *Home Improvement* during the Golden Age of sitcoms. Because of its longevity, going to work was like working with family. It was well organized. It was a happy time. And I was *solvent*! Wow. I got to buy my first house because of this show (when we were picked up for three seasons).

There were two "least favorite" jobs. One had a showrunner who was schizophrenic and badly in need of therapy and/or chemical intervention. You never knew when this person would be kind and loving or turn and scream at you in front of whoever was around. One time the screaming got so bad, I excused myself from the casting room because the attacks got so personal that I started to cry. When I returned, I was told, "If you had any self-esteem, you wouldn't have cried." I cannot tell you the amount of self-control it took not to scratch this person's eyes out. All I said was, "You claim to have such a bleeding heart for all the bad things actors have to go through, and yet you just reamed me loud enough for every actor in the waiting room to hear." The pilot was not picked up, but I would not have done the series had it been.

The second involved a director on a different pilot. He would assess an actor as he walked through the door, and if he didn't like his "look," he would not pay attention to the audition *at all*. Sometimes he'd talk to the producer as the actor read. Some actors were so offended that they slammed the door when they were leaving. I got phone calls every day from agents complaining about how this director was treating their actors. It got so bad that I called the head of casting about this behavior—she was as upset as I was and spoke to the director about it. After that, the director would not speak to me, look me in the eye, or answer a direct question. And who wound up being cast after jumping through every hoop the director asked us to? Every single person the producer and I had selected *prior to the director's arrival.* We had spent two horrible weeks working fifteen- to eighteen-hour days because of him for no reason. I passed on a subsequent pilot when I found out this director had been engaged for it.

◆◆◆

THE MOST MEANINGFUL MOMENT of my career was the day I won the Emmy for casting *Arrested Development.* The night of the awards, when the first syllable of my first name was announced, I screamed! I was so ecstatic that when I went backstage to have photos taken, I nearly ran smack into Bob Newhart.

There are also the little, daily moments. When an actor I believe in books his first SAG job, whether I've been the one hiring or not; when an actress I've campaigned for not only books a role but soars in it; when a producer hires me repeatedly; when a director calls me from another project to get the name of an actress I introduced him to; when a producer or actor remembers the contribution I've made to his career after being hired.

◆◆◆

THE BUSINESS IS HARDER than it used to be. Part of the reason is how damned intrusive the studios and networks have become. In the first twenty-ish years of my TV career, the only time the studio or network got involved was if I was hiring a major recurring character (but usually we would just have to let them know who we wanted prior to hiring), or if we were stunt-casting a role. But here's how it goes now. All producer casting sessions need to be taped. Then we must send edited tapes first to the studio. Once the studio has approved, we send to the network casting departments for approval. All roles must be approved before I can hire, even if it's a small role with one line. This process can take one to two days. When we have only a five-day prep for an episode, this really cuts into all our prep time. One network started doing this in the early 2000s, and then all of them followed suit. It's particularly galling when a young exec has no casting experience, or doesn't know how to judge a performance from a taped audition, and calls the casting office asking for additional tape on actors with twenty- or thirty-year careers behind them. I also think it's disrespectful to the producers and showrunners. In my opinion, this casting change began when the competition grew from four major networks to myriad platforms for audience viewing. I think that fear regarding more competition also instilled fear about job justification, which is why so many dang people have to weigh in on these decisions.

The other large change has been the transition to digital recording of casting sessions. Prior to the mid-2000s, when we taped auditions they were on half-inch video, which were difficult to edit and could not be sent electronically. With digital, it is not only possible to stream an audition in progress, but said audition can be uploaded and viewed within minutes. More and more producers are not in the room during the audition process due to this convenience. Also, because of the growing absence of producers in the room, actors are able to do more self-taping for auditions, and knowing how to do this well is an important skill for actors to learn.

Casting has much more visibility now than it did when I started my career in 1981. What this means is that jobs—especially entry-level jobs—are difficult to find because more people are interested. When I started, I got my first job as a casting coordinator and received on-the-job training. No casting office wants to train someone from the ground up anymore. You have to intern in a casting office first. If you are attending college/university, find out if your program offers internships for credit. Some studios and networks also offer casting internships. I used to be able to use "free" interns, but because of lawsuits concerning internships in our business, those are now either illegal or greatly frowned upon. If you are interested in casting, I think some of the prerequisites are: the ability to multitask and function in an office where the phone never stops ringing; being comfortable with reprioritizing in a moment when casting or production requirements change; a team-player attitude; great phone etiquette; a knowledge of basic office and computer skills; a love of actors and the creative process; a good memory; and finally, the ability to take all the seemingly disparate pieces of information you collect on the job and start connecting the dots into a cohesive whole.

◆◆◆

ONE OF THE THINGS I've always loved about this career is getting to meet people you've only known about from afar as a fan. Early in my career, it was a kick meeting Ed Asner, who was always so kind to me. When I got married, I brought my parents to the set. Ed made such a big deal about meeting my mom that I often said the highlight of her LA trip was not my wedding, but meeting Ed Asner.

Another unique aspect of my job is that no two days are the same. Of course, there are routines and deadlines, but we are always looking for different types of actors, the production challenges we face can vary vastly, and we are perpetually digging up new leads in our effort to make the stars align. There is nothing more satisfying than seeing our piece of the puzzle become part of a successful whole. If I could live my life over, I would definitely still pick this career.

Deborah Barylski, *a St. Louis native, is an Emmy Award–winning casting director. In a thirty-five-year career, some of her most recent credits include* The Middle, Arrested Development *(for which she won an Emmy),* Life with Bonnie, Still Standing, Home Improvement, *and* Just Shoot Me, *as well as past favorites* Frank's Place, The Famous Teddy Z, *and* Doctor, Doctor. *She also cast the feature,* Pastime, *which won the Audience Award at Sundance in 1990. She was nominated for the Artios Award for excellence in casting seven times, and won the Artios in 2003 for* Arrested Development.

BERNIE KOPELL

Actor

"As you mature in the business, you realize that the audition process is both an opportunity and a necessary evil. There are many deciding factors, few of which have any relationship to your value, your talent, or even your best reading."

M Y FRIEND RONNIE SCHELL used to say that the primary qualification for a comedic actor is a troubled past. If this is the true barometer for success, my calling was cemented at an early age. I had an abusive and domineering father, who, for as far back as I can remember, made me feel as if I had no value. I rebelled to survive, drinking and cutting classes all through high school. Eventually, I was lucky enough to have an English teacher who was able to identify some talent in me, and before I knew it, I had joined what they called "verse choir" (an extracurricular class where students read poetry and prose). After that, I managed to make my way to the all-city radio workshop at WNYE. These minuscule yet ego-boosting successes encouraged me to seek formal drama training at NYU, where my immediate connection with the theatre confirmed that I had chosen the right path. As life-changing as that was, my budding performing skills still didn't stop my parents from walking out of my first play at intermission—in front of the entire audience. I managed to pick myself up, dust myself off, and press onward, my drive for success a combination of wanting to master the craft and spite.

I have always called acting a privileged business. You get to use your right brain and play like a kid in the sandbox. But you'd fucking well better be a professional and a grown-up if you want to sustain. Yes, you have your creative "magic time," as Jack Lemmon used to call it, but you also must be reliable, responsible, and have the necessary work ethic. It's a combination of being inventive and "works and plays well with others." Case in point, my old friend George Peppard was cast as Blake Carrington in *Dynasty*. George had a habit of telling everyone—cast, crew, etc., how to do their jobs. A no-no. He was let go. They brought in John Forsythe, a pro's pro.

The greatest actor of his time, Sir Lawrence Olivier, was once asked why people become actors, and he replied: "Look at me, look at me." Yes, actors love attention, but there's another part of the equation: "Who is it that's looking at me?" One of the most rewarding aspects of doing what we do is getting respect from fellow performers whom we trust and admire. Not long ago, I got a lovely email from character actor, Stuart Pankin, regarding my role as a concentration camp survivor in the reimagined version of *Hawaii 5-0*. Ironically, on the morning of that very shoot, the remarkable actor Chi McBride strolled in at seven in the morning, while I was in hair and makeup, and said: "Mr. Kopell, my call isn't until much later, but I came in early to see you, because I wanted you to know that my family and I couldn't wait to sit together and watch you as Siegfried on *Get Smart*. Thank you." Then he gave me a big hug. Now, that meant something.

◆◆◆

THE PRESSURE OF HAVING to go from job to job is less pressure than the necessity of auditioning to *get* the job. You arrive at the audition, sign in, take a seat next to a guy who's up for the same part that you're up for. To compensate for your shoulders tightening, you put on a friendly attitude while fantasizing the earth opening up and swallowing everyone who's up for the role except you. As you mature in the business, you realize that the audition process is both an opportunity and a necessary evil. There are many deciding factors, few of which have any relationship to your value, your talent, or even your best reading. It might have to do with how you fit in with the other actors who've been previously cast, or the producer or director's on-the-spot perception of you, possibly based on the bad lunch he had or the fight he had that morning with his significant other.

Heaven, for an actor, is being handed a role without having to go through the audition process. The producer or director is a fan of your work, and he or she has enough faith that you will "kill" in the particular part. That was my experience with one of television's most brilliant producers, who, on the basis of seeing one performance, became my mentor and friend of forty-seven years.

It was my first starring gig, the most memorable role of my life, because it proved my father wrong. He had always contended that the only way I could make money as an actor was if he paid off the producers to cut me a check. But there I was, twenty-eight years old, with the leading role in *The 49th Cousin* at the Intimate Players Ring Theater (158 seats) in Los Angeles. I played a young Russian immigrant with a thick accent who went door to door selling kitchen utensils. The audience seemed to enjoy what they saw, the children of immigrants returning two or three times to see the show. I was pleased to be able to authentically and comedically sustain a Russian accent for two solid acts, and the run lasted eleven months. The pièce de résistance was the actual check. I cleared $33.35 weekly. I would finger the perforated

120

numbers, the 33 in red, the 35 in black, the blissful sensation a tactile affirmation of my worth, my value. The added bonus occurred one night when an elegant gentleman came backstage looking for me. He extended his hand and informed me that we were going to work together. The man turned out to be none other than Leonard Stern, my future mentor, who would go on to hire me for *Get Smart.* Most people assume that my favorite role was playing Dr. Adam Bricker on 250 episodes of *The Love Boat,* but without *The 49th Cousin* and Leonard Stern sitting in the audience, I might never have boarded that ship.

Of course there are always those jobs you wish you hadn't taken. One that comes to mind was a cigarette commercial I did in the sixties. God forgive me for persuading anyone to breathe in those damned deadly things. I may have made some sort of amends when I did a successful five-year TV campaign for an anti-smoking product called Cig-Arrest in the eighties. A cynic might see it as profiting off getting people to smoke, so I could later profit off getting them to stop, but I like the "amends" interpretation much better.

◆◆◆

AS FAR AS ADVICE to people breaking into the business today, I tell them to remember that no two careers are alike. Learn, and never stop learning about the profession you've chosen, and what your "marketability" might be. When I studied acting at NYU, the department chair's first word was: "re-matriculate." As in, "find something else to do with your life because this is too difficult." At the time, nobody moved. The reality was, only two students made a career: James Drury, who starred as "The Virginian," and yours truly. Despite the odds, don't forget that if there were no success stories, there would be no entertainment. I've been a professional since 1961, and I'm still at it. Thanks, Dad, for the motivation.

Bernie Kopell *was born in Brooklyn, drafted into the Navy, sailed all over the world on the storied battleship, the USS Iowa, drove a taxi, sold Kirby vacuum cleaners, and finally got on the TV map with* The Jack Benny Show. *Subsequently, in addition to hundreds of guest-starring roles, he became a series regular on* Bewitched, The Doris Day Show, That Girl, *as Siegfried on* Get Smart, *and for ten years on* The Love Boat *as Dr. Adam Bricker.*

JAMES MORRISON

Actor

"Like Olivier said, 'You're not a real actor until you've been fired at least three times.'"

WHEN WE WERE PUTTING together *Showing Up*, a documentary about the actor's audition process, Riad Galayini (wife, actress, coproducer) and I decided we would not appear in the film. It was more important for us to simply be the messengers: the "invisible" characters in the telling of our story, whatever form the narrative took. Several people have asked since it was released why I didn't tell my audition stories or share how I feel about the process and the answer has always been the same: I told it through the actors I wanted to honor in the film. We also didn't want to be tasked with the added burden of deciding which and how many of our contributions were worthy of inclusion. It was hard enough to cut a hundred hours of actor interviews down to eighty minutes. Like any other actor who has been at it for a while, I've got my "war stories" and moments of inspiration, success, and failure, and I'm certainly not shy about relating them. But I felt it was more important to be the listener in the conversation, one of the most important things a person must be as an actor—as those who do it well know. It turned out well for the film but I do have one war story I've always wanted to share.

In 1989, I auditioned for and was cast in what I was told would be a recurring role on the series *L.A. Law*. I was to be the lawyer in the divorce trial of a couple of married series regulars. In a nutshell, the job went like this: I showed up for work on the first day and found the director to be in way over his head. Many guest episodic directors are put under the added stress of series regulars and producers treating them with disdain and they pick guest actors or crew members to take it out on. After each of my takes, the director would approach me with the most absurd and impossible notes to incorporate, and it soon became clear I was his scapegoat for the day. On a couple of occasions, after I'd realized what he was doing, I actually laughed at him—my "defense mechanism"—which didn't help matters. Finally, after a few takes, one of the producers approached me and said, "We're going to have to cut your hair. It's too long." That's when I knew it was over. So I said, "Why didn't we decide this when I was in the makeup chair before we started shooting? Now it's not going to match."

"You let us worry about that," he replied.

"No, I'm happy with it the way it is."

To which he replied, after a long look of disbelief, "Okay."

And he walked away. Next thing I knew, I was wrapped for the day and sent home to find a message from my agent. They'd fired me. And who could blame them, really? It was one of the worst days I've ever had on a set. And I'd kind of asked for it. In a way I was relieved, but mostly I was devastated. Lost income aside, it was the first time I'd been fired and my ego was shattered. Dann Florek, one of the actors playing my character's clients in the episode, called me and was very sweet about how he thought the day went down, assuring me it had nothing to do with my work, that the director was taking his frustrations out on me, and that "like Olivier said, 'You're not a real actor until you've been fired at least three times.'" (Since then, according to Olivier, I have become a "real actor" and then some.) I felt better after Dann's call and will always be grateful to him for putting that in perspective for me. But the story gets better.

◆◆◆

THREE YEARS LATER, 1993, I got an audition for *L.A. Law*, this time to play an incarcerated marijuana farmer on trial for murder. I briefly considered the possibility that they must have made a mistake. I thought, "Why would they ask someone they'd fired to audition for them again?" But since, in war and auditions, our job "is not to reason why," I took the appointment, went in to audition for them, and got the job. It was a great experience and I enjoyed working with Broadway director, Tom Moore—someone who appreciates actors, knows what we do and how to talk to us, which is always a treat no matter where or when it happens.

◆◆◆

AFTER THE JOB WAS over, I was talking to my friend, mentor, and spiritual advisor, the late, great Jack Kissell, about how, as I put it, "the circle had been completed" by getting and completing a job from people that fired me.

"Getting the job and completing it didn't complete the circle," he said.

"What do you mean? I was fired before I could finish the first one and was able to get through the second—"

"No, it had nothing to do with getting the jobs or doing them."

"What was it then?"

"It was having the humility to audition for people you felt had wronged you. You put your resentment and your ego aside long enough to forgive them and do what it is you're meant to do. You let go, saw it another way, saw what your job was, and it set you free. You set yourself free. That's the circle."

◆◆◆

I'LL NEVER FORGET THAT. Whenever I feel constrained, inhibited, resentful, or bound by what I or others think about what my real job as an actor is—or far more importantly, what being a human being is—I remember that completed circle. It saves me from myself, keeps me going to the next stop on this journey. It sets me free.

James Morrison *has been on the professional stage since the early 1980s and has won awards such as the Los Angeles Drama Critics Circle Award for Outstanding Performance. He played Counterterrorist Unit Director Bill Buchanan on 24, and has guest starred in series such as* Frasier; Quantum Leap; The X-Files; JAG; Murder, She Wrote; The West Wing; and Six Feet Under. *He was a main cast member of the 1995 series* Space: Above and Beyond. *Morrison and his wife, Riad Galayini, codirected and produced the feature documentary* Showing Up. *He is a published poet, yoga teacher, and a singer/songwriter. He has composed two albums to date, which can be heard and purchased on his official website,* jpmorrison.com.

RENA STROBER

Actress

"I have a feeling that people in other fields may not have experienced sharing the stage with a singing/shitting sheep."

MY VERY SUPPORTIVE PARENTS put me in dance class when I turned four years old, and the second I stood on stage in my tiny tutu and even tinier ballet slippers, I was hooked. I danced till my teens and at the same time started training in musical theater at the famous summer camp, Stagedoor Manor, in the Catskills. After college, I made my Broadway debut in *Les Miserables,* and have been on and off stages and TV screens for almost twenty years. I was a recurring guest star on Disney's *Liv & Maddie,* appeared in *Veep* on HBO, and continue to voice roles for Disney animation, feature animated films, and dozens of video games. When I'm not working as an actor, I teach voice at a music school for blind children ages four to eighteen.

I think working in the arts is like never having to work in the "real world"—that world where people get up super early at the same time every day and go to the same place till the end of the day and then do this for years and years and years. I get to go to different places with different people and continually have new adventures. Because I'm doing what I've done since I was four, it never feels like work. When I'm dressed up in character, I definitely have Peter Pan moments of never growing up! But this also comes with its share of heartache. No certainty, no security, and weeks where you don't know what's next. I try to surround myself with people who understand the life of an artist so I don't feel awful about not having a "real job."

As a girl who started on the stage, I can strongly state that there's *nothing* like the theater community. We are a strong bunch of oddballs who sing and dance and dress up. We also have a tendency to break into song at inappropriate moments. Therefore we must stick together, which creates very strong communities. I've also been on sets of TV shows and can say that the series' regular casts get very close. Unlike "normal jobs," people in the arts spend many more hours together and in closer quarters. Some days can be twelve to sixteen hours of rehearsing, eating and shooting scenes together. This definitely creates a bond like no other (It can also create drama and friction).

After every show, I feel sad for a few weeks, because it's as if a romance has ended. I think that's why actors are always in therapy. We create such strong relationships and then they're over when the job is done. I've gotten better at keeping in touch with former co-workers, but I've never gotten used to the sadness I feel when a long run of a show is over.

My best job was either doing *Les Miserables* on Broadway or spending a day as a guest star on *Veep*. Broadway was like no other experience. I spent my days wandering around New York City, knowing I had a wonderful job to go to that night. I'd arrive at work at seven in the evening, cover my face with dirt, catch up on local gossip, and sing an incredible score for three hours. The cast would often go out for drinks post-show. I also joined the Broadway Softball League at this time and, because *Les Mis* was such a masculine show, we kicked ass on the field.

Spending a day on the set of *Veep* was also incredible. I was around consummate comedic actors and was asked to improv most of my scene. One of my idols, Julia Louis-Dreyfus, sat fifty feet away at the monitors, thinking up new funny lines for me… which was a dream.

My worst job was working as a singing waitress at a family restaurant in Burbank. Straight out of college with my sights set on Broadway, this "stop along the way" hurt my soul. I had to dress up like Scarlett O'Hara and sing horribly written birthday songs to senior citizens at 5:00 p.m. and to screaming kids at 6:00 p.m. I was covered in ketchup and always smelled of prime rib.

An experience that might not happen in any other business—I was cast to play Louise/Gypsy in a regional production of *Gypsy* a year after I graduated college. It was my first lead role in a professional production. In Act One, Louise sings the famous lullaby "Little Lamb" to a real lamb that another character gives her for her birthday. It's a beautiful song and I was excited to sing it. Because the show was in December, there were no lambs to be found, so the director got a sheep instead. Opening night, the sheep was walked out on stage in a huge white diaper. As I held its leash close to me and started to sing, "Little Lamb, Little Lamb my birthday is here at last," the lamb opened its mouth and started to *BAAAAA* directly into my microphone! The audience began to laugh. Just when I thought things couldn't get worse or more awkward, the sheep lowered its hind legs, squatted, and tiny round pellets suddenly fell from the giant diaper. Suddenly this sweet/sad ballad that Sondheim wrote became the comic number for Act One. I have yet to meet a stockbroker who has shared the floor with a singing/shitting sheep.

The most meaningful moment in my career was taking the stage with a young blind boy named Gavin. I met him when

I was invited to his school, the Academy of Music for the Blind, and he asked me to sing a duet with him. We sang "Time To Say Goodbye," and for the first time I realized just how deeply music can affect us. Gavin was born blind and sang from such a deep place that I was forever changed. I went on to become his voice teacher and perform with him and his fellow students all over California. Sometimes it takes a tiny kid to make us realize just how lucky we are to understand music.

The business today is much more competitive than it was when I started, and there are more people doing it. Shows like *Glee*, *Smash*, and every singing reality show have made people think they can just walk into the entertainment world. I started studying at the age of four and never stopped. Now all it takes is one reality or YouTube show to make someone "famous," because that's what people think success is. So producers turn around and want someone "famous." It's all backward and much harder to get acknowledged for your hard work and the dues you've paid over the years.

My advice to people breaking in today who aspire to a career like mine? Do something else. Seriously. Every day is hard work. I'm always asking people to give me a chance and have to prove myself over and over again. It's *never* easy. There are ways to perform for fun and still be fulfilled. The fight to work in entertainment just keeps getting harder and harder. Do it for fun and then get a job with some kind of security that still gives you a sense of accomplishment.

As for me? Sad to say, I can't imagine doing anything else with my life.

Rena Strober *began her career on Broadway in* Les Miserables *and spent a decade singing on stages both in NYC and around the world. She now lives in Los Angeles where she has appeared on popular TV shows such as* Veep *and* Shameless *and recurs on Disney Channel's* Liv & Maddie. *Rena also voices dozens of cartoon and video game characters and has sung on animated films such as* SpongeBob SquarePants *and* Sausage Party. *When Rena isn't working on TV, she teaches voice at the Academy of Music for the Blind where she works with children ages four to eighteen years old.*

IT'S A WHITE INDUSTRY

By Chris Rock

"True Detective? I never heard anyone go, 'Is it going to be Amy Adams or Gabrielle Union?' for that show. I didn't hear one black girl's name on those lists. Not one. Literally everyone in town was up for that part, unless you were black."

I WAS PROBABLY NINETEEN when I first came to Hollywood. Eddie Murphy brought me out to do *Beverly Hills Cop II* and he had a deal at Paramount, so I remember going through the gates of the Paramount lot. He's in a Rolls-Royce, and he's not just a star—he's the biggest star in the world. Don Simpson and Jerry Bruckheimer's office was in the same building as Eddie's office, and they would come to work every day in matching cars. Some days it would be the Porsches, and the next day it would be Ferraris. I was like the kid in *A Bronx Tale*. I got to hang around when the biggest parts of show business were happening. I was only there a couple of weeks, but I remember every day Jeffrey Katzenberg would call Eddie Murphy—I don't even know if Eddie was calling him back—but it was like, "Jeffrey Katzenberg called again." "Janet Jackson just called." "Michael Jackson called." It was *that* crazy. I've still never seen anything like it. I had a small part in the movie, but my dream was bigger than that: I wanted to have a convertible Rolls-Royce driving down Melrose blasting Prince with a fine girl.

Now I'm not Murphy, but I've done fine. And I try to help young black guys coming up because those people took chances on me. Eddie didn't have to put me in *Beverly Hills Cop II*. Keenen Wayans didn't have to put me in *I'm Gonna Git You Sucka*. Arsenio didn't have to let me on his show. I'd do the same for a young white guy, but here's the difference: Someone's going to help the white guy. Multiple people will. The people whom I've tried to help, I'm not sure anybody was going to help them.

And I have a decent batting average. I still remember people thinking I was crazy for hiring Wanda Sykes on my old HBO show. I recommended J. B. Smoove for *Saturday Night Live*, and I helped Leslie Jones get on that show. She's about as funny as a human being can be, but she didn't go to Second City, she doesn't do stand-up at The Cellar, and she's not in with Judd Apatow, so how the hell was she ever going to get through unless somebody like me says to Lorne Michaels, "Hey, look at this person"? I saw her at a comedy club four or five years ago, and I wrote her name down in my phone. I probably called four managers—the biggest managers in comedy—to manage her, and all of them said no. They didn't get it. They didn't get it until Lorne said yes a few years later, and then it was too late.

Some of these younger black guys just want me to see their act. Some come to me for advice. They want to know about agents and managers and the business; this kind of deal and that kind of deal; dealing with the media and dealing with family; money crap and where they should live. It's big brother shit, and they ask because there aren't that many black people to turn to. Who do you hire? Where's the big black PR agency? Where are the big black agents? Where's the big black film producer? That's why I've been all over Steve McQueen. I put a microchip in Steve's pocket and track him like an Uber driver. Steve thinks we keep bumping into each other by accident. "Hey, Steve, my man!" I don't care if I have to play a whip, I'm going to be in a Steve McQueen movie. But I digress.

It's a white industry. Just as the NBA is a black industry. I'm not even saying it's a bad thing. It just is. And the black people they do hire tend to be the same person. That person tends to be female, and that person tends to be Ivy League. And there's nothing wrong with that. As a matter of fact, that's what I want for my daughters. But something tells me that the lives my privileged daughters are leading right now might not make them the best candidates to run the black division of anything. And the person who runs the black division of a studio should probably have worked with black people at some point in their life. Clint Culpepper [a white studio chief who specializes in black movies] did a good job at Screen Gems because he's the kind of guy who would actually go see *Best Man Holiday*. But how many black men have you met working in Hollywood? They don't really hire black men. A black man with bass in his voice and maybe a little hint of facial hair? Not going to happen. It is what it is. I'm a guy who's accepted it all.

We cut it out in *Top Five*, but there had been a scene where Kevin Hart, who plays my character's agent, is in his office talking to me, and he finds out that "Zoolander" (Ben Stiller) is down the hall and he's mad because none of the agents called him. He's the only black agent at the agency, and there was a line in the movie like, "I'm the only black agent here. They never invite me to anything, and these people are liberals. This isn't the Klan."

But forget whether Hollywood is black enough. A better question is: Is Hollywood Mexican enough? You're in LA, you've got to *try* not to hire Mexicans. It's the most liberal town in the world, and there's a part of it that's kind of racist—not racist like "F— you, nigger" racist—but just an acceptance that there's a slave state in LA. There's this acceptance that Mexicans are going to take care of white people in LA that doesn't exist anywhere else. I was renting a house in Beverly Park while doing some movie, and I saw a bunch of Mexican people at eight o'clock in the morning in a line driving into Beverly Park like it's General Motors. It's a weird town.

You're telling me no Mexicans are qualified to do anything at a studio? Really? Nothing but mop up? What are the odds that that's true? The odds are, because people are people, that there's probably a Mexican David Geffen mopping up for somebody's company right now. The odds are that there's probably a Mexican who's that smart who's never going to be given a shot. And it's not about being given a shot to green-light a movie because nobody is going to give you that—you've got to take that. The shot is that a Mexican guy or a black guy is qualified to go and give his opinion about how loud the *boings* are in *Dodgeball* or whether it's the right shit sound you hear when Jeff Daniels is on the toilet in *Dumb and Dumber*. It's like, "We only let white people do that." This is a system where only white people can chime in on that. There would be a little naivete to sitting around and going, "Oh, no black person has ever green-lit a movie," but those other jobs? You're kidding me, right? They don't even require education. When you're on the lower levels, they're just about taste, nothing else. And you don't have to go to Harvard to have taste.

Fifteen years ago, I tried to create an equivalent to *The Harvard Lampoon* at Howard University, to give young black comedy writers the same opportunity that white comedy writers have. I wish we could've made it work. The reason it worked at Harvard and not at Howard is that the kids at Howard need money. It's that simple. Kids at Harvard come from money—even the broke ones come from money. They can afford to work at a newspaper and make no money. The kids at Howard are like, "Dude, I love comedy, but I've got f—ing tuition that I've got to pay here." But that was fifteen years ago; it might be easier to do it now because of the Internet. I don't know.

I really don't think there's any difference between what black audiences find funny and what white audiences find funny, but everyone likes to see themselves onscreen, so there are some instances where there's a black audience laughing at something that a white audience wouldn't laugh at because the black audience is really just happy to see itself. Things that would be problems in a world where there were a lot of black movies get overlooked. The same thing happened with those *Sex and the City* movies. You don't really see that level of female movie that often, so women were like, "We're only going to get this every whatever, so f— you, f— the reviews, we're going, we like it."

And you should at least be able to count on your people, and then it grows from there. If someone's people don't love them, that's a problem. No one crosses over without a base. But if we're going to just be honest and count dollars and seats and not look at skin color, Kevin Hart is the biggest comedian in the world. If Kevin Hart is playing forty thousand seats in a night and Jon Stewart is playing three thousand, the fact that Jon Stewart's three thousand are white means Kevin has to cross over? That makes no sense. If anybody needs to cross over, it's the guy who's selling three thousand seats.

But here's one thing I've noticed in the last five to seven years, and I didn't think I'd live to see this day. There used to be black film and Eddie Murphy, and the two had nothing to do with each other. Literally nothing. And in the world of black film, everything was judged on a relative basis—almost the same curve that indie films get judged on. It was, "Hey, *House Party* made a lot of money relative to its budget," or "Oh, we only paid $7 million for *New Jack City* and it made $50 million." Now, not only are black movies making money, they're expected to make money—and they're expected to make money on the same scale as everything else.

I think they've been better in the last few years, too—a little more daring, a little funnier. But look, most movies suck. Absolutely suck. They just do. Most TV shows suck. Most books suck. If most things were good, I'd make fifteen dollars an hour. I don't live the way I live because most things are even remotely good. But when you have a system where you probably only see three African American–led movies a year, they're going to be judged more harshly, and you're really rooting for them to be a little better than the 140 movies starring white people every year.

The best ones are made outside of the studio system because they're not made with that many white people—maybe one or two, but not a whole system of white people. I couldn't have made *Top Five* at a studio. First of all, no one's going to make a movie with a premise so little and artsy: a star putting out a movie and getting interviewed by a woman from *The New York Times*. I would have had to have three two-hour meetings explaining that black people also read *The New York Times*. A studio would've made it like *Malibu's Most Wanted*. And never in a million years would they have allowed a scene where the rich guy comes back to the projects and actually gets along with everybody. No way. In most black movies—and in most black TV shows and even in most black plays—anyone with money or an education is evil, even movies made by black directors. They have to be saved by the poor people. This goes back to *Good Times* and *What's Happening!*

Now, when it comes to casting, Hollywood either decides to cast a black guy or doesn't. We're never on the "short list." We're never "in the mix." When there's a hot part in town and the guys are reading for it, that's just what happens. It was never like, "Is it going to be Ryan Gosling or Chiwetel Ejiofor for *Fifty Shades of Gray*?" And you know, black people f—, too. White women actually want to f— black guys, sometimes more than white guys. More women want to f— Tyrese Gibson than Jamie Dornan, and it's not even close. It's not a contest. Even Jamie would go, "Okay, you got it."

Or how about *True Detective*? I never heard anyone go, "Is it going to be Amy Adams or Gabrielle Union?" for that show. I didn't hear one black girl's name on those lists. Not one. Literally everyone in town was up for that part, unless you were black. And I haven't read the script, but something tells me if Gabrielle Union were Colin Farrell's wife, it wouldn't change a thing. And there are almost no black women in film. You can go to whole movies and not see one black woman. They'll throw a black guy a bone. Okay, here's a black guy. But is there a single black woman in *Interstellar*? Or *Gone Girl*? *Birdman*? *The Purge*? *Neighbors*? I'm not sure there are. I don't remember them. I go to the movies almost every week, and I can go a month and not see a black woman having an actual speaking part in a movie. That's the truth.

But there's been progress. On *Saturday Night Live*, we did a sketch where I was Sasheer Zamata's dad and she had an Internet show. Twenty years ago when I was on *Saturday Night Live*, anything with black people on the show had to deal with race, and that sketch we did didn't have anything to do with race. That was the beauty: the sketch is funny because it's funny, and that's the progress. And there are black guys who are making it: Whatever Kevin Hart wants to do right now, he can do; I think Chiwetel is a really respected actor who is getting a lot of great shots just because he's really good; if Steve McQueen wants to direct a Marvel movie, they would salivate to get him. Change just takes time. The Triborough Bridge has been the Robert F. Kennedy Bridge for almost twenty years now, but we still call it the Triborough Bridge. That's how long it takes shit to change. We're not going to be calling it the Robert F. Kennedy Bridge for another ten, fifteen years. People will have to die for it to actually be the Robert F. Kennedy Bridge.

Chris Rock *is a comedian, actor, writer, producer, and director. After starting out as a stand-up comedian, Rock became a cast member of* Saturday Night Live *and went on to star in* Down to Earth, Head of State, *the* Madagascar *film series,* Grown Ups, Grown Ups 2, Top Five, *and a series of acclaimed comedy specials for HBO. He developed, wrote, and narrated the sitcom* Everybody Hates Chris *(2005–2009), which was based on his early life.*

SASSY FRIEND #1

By Gabrielle Union

"How we gauge what success is supposed to look like is different for white actors than it is for black actors."

HOLLYWOOD IS EXTREMELY SEGREGATED. The whole idea of Black Hollywood, Latino Hollywood—it's very real. And it all depends on who is with you in the audition rooms as you are coming up. Because you are generally auditioning with people who look like you, over and over again, simply because of how roles are described. When it got down to the wire for the role of "Sassy Friend #1," these were the people I saw. That's how I got to know Zoe Saldana, Kerry Washington, Essence Atkins, Robinne Lee, Sanaa Lathan and all the Reginas. Sassy Friend #1 was a black girl between x and y age, and that meant a very shallow casting pool. When it came time to cast a family, I would meet an array of actors who all looked like me. Sitting in those rooms for hours at a time, multiple times a week, you get to know people.

As you all start to rise, it's the same people, who are now deemed the "it folk," who you sit in better rooms with. And those people become your community; they know the struggle you went through, because they went through it, too. And the rooms pretty much stay that way, no matter how high you rise, because for the most part Hollywood doesn't really subscribe to colorblind casting. What Lin-Manuel Miranda did with *Hamilton* is literally unheard of. We black actors meet in the room into which we are invited, but we are often barred from, to steal from Lin, *the room where it happens.* The spaces where deals get made and ideas get traded. Half the time you get picked to do something in Hollywood, it's because someone cosigned for you. "Oh yeah, she's talented, but more important, she's cool," someone with more pull than you will say, "I hung out with her this one time."

But how do you hang when you're not at the same parties? The biggest award show parties come with very rare invites, and the brown people you see there are the same brown people that have been starring in things forever. Unless you spend at least five grand a month on a power publicist to help land a spot, it's not gonna just "happen." Black actresses are rarely deemed the ingénues, or even the up-and-comers. So your work or even a spark of public interest isn't a guarantee. But let's say you make it into the room, whether through pay-to-play or luck. You're in. You got the golden ticket.

So let's go in together. First off, the light is amazing, but you're too wired from the Red Carpet to do anything but rush to find the closest drink. Those Red Carpet appearances are timed to the second, so that there won't be a big collision of big stars. Performers are scheduled and served up like courses at a meal. If your entrance is set for eight thirty and your car gets there at eight? Circle the block, bitch, because someone more important than you has a better call time. And unfortunately, if you have a late call time, a lot of people will have left the party by the time you cross that threshold. That feeling though, when this wall of cameras fires at you and you hear the machine-gun rat-a-tat of clicks, is exhilarating. Your every move creates a new wave of shots.

Once inside, you're just another beautiful person in this beautifully lit room full of writers, producers, directors, and studio heads. Yes, this is a great chance to network and get to know people, but if you are one of only a sprinkling of black folks in the room, how does that even happen? Just because you're there doesn't mean anyone's gonna talk to you—trust me. You feel like an interloper, and you go for the familiar. Because you know who is for sure going to talk with you? The other brown people.

Here's the thing about the #OscarsSoWhite discussion. Hollywood films are so white because their art happens in a vacuum. It is made by white filmmakers, with white actors, for imagined white audiences. No one even thinks of remedying the issue through communal partying. Inviting one black actor to the party isn't enough—sorry, folks. We all know you can create even better art by truly being inclusive, but you're never going to get inclusive in your work if you can't figure out how to get inclusive in your social life. If you're an actor of color and you've never had the chance to hang out with somebody and show them you're talented and fun and enlightened and deeper than what you can submit on a résumé, you never have the opportunities to be included. Prince created those opportunities just by throwing a better party. When he included you, you literally found yourself in the bathroom line with some of the world's biggest names in entertainment. How we gauge what success is supposed to look like is different for white actors than it is for black actors. And I am aware that half my résumé looks like crumbs to white actors.

The films *Deliver Us From Eva* and *Two Can Play That Game*—these are hood classics, if not cult classics like *Bring It On*. A lot of people appreciate these films, but because there aren't any white people in them, they get marginalized and put on a separate shelf. They are underappreciated, but they never lost money. And I will continue to do these movies—the ones I call FUBU, For Us By Us—because I love them and I am grateful for them.

I made lifelong friends on the sets of these films. The black Hollywood community is so small that we all came up together and created opportunities for each other. These movies set the stage for twenty-plus years of careers. It's a testament to the community that we, over the years, have always looked out for each other and pitched each other for jobs. I am incredibly grateful for that love we have for one another and the mutual respect of talent that we bring to the table. None of us benefit from tearing each other down. There aren't enough of us. We need each other to lean on.

Gabrielle Union *has starred or appeared in over eighty films and television shows, among them* Bring It On, Top Five, Being Mary Jane, *and* Breaking In.

FIVE

THE SHOOT

"Location, location, location," the barometer for real estate prices…and the gateway to memorable Hollywood experiences.

IN THESE TALES FROM *the set: Lowly DGA trainee and fallen Orthodox Jew* **Herb Adelman** *is charged with teaching Gene Wilder how to act more Jewish on* The Frisco Kid. *Director* **John McNaughton** (Henry: Portrait of a Serial Killer*) shows us the Peter Principle in action during the filming of his second movie,* The Borrower. **Rocky Lang** *details the troubled relationship between Dustin Hoffman and director Sydney Pollack during the filming of* Tootsie. *And documentary filmmaker* **Maria Berry** *recounts a trip to Gaza, her assignment being to interview the cofounder of Hamas.*

THE YESHIVA GOFER

By Herb Adelman

*"I was caught between an expectant movie star and my Orthodox Jewish
father who never went to the movies, had no idea who the man was, and
might not have cared even if he did know."*

OBSERVING THE PIOUS RITUALS of Orthodox Judaism as
training for Hollywood success is tantamount to flipping
burgers in the hope of becoming a brain surgeon. The pathways
just don't line up. Yet for me, the worlds of *davening* (praying)
and moviemaking were destined to collide in a perfect storm,
affecting my young life in ways I could never have imagined. How
did an Orthodox Jewish boy from Brooklyn become the DGA
trainee and location religious advisor on the multimillion-dollar
Western, *The Frisco Kid*?

Naturally, by way of Bogotá, Colombia. Yes, it was a circuitous route…

I grew up in a one-bedroom apartment in the Flatbush
section of Brooklyn, New York, sharing the living room with my
educationally challenged, schizophrenic older brother. I prayed
every day and went to synagogue Friday, Saturday, and Sunday
nights. I was kosher and never ate in a non-kosher restaurant.
I went to Yeshiva Rambam elementary school and Yeshiva
University High School for Boys in Brooklyn, and flunked out of
the Architecture School at Pratt Institute where I had a New York

State Regents scholarship...and lost the scholarship. That was my early education.

Luckily, I got hired by an architectural firm in Manhattan where, during the day, I worked on the lighting system for the main terminal at the new Dulles International Airport (designed by Eero Saarinen). At night I attended classes at Brooklyn College. After a year, I was accepted into the day school.

As happy as I was to be back in college, like many young people trying to figure out their lives, I found myself adrift. Finally, I discovered the Radio and Television Department, which was a part of the Speech and Theater Department at Brooklyn College. Did I want to be a film director in Hollywood or a set designer on Broadway? I didn't know for sure, but I was interested enough to pursue the field.

Upon graduating, I won a teaching fellowship for graduate work in the Radio and Television Department and went on for a master's degree in...who knows what? It was the sixties.

One of my professors turned out to be a working Broadway set designer and asked me to assist him while I was in school. In addition to the Broadway tasks, I helped design and oversee the installation of decorations for the Golden Trumpet Ball, an annual gala supporting the Boston Symphony. I suddenly found myself amongst the Cabots, the Lodges, and the Saltonstalls—the elite families of Boston. Not bad for a kosher kid from Brooklyn.

At some point during my graduate work, one of my other college professors was recruited by the Peace Corps to head the Educational Television Project in Colombia. He asked if I would be interested in joining him. If the world of Cabots and Lodges and Saltonsalls was foreign to an Orthodox, kosher, Jewish kid from Brooklyn, how was he supposed to live in Bogotá, Colombia?

What would his Orthodox, kosher, Jewish parents think? Would they even allow it?

They quickly realized that their alternative was much worse—sending their son off to the Vietnam War. From my point of view, the opportunity to serve in John F. Kennedy's Peace Corps now seemed like a godsend (or "G-dsend," as the Orthodox write). I was beyond excited. Like many of my generation, I'd been inspired by Kennedy's inaugural address when he said, "Ask not what your country can do for you, ask what you can do for your country." The words had been ingrained in me for five years, and now I had the opportunity to actually act on them.

By September 1966, I was in the Colombian Educational Television station in Bogotá, Colombia, supervising Peace Corps volunteers and training Colombian workers...while living in an apartment with the only kosher butcher in Colombia. Suddenly, on June 5, 1967, my pro bono television career was interrupted by the news that Israel had been invaded by Egypt, Saudi Arabia, Jordan, Syria, and Lebanon. A lifelong supporter of the Jewish State, I (along with fellow volunteer, Bob) asked the Peace Corps to release me so I would be free to help with the war effort. They informed us that Americans were now banned from travel to the Middle East. Two days later, however, we got a call to help protect the Jewish community of Bogotá from the threat of possible anti-Semitic attacks. Bob and I, the two Peace Corps volunteers, were offered our choice of guns or clubs. We took the clubs and holed up with thirty Colombian Jews in a townhouse that served as the Israeli embassy. Thankfully, there turned out to be no disturbances on the streets of Bogota, but inside the embassy, it was chaos—massive quantities of pent-up testosterone with no outlets except smoking, drinking, playing cards, listening to the latest news on shortwave radios, and making a colossal mess. Bob and I wound up cleaning up the place and answering phones, taking multiple calls from Colombian Air Force pilots who wanted to volunteer for the State of Israel. By the next morning, Bob and I were the only ones left of the "security detail" to turn the embassy over to an arriving Israeli diplomat. He thanked us, in Hebrew, for our service.

Yes, this is a *very* circuitous route to *The Frisco Kid*. But we're getting there…

I finished my two years in the Peace Corps in July 1968 and spent roughly three months traveling around South America with three women…mostly by land and water.

Suddenly, the exotic adventures were over. I was back in the one-bedroom apartment in Brooklyn, sharing the living room with my older brother. Eventually I got a job at an advertising agency in Manhattan. I wasn't happy—neither with my living situation nor with working as an assistant on commercials that advertised products and values I considered to be bullshit.

So, I left New York to work as a copywriter at an advertising agency in Washington, DC. After a year, I quit that job to take a three-week temporary gig as a contractor in Lyndon Johnson's War on Poverty—which would last five years.

By 1973, I had gone two years without a vacation when opportunity knocked. My next-door neighbor, who worked at Arena Stage, told me about a movie that was coming to Washington for a couple of weeks and needed crew. I applied and got a job as the production assistant to the prop master. I took two weeks' vacation and on that project I learned about the DGA Second Assistant Director Training Program.

Then, in 1977, at the ripe old age of thirty-five—and after four years of trying—I was accepted into the Directors Guild of America Second Assistant Director Training Program and moved from Washington, DC to Los Angeles. Basically, the DGA program trained you to be a gofer with very significant responsibilities. One screw-up could cost a movie production tens of thousands of dollars.

My first assignment was on the Irwin Allen disaster movie, *The Swarm,* where I had the opportunity to work with such legends as Michael Caine, Henry Fonda, Olivia de Havilland, Patty Duke, and Richard Widmark, among others. This was a big movie, filled with extras, stunts, special effects, and millions of live bees. It was great training for a future assistant director.

The shoot ended in November, and thankfully I was immediately assigned to another feature film, *American Hot Wax.* It was loosely based on the story of Alan Freed, the radio disk jockey who popularized American rock 'n' roll and got caught up in the payola scandal of the early 1960s. This movie gave me the experience of working with thousands of extras, filming many scenes with music, hanging out with up-and-coming comedian Jay Leno, and working with such rock 'n' roll legends as Chuck Berry and Jerry Lee Lewis.

After finishing *American Hot Wax* and another, less memorable project, I got the call to interview for a feature film called *The Frisco Kid.*

I drove to Warner Bros. to meet with Mel Dellar, who was the first assistant director on the film and would become my principal mentor in the business. I also interviewed with the second assistant director, Peter Bergquist, who eventually would become a lifelong friend.

The Frisco Kid starred Gene Wilder and Harrison Ford. It was about a Polish rabbi traveling from Poland to San Francisco in the 1880s who, on the way, happens to hook up with a bank robber. Gene Wilder had starred in *Blazing Saddles, Young Frankenstein,* and *Silver Streak*—and Harrison Ford had just starred in *Star Wars*. You can guess who played which role. These were the biggest movie actors I had ever worked with but I wasn't particularly starstruck. My excitement had to do with being employed and accumulating the four hundred days needed to graduate from the training program. Then I would be able to work as a union second assistant director and get paid a decent salary with benefits.

While *The Swarm* and *American Hot Wax* were shot on stage and at local locations in and around Los Angeles, *The Frisco Kid* was to be filmed at many distant locations in addition to the Western streets and stages at Warner Bros. and the MGM Studios in Culver City. We'd be shooting outside of Greely, Colorado, on the beaches north of Santa Barbara, and at several spots in southern Arizona. This would give me much needed experience in location production and add significantly to my résumé.

Although *The Frisco Kid* had a rabbi as a religious advisor in Los Angeles, the film's budget couldn't accommodate rabbinical oversight on location. It seemed that in Greely, Colorado, the cast and director would be left to their own devices.

On one of the first days in Colorado, Gene had to put on *tefillin*. *Tefillin*, or phylacteries, are a set of two small black leather boxes containing scrolls of parchment inscribed with verses from the bible, which are worn by observant Jews on their foreheads and left arms during weekday morning prayers. One of the leather boxes is placed on the upper left arm, and a strap from the box is wrapped around the arm seven times down to the hand, and in a very specific way around the hand and fingers. The head *tefillin* is placed above the forehead with two more black straps hanging down the front. The Bible commands that they should be worn to serve as a "sign" and "remembrance" that God brought the Children of Israel out of Egypt.

But we were not in Israel now…or Los Angeles. We were in the rural outskirts of Greely, Colorado, where Vic Petrotta, the great second-generation prop master of Italian heritage, was the keeper of the *tefillin*. Our director, the primarily action-oriented Robert Aldrich, who was related to the Rockefeller family, knew as much about phylacteries as I knew about performing a kidney transplant. And finally our star, Gene Wilder, born Jerome Silberman to Russian Jewish immigrants, had not a clue what to do with those strange black leather boxes and straps. (Most non-Orthodox don't.) *If only there were an observant Jewish crew member….*

Enter Herb Adelman, the fallen Orthodox Jew and now agnostic DGA trainee, who steps in and tries to save the day. From the time of my *Bar Mitzvah* until I went off to the Peace Corps, I had strapped on the *tefillin* every day from Sunday to Friday as part of my daily prayers. Saturdays were exempt—a day of rest. Since the Peace Corps, I hadn't been anywhere near them.

At the risk of comparing a solemn religious ritual to riding a bike, it comes back. Without hesitating, I offered my expertise. Vic, Gene, Bob, the director, and probably the entire crew, were dumbfounded to learn that their lowly DGA trainee knew exactly what to do with those strange black boxes and straps, enabling the production to continue on schedule and budget. From that point forward, in addition to all my other gofer responsibilities, I became the movie's de facto religious advisor on all location shoots, with, of course, no further compensation or screen credit. So goes the movie industry.

The drill was that I would regularly be summoned to Gene's motor home or the set to advise the star on one Jewish detail or another. Many times it would be about Hebrew pronunciation. Mostly, Gene listened and spoke the words the way I advised. For the times Gene didn't follow my advice and mispronounced the Hebrew words, I take no responsibility.

One day, somewhere in Colorado, I was informed that Gene needed to see me immediately in his motor home. I knocked on the door and the star opened it.

"Thanks for coming, Herb. You know the scene where I have to chase a prairie hen?"

"Sure."

"Can you give me some curse words in Yiddish?"

"I don't know Yiddish."

"What do you mean you don't know Yiddish?"

"I never learned it. I know Hebrew…but very little Yiddish. But I'll tell you what. I'll call my dad. He speaks it fluently."

"That would be wonderful."

I grab the phone and call New York. The phone rings and my mother picks up. "Hey, Mom. How are you?"

"I'm fine. So, why don't you call more?"

"Well, because I'm somewhere in the middle of Colorado and it's not easy to get to a phone."

"So what's that you're calling on now?"

I'm with the star of a multimillion-dollar movie. My mother is wasting his valuable time on guilt-tripping me. This can't go on.

"Listen, is Dad there?"

"Hold on. Sruel? It's Chaim. He wants to talk to you….I don't know why. He just wants to talk to you….So, just come to the phone and you ask him! Okay?"

There's a *pause…then…*

"Chaim?"

"Hey, Dad, how are you?"

"So, why don't you call more?"

"Well, I'm on this movie in the middle of Colorado and I work long hours and it's not easy to get to a phone."

"So? From now on try harder."

"I will. But listen. I'm working on this movie about a rabbi who's played by Gene Wilder and he wants to learn some curse words in Yiddish and I thought you could help."

"Gene who?"

I was caught between an expectant movie star and my Orthodox Jewish father who never went to the movies, had no idea who the man was, and might not have cared even if he did know. Plus, how was I supposed to explain to my father who a famous actor was with the actor standing right there? Think fast, Herb.

"You know, Dad, he did *Blazing Saddles*...and *Young Frankenstein*...and *Silver Streak*..."

"Silver who?"

I just had to move on.

"Listen, Dad, this is a movie about an Orthodox Polish rabbi and in the movie he's hungry and chasing a prairie hen to eat and he's frustrated and...Gene, the actor, thinks it might be good if he uses some Yiddish curse words to show his frustration...."

"But you know I don't use those kinds of words."

"I know, Dad. But let's just say you were in that kind of frustrating situation, and things got to you, what would you say... in Yiddish?"

"I told you I don't talk like that."

"I know, Dad. I know."

I'm dying. I've got to pull something out of my hat.

"How about this, Dad? What if it were someone else? Say, that furrier down the street you're not crazy about. If he started cursing, what would *he* say in Yiddish?"

There's a very long pause...finally...

"Okay, here's what I would say...."

And he proceeds to give me several phrases that I don't understand, but copy down phonetically.

"That's great! Thanks, Dad. I'll try to call more often. I promise."
And off we went to shoot the scene.

It was an ironic twist. After having left the Orthodoxy, presumably forever, to travel from Brooklyn to Bogotá to Washington to Los Angeles, with many stops in between, I needed to make a virtual pilgrimage to my religious roots in order for a Hollywood dream to come true. Circuitous? Maybe. Or perhaps it was *bashert*—the profound Yiddish word denoting an outcome that was meant to be. It certainly seems that way now.

If you search YouTube, you can watch the scene that takes place somewhere in the wilds of 1880s America, in which Gene Wilder plays a Polish Orthodox rabbi cursing a prairie hen in Yiddish. The words were written by my father, who didn't get a screen credit, a writer's fee, or any residuals. Nevertheless, and even though he had agreed to the task reluctantly, the memory of my father getting to participate in my work remains one of the fondest of my career.

(*EDITORS NOTE:* When I went to view the *Frisco Kid* prairie hen scene on YouTube, the first video that came up turned out to be dubbed in Italian. It somehow seemed fitting that Sruel Adelman's unlikely, impromptu leap into off-color Yiddish screenwriting had reached an even bigger audience than he, or his son, might have ever imagined.)

Herb Adelman *moved to Los Angeles after serving two years in the Peace Corps in Colombia and working in Washington, DC on federal poverty programs. He was first assistant director on the TV series* Hill Street Blues *and the feature films* Hoosiers *and* No Way Out. *He was the unit production manager and/or coproducer on the TV series* In the Heat of the Night, Sabrina the Teenage Witch, *and the first season of* Criminal Minds. *In 2006 he was awarded the Frank Capra Achievement Award by the Directors Guild of America for his career achievement and service to the Guild.*

MAKING *THE BORROWER*

By John McNaughton

"A script about a monster from outer space, tearing the heads off humans and wearing them as its own, was not considered an A-list project by the Hollywood community."

O N A DISTANT PLANET inhabited by superintelligent giant insects, an arch-criminal is sentenced to the worst punishment known to its kind. The creature is genetically modified into human form and sent to earth. Two hunters, a man and his son, witness the alien's arrival. When the hunters approach, the alien's transformation fails and its head explodes! Believing the creature will bring him riches and fame, the father means to take possession of the corpse when it rises and tears the father's head off, assimilates it, and is reborn as The Borrower.

After directing *Henry: Portrait of a Serial Killer*, I got an agent. Scripts were sent to me; lots of them. Your first success will brand you in Hollywood. If it's a love story, they'll send you more love stories. If it's horror, they'll send you horror. Bad horror. So I waited. Then one day I got a script that interested me, *The Borrower*. I always look for something I haven't seen before and this one fit the bill. A monster walks the earth, tearing the heads off human beings. It seemed to me a metaphor for what actors do—take the heads of other human beings and inhabit their lives. I agreed to direct. Little did I know…

I was flown to LA and walked straight into a meeting with Donald Kushner and Peter Locke, whose company, Kushner-Locke, was producing the film. They gave me a car, an apartment in Westwood Village, and an office in a high-rise on Wilshire Blvd. After weeks of working on the script and interviewing numerous special effects practitioners, my benefactors decided to defer production and shoot a special effects test to determine if the project was feasible at the proposed budget.

They hired a production manager to produce the shoot. His one credit was a film called *Surf Nazis Must Die*. He scheduled three big special FX scenes to be shot in one twelve-hour day.

We shot the scenes against a painted backdrop that looked like shit. The FX crew had not completed the various prosthetics, props and gags necessary for the scenes and were cobbling them together as we shot. The cinematographer's main claim to fame was shooting lens tests for Panavision, and his primary interest on this day was shooting focus and color charts and taking endless meter readings off the pathetic backdrop. The only saving grace was having cast Tom Towles (who'd played Otis in *Henry*) in the lead, the lead being the only actor on set that day.

After twenty-six hours, we stopped. The day was a complete disaster. Certainly one of the worst of my life. I went home and slept for a few hours and late that afternoon, went to a projection room to see what we'd wrought. My only memory of the screening is Peter Locke talking fast and proposing to put up an additional $20,000 for some kind of whiz-bang effects tricks to somehow save what we'd just seen. Personally, I was not hopeful and returned to my apartment in disgrace and most likely got drunk. The next day at the office, I was informed that they had decided not to waste the additional $20,000 on effects and was asked to turn over the keys to my apartment and car. *The Borrower* was shut down. I had a plane ticket back to Chicago but no place to stay when I got there. I prevailed upon Steve Jones, the producer of *Henry*, and he offered his couch. It was almost Christmas.

Like its headless namesake from outer space, *The Borrower* refused to die. After my return to Chicago, I got a call. Another company, Atlantic Releasing, was interested in resurrecting *The Borrower*.

Enter William Tennant. William "Bill" Tennant was the head of production at Atlantic Releasing. He was at one time an agent representing, among others, Stanley Kubrick, Roman Polanski, and Sharon Tate. He was called off the tennis court one morning by the police and asked to identify the body of Ms. Tate at the infamous house on Cielo Drive where she was murdered by the Manson Family. He eventually had a fall from grace and was found "sleeping in a doorway on Ventura Boulevard," wrote Peter Bart in a 1993 article for *Variety*.[1]

But now he was back in the game and my new boss. We talked about the film and agreed the script needed work. I suggested Richard Fire, cowriter of *Henry*, to rewrite the script. Bill signed off and soon Richard and I were on a plane to LA. We were booked into rooms at the Chateau Marmont, which became my LA base for the next few years. After we were settled, Richard and I met Bill Tennant at a French restaurant nearby on Sunset. I don't really remember what was said at lunch, but I do remember that as we walked back to the hotel, Richard and I said nothing until we parted with Bill. Then, once he was out of earshot, we looked at each other and said in unison, "It was the devil." Why we would both have the identical thought simultaneously, especially when neither of us was particularly religious or spent much time thinking about the devil, tells you a lot about Bill Tennant.

---

1   *Peter Bart: Exec Comes Full Circle after Descent into Despair, (*Variety*, 2/7/93).

It was agreed that we would shoot the film in Chicago. Richard and I flew back to work on the script. Steve Jones was hired as producer. Frank Coronado also came on board to draw storyboards and we started the search for cast and crew.

Eventually, Bill Tennant came to Chicago to survey our progress and soon decided to move the production back to LA, where he and Atlantic could keep a closer eye on us. When I look at the original storyboards and see all the great Chicago locations and details Frank drew, it breaks my heart knowing how cool the picture would have been had we shot in Chicago. Yet, with time I've come to appreciate the LA setting, which, in the end, worked quite well. As my mother used to say, "everything happens for a reason."

So back to the Chateau Marmont and a cozy little cottage all my own…. We set up offices in the building Atlantic occupied on Sunset Blvd.—a converted motel about a block west of Chateau Marmont, which allowed me to walk to work. A line producer was hired, Steve Jones came to LA and we began to cast and hire a crew.

A script about a monster from outer space, tearing the heads off humans and wearing them as its own, was not considered an A-list project by the Hollywood community.

Our casting director made it known that she was slumming and doing us a big favor and not to set our sights too high, thereby embarrassing her around town. Despite her lack of enthusiasm, we managed to put together a very cool cast…for the most part.

What was becoming clear to me was that although Steve Jones, a small core of friends and collaborators, and I believed we were going to make an original and outrageous film with a lot of tongue-in-cheek humor, the town thought otherwise.

We interviewed cinematographers who all submitted sample reels. All save one, who didn't bother and behaved as if he already had the job. We showed him the door and hired Julio Macat who would do a great job for us until Bill Tennant fired him. But I'm getting ahead of myself…

The cast was coming together. Tom Towles was hired to play the hunter who finds the monster, and Bentley Mitchum, grandson of Robert, was cast as his son. Antonio Fargas, aka Huggy Bear from *Starsky and Hutch*, was cast as Julius, the homeless guy who is The Borrower's second victim. Mädchen Amick, would play the teenager, Megan. Tony Amendola—Dr. Cheever. Neil Giuntoli—Scully. Tamara Clatterbuck—Officer Chodiss. For the two leads, we chose Rae Dawn Chong as Detective Diana Pierce and Don Gordon as her partner, Detective Charles Krieger. Gordon, a veteran actor whom I'd seen in a hundred films and TV shows growing up, was best known for playing Steve McQueen's partner, Delgado, in *Bullitt*. Rae Dawn Chong, daughter of Tommy Chong, had made a splash in *Commando* with Arnold Schwarzenegger and *The Color Purple*, directed by Steven Spielberg.

Immediately, Rae Dawn Chong wanted script changes and Richard Fire and I were dispatched to her home in Upstate New York to make them. Richard and I had come to refer to her character, Diana Pierce, as Dirty Harriet. She was a woman of few words and much action. She kicked ass and took names while her partner, Krieger, the older, wiser cop, had all the funny lines. In our first meeting, Ms. Chong didn't mince words. She resented the fact that Krieger got all those good lines and she wanted them. All we had to do was give his character's lines to her and the script would be greatly improved in her opinion, even though they were completely out of character for Diana Pierce. So that's what we did. Unfortunately, no one bothered to send Don Gordon the revised script. He came to the first rehearsal, was handed the new script and I watched as he skimmed the pages, and slowly realized what had happened. As he heard her read what had formerly been his dialogue, he finally reached critical mass and exploded. About ten minutes into our first rehearsal, they were up and screaming obscenities at each other. I calmed them down and got them to read again, but before long they were back to shouting insults at each other, which set the tone of their relationship for the rest of the film.

At one point, during a lull, Rae Dawn looked up from her script and said, "John, do you realize, the monster is the star?" I certainly did but kept it to myself. One of the things I liked about the script was that the cops never believed there was a monster from outer space running amok. What real cops would? In this case, the cops were clueless, faced with a series of grisly murders but never believing the truth until it was too late.

The first scene we shot was of the homeless guy, Julius, played by Antonio Fargas, pushing his shopping cart along the beach. Antonio was a little edgy at first, not sure what he had gotten himself into, but once he realized there was a core group trying hard to make a good movie, he joined the team and gave a lovely and very funny performance. On my first film, *Henry*, we worked with a crew of between three and five people. Now I had a crew of about sixty-five and had no idea what most of them did. I was to learn the hard way that some of them did very little. There was a parking lot near the beach where the trucks and trailers were parked, but there was only one way in and out. When we finished the scene and were ready to move to the next location, a teamster made a miscalculation and wedged his truck in, blocking the entrance/exit, and we were stuck for two hours until a tow truck pulled him out. Not an auspicious start.

As the production proceeded, two factions formed. On one side, those of us who were trying to make the best film possible; on the other, those who were there to collect a paycheck. One night, we were shooting in Downtown LA. Tom Towles was walking down the street, covered in blood, with a huge gash across his neck, ostensibly where his head had been attached to the Borrower's body. We chose a 400mm telephoto lens to shoot his walk through the crowd of real folks so that the camera would not be seen by the crowd and we would get real reactions from real people. I was standing with the line producer, who turned to me and said, "I hate this kind of filmmaking." I just looked at him and said, "Oh yeah, well I love it." And still love it every time I watch the scene and see the amazing reactions and non-reactions from real people on the street.

For the most part, the actors were great, but my relationship with Rae Dawn Chong was a sore point. An actor needs to open up and let the director in if there is to be a good working relationship, but Rae Dawn never opened up to me, never let me in. It soon became apparent that we just plain didn't like each other and she was not interested in taking my direction. It got so bad that when we were shooting her scenes, my mind would wander, trying to figure out how to cut around her and still have a viable scene. I learned from her that when you go into open conflict with your lead actor, the film is in trouble.

One day, the inevitable happened and she refused to come out of her trailer. I had no idea what to do, at which point Bill Tennant arrived on set and I learned. He walked up to her trailer, knocked on the door, and when she answered, he simply said, "Call your agent, call your attorney, you're in breach of contract," and shut the door. Five minutes later she was on set.

For all the hell we went through on a daily basis, the film was looking very good. Cinematographer Julio Macat and his crew were doing some very innovative work, which, of course, got under the skin of the payday faction who sniped at and undermined Julio as best they could. Thanksgiving fell at the halfway point of our shoot and although we had been behind schedule since the mishap on the first day, we'd worked very hard to catch up and were only half a day behind by Thanksgiving. It was great to have a break, and I was feeling pretty good until Thanksgiving evening. I had gotten together with some old friends for dinner and drinks. At about 8:00 p.m., I got a call from Bill Tennant. He gave me an ultimatum. Either agree to fire Julio and his entire crew or he would shut down the film. If I had it to do over, I would have called his bluff and told him to go ahead and shut it down, resulting in a total loss for Atlantic Releasing, which would make no sense. Eventually, I learned that Bill Tennant had learned a nasty trick from a former mentor, an old school producer who would fire the director of photography on the first week of production and hire someone loyal to himself, thereby taking control away from the director.

So it came to pass that Julio and his crew were fired and I was handed the very guy who showed up for his interview without a sample reel. He was a friend of the line producer, and that's who he intended to work for, not me. With Julio went the entire grip and electric crew and their replacements were not embraced by the rest of the crew, most of whom had grown fond of Julio and his team. From this point on, every day was a battle. The new DP was lazy and recalcitrant. Rae Dawn Chong was uncooperative and unhappy to be in the film at all. One evening, the owner of Atlantic appeared and presented Rae Dawn with a beautiful pin from Cartier, a solid gold panther with a ruby eye, costing $7,000 that we could have sorely used to actually make the film.

The last week of the shoot took place on stage. I remember standing in the middle of the bedroom set with the line producer. I was looking up into the rafters, figuring where to place the camera and how to shoot the scene, and noticed that he was looking at the floor. I realized he was looking at the brand-new rug, imagining how it would look in his house.

Things got really ugly on the last week. No one had been paid. Since we were shooting nights, I got up early one day and drove over to Atlantic's offices to ask why. I pulled into the lot behind the building where there would normally be twenty-five or so cars and it was empty. When I approached the back door, it was open and swinging on its hinges. Inside, the place was cleaned out. Atlantic Releasing had literally disappeared in the middle of the night.

Enter the completion bond company. Since Atlantic Releasing was no more, it was up to the bond company to fund the completion of the film. This is never a happy situation for anyone. The good news was that by allowing us to finish the film in Chicago, we were able to use local contacts and call in favors and finish the film for a good deal less than it would have cost in LA. After we wrapped shooting, producer Steve Jones, editor Elena Maganini, and I packed our bags and headed for LAX, where we had a celebratory drink before our flight departed for home. Elena had a bad feeling and called her assistant, who was responsible for handing the film and sound elements over to FedEx for shipment to Chicago. As it turned out, the line producer had waited until we left for the airport, then cancelled the pickup and tried to seize the film so that he would be in charge of postproduction, thereby extending his employment for a few months. Fortunately, we were able to contact R. P. Sekon, an ally from the production team, who loaded the elements into his own van and delivered them to the airport where they were successfully shipped to Chicago. Victory! We had won the battle if not the war.

Although *The Borrower*'s travails were far from over, I'll save that part of the story for another day. We managed to finish the film in Chicago. That there were no housing and/or living expenses allotted for the director, producer, and editor accounted for a considerable savings, keeping the bond company as happy as could be expected.

On Halloween, a few years ago, the Music Box Theatre in Chicago screened *The Borrower* on LaserDisc (the best "hard copy" format in which it currently exists). I hadn't seen the film in years and was proud of how true it was to our original vision and amazed at the reception it received.

The Borrower is now owned by Warner Bros. and can be found on YouTube Movies. It is offered in the 1:33 TV format, but hopefully, sometime soon, it will be restored and reissued in the original 1:85 format.

Before becoming a filmmaker, **John McNaughton** *worked for Encyclopedia Britannica, Chicago Bridge and Iron, Republic Steel, Pullman Bank, Campbell Mithun Advertising, as a carnival barker, silversmith, sailboat builder, bartender, carpenter, and operator of a laser light show. In 1986, McNaughton directed, cowrote and coproduced his first feature,* Henry: Portrait of a Serial Killer. *Among his many other credits are* Mad Dog and Glory, *starring Robert De Niro, Bill Murray, and Uma Thurman;* Wild Things, *starring Matt Dillon, Kevin Bacon, Bill Murray, Neve Campbell, and Denise Richards; and* Lansky, *written by David Mamet, starring Richard Dreyfuss and Anthony LaPaglia. Most recently he directed* The Harvest, *starring Academy Award nominees Michael Shannon, Samantha Morton, and Peter Fonda. He is currently working with novelist and screenwriter Irvine Welsh (*Trainspotting*) on an adaptation of his book,* The Sex Lives of Siamese Twins, *and re-teaming with Michael Rooker on a film version of Flannery O'Connor's short story, "A Good Man is Hard to Find."*

TOOT TOOT TOOTSIE

By Rocky Lang

"The star and the director were using my documentary to voice their displeasure with the difficulties and disagreements they were having with each other."

D USTIN HOFFMAN AND I stood side by side at the urinals at Columbia Pictures, located on the Warner Bros. lot in Burbank. The actor was not only pissing, he was pissed! Dustin, along with his wife Lisa, and I had just viewed Sydney Pollack's rough cut of the 1982 comedy *Tootsie*, and he hated it. I had seen the cut a day earlier, but Sydney asked me to sit with the film's star while he watched it because Sydney anticipated an explosion and wanted a neutral witness. As Dustin peed, he muttered incoherently, his veins popping out of his neck. He turned to me, nearly spraying my shoes, and said, "Next time we will do a real documentary about the real bullshit that goes on during the making of a movie!"

It was nearly a year earlier when I pitched the idea of documenting the making of *Tootsie* to Sydney, one of my favorite directors. He'd already directed popular screen masterworks such as *The Way We Were*, *Absence of Malice*, and *The Yakuza*. I was twenty-two years old, and with a year at AFI fresh on my résumé, I asked my screenwriter friend Eric Roth to introduce me to Sydney, for whom he was penning a script.

Sydney's second-floor office overlooked the Columbia Pictures parking lot, and the first thing he said when I walked in to see him was, "You know, I asked your dad to fire me off my first television show, *Shotgun Slade*, because I had a horrible case of hemorrhoids." After discussing hemorrhoids, I told Sydney I wanted to do a film that examined the actor-director relationship, and *Tootsie* afforded the perfect canvas for that. Sydney, who had started his career as an actor and had been a student of the legendary acting coach Sandy Meisner at the Neighborhood Playhouse, loved the idea.

We agreed that there would be no secrets and I would have complete access, and so I did…almost. At the time, no one could know that this gender-bending classic-in-the-making would also be one of the most contentious shoots of all time. Strapping in with a $250,000 budget, a nice expense account, a first-class ticket to New York City, and an Eastside apartment on Seventy-Third Street, I was about to begin the ride of my life.

Sydney was staying in a massive and richly appointed apartment at the Sherry-Netherland in Midtown Manhattan. And it was there, as I set up my cameras to document an informal rehearsal, that I first was able to observe him and Dustin together in creative focus. Dustin, in a blue polo shirt, sat at a dining room table running dialogue lines with Sydney. The actor had recently convinced the filmmaker to play the part of George Fields, the agent of Dustin's actor/actress character, Michael Dorsey/Dorothy Michaels, in *Tootsie*. Sydney had resisted acting in any project he was directing, but Dustin sent him flowers and was relentless.

At this rehearsal, I noted how close the director and star seemed to be and had no idea that in a few short weeks they would be at each other's throats, production would stop, and Sydney would threaten to leave the picture.

Tootsie presented a number of challenges. The first was that Dustin had to be convincingly female in order to play Dorothy. Many makeup tests were performed and variously sized denture fittings undertaken, as women's teeth are longer than men's. And of course, there was the complete shaving of Dustin's body hair, which he had to do in a sauna each day. The bigger problems— those of ego and control—were festering below the surface.

Tootsie was originally Dustin's idea, based on watching the transgender tennis player Renée Richards enter the professional women's tennis circuit (the project was initially titled "Shirley"). Richards, formerly Richard Raskind, was an eye doctor from New York who was never successful at the pro level as a man but excelled on the court as a woman. It was a societal norm-shaking theme Dustin wanted to explore.

"Shirley" went through several incarnations with different writers, ultimately becoming *Tootsie*. It centered on a struggling actor, and it became even more important and personal to Dustin because it touched on his early days in the profession. As he told me: "In our salad days, Gene Hackman, Bobby De Niro, and I just wanted to get into a fight because we were so frustrated about not getting the work. It's the frustration of the inability to work, and the inability to generate it for yourself, and you just want to go out and hit somebody." This very frustration would motivate Michael Dorsey to put on the dress to get the work.

Sydney had a different perspective. His premise was that by putting on the dress and experiencing life as a woman, Michael is given the unique opportunity to see himself and his relationships—both personal and career—from a fresh (i.e., opposite sex) viewpoint. While the professional frustrations of acting remain the key plot driver in the film, the story delivers a lot more on the nature of gender roles—as evidenced in the last scene, when Michael says to his soap opera co-star/would-be love interest Julie Nichols (Jessica Lange): "I was a better man with you as a woman…than I ever was with a woman as a man." The thematic tension at play in the script fueled some creative issues between Sydney and Dustin; that, and the fact that when Sydney signed on to direct, Dustin relinquished control of the project.

Leaving my apartment on a crisp day with a perfectly robin's-egg-blue sky, I accompanied Nan Bernstein, the associate producer and production manager on *Tootsie*, via subway to the National Video Center at 460 West Forty-Second Street. This was going to be our main base for the duration of the film. What became clear to me quickly was that the cast members of *Tootsie*, all very talented, had completely different approaches to acting. Dustin and Teri Garr came from a Method background and liked to immerse themselves in character by studying each action, each feeling, and each emotion. Jessica Lange, on the other hand, didn't want to rehearse, didn't want to think about the part, and would just act. So naturally gifted, she had a way of pulling it off. And then there was Bill Murray, an instinctual actor hailing from Chicago's Second City theatre troupe and *Saturday Night Live*, who never read the same line twice; he loved to improvise and did it regularly. Dustin could do anything and, being immersed in character, he could go with it whenever Bill went off script. Other actors had more difficulty when Bill strayed, but it always made things interesting. And I realized how brilliant Sydney was in balancing these actors with different styles and massive egos.

At first, there were the usual difficulties of making a film, but no major problems. Dustin, however, was getting increasingly agitated over the subtle thematic crosscurrents in the script: what the intention and inflection of each line delivery meant, and ultimately what the picture was really about. It was taking longer to shoot scenes as Dustin and Sydney would have longer and longer discussions prior to rolling cameras. Many times, Sydney would shoot a scene both ways so he could placate Dustin—the director knowing he had his own version to use later.

As a neutral presence on the set, I found myself being pulled in two directions by Dustin and Sydney. The star and the director were using my documentary to voice their displeasure about the difficulties and disagreements they were having with each other. Dustin, in particular, seemed to be using the documentary as a way of getting his point on the record so that he would have it if it were needed later. It occurred to me that my footage could be used as an exhibit in potential future arbitration or litigation.

As the crew was preparing to shoot the shower scene, in which Dustin runs around the table trying to get out of the Dorothy makeup and into the Michael character as Teri Garr bangs on the door to come in, people were on edge. Lighting was set, and everyone was in place except Bill Murray, who arrived late.

I approached Sydney and asked if it was okay if I filmed as Bill came through the door. Knowing that he had kept everyone waiting and tensions were high, I anticipated that something would happen. Sydney, keeping his word to me that I would have complete access, agreed but warned me not to get in Bill's face. He told me to shoot with a long lens and stay in the background.

When Bill came through the door, nothing happened. He walked in and went into wardrobe, then came out and shot the scene. My cameras rolled and we got zilch. No drama, no yelling, nothing.

The next day, I was standing with David McGiffert, the assistant director, when Bill strutted across the set, grabbed me by my neck, and pushed me into a wall. His face was two inches from mine and his eyes bulged out. He said he was going to beat the shit out of me for filming him. He pulled his arm back, closed his fist, and then dropped it. He accused me of working for some tabloid TV show, and when I told him Sydney approved me to shoot, he didn't believe me. Bill stormed off and approached Sydney. After about thirty seconds, he dropped his head and slunk back to me, apologizing. No harm, no foul—but I had a great story to tell.

Tensions continued to mount and everyone was filled with expectation. By this time, Sydney and I had developed a friendship and trust; I loved the way he worked and ran a set. To me, he was the consummate director. He understood story, character, the actor's neuroticism, and the technical and visual aspects of filmmaking, plus he had the ability to lead. But the atmosphere was not good, and he knew it. A sort of cold war had developed between him and Dustin.

Sydney confided in me: "We have problems and they are very hard to reconcile. Sometimes we get along, and sometimes not. And when we're not, it's a terrible problem and then we fight like hell with each other, and yell and scream and insult each other. Sometimes it looks really grim."

Sydney was tied up in knots over this and lived on antacids. He told me as I interviewed him for the documentary, "Legally, I have control of the picture, but that's only legally. That doesn't mean that I don't owe him a lot morally, which I do. Besides that, I can't whip him over the head and make him do a scene my way, and when that happens we go into my trailer or his and scream and yell at each other and then we come out and do it my way."

The shit hit the fan on the day that Dustin, in character as Dorothy Michaels, was to reveal himself as Michael Dorsey. The scene called for the appearance that Dorothy was making up an excuse for revealing herself to be a man on live TV. Sydney changed the text the night before the shoot and presented it to Dustin the next morning.

Dustin was furious. He didn't like the changes, especially so late in the game. Dustin accused Sydney of deliberately changing the script to unsettle him as he did the scene. He then pulled me aside and, on camera, again accused Sydney of this.

Sydney, on the other hand, felt adjustments needed to be made for the integrity of the scene. He thought Dustin was being a baby and it was no big deal. I spoke with Lee Gottsegen, Dustin's brother-in-law, who was also the actor's assistant, and he told me Dustin was fed up with everything—that as soon as he got out of the Dorothy character and became Michael, the gloves would come off and heads would roll. Because Dustin was a Method actor, his frustrations would finally be unleashed on Sydney via the chauvinistic character of Michael Dorsey.

But Dustin and Sydney were at an impasse, unable to communicate, and the movie shut down. Mike Ovitz, the Creative Artists Agency mega-agent who represented both men, flew in from the coast. Ovitz, Sydney, and Dustin walked in circles on the set while the crew was released. I stayed and watched this unfold from the TV control room; it was the one time Sydney told me I couldn't film. Sydney wanted out. He had had it. He had already called his friend, Robert Benton, who'd directed Hoffman in *Kramer vs. Kramer* a couple years earlier, and asked him to take over.

Each day of filming cost about $85,000 and two days had gone by without any production. Finally, tempers cooled as Ovitz brokered a peace deal, and the movie went on and was completed without further incident. I never saw Dustin and Sydney close again—and it was sad, because the first time I saw them together at the Sherry-Netherland, they seemed in sync and were greatly enjoying each other; excited about embarking on this project together. It was a good relationship gone bad. Movies are sometimes like that. People fall in love with the material and then each other, and then as the movie progresses—as in life, but in a more compressed time frame—relationships become frayed, ideas and people change, and the pressure gets to everyone.

After the last day of shooting on *Tootsie*, I returned to LA. I got into the editing of my documentary—wading through hundreds of hours of footage—and began putting the best of it together. I was nervous about showing Sydney the first cut because it fully examined the creative tension dogging the production, and especially the combustible script-changing incident.

I arrived at Sydney's office at Columbia Pictures with a copy of the rough cut and watched it with him. He was enjoying it until Dustin came on and talked angrily about how Sydney changed the text.

Sydney stopped the tape and, with fire in his eyes, turned to me.

"That's a shitty thing to do. How could you put that in after everything I've done, and I protected you from Murray? It's not even what happened. Dustin is nuts."

I told him he should watch the rest of the film and reminded him this was to be an honest document of the making of a movie. So we watched the rest of the film, and I felt horrible. I loved Sydney and respected him and wanted to be the type of filmmaker he was. I just thought I was doing the right thing, and I felt I had presented both sides fairly.

After the documentary was over, Sydney told me to do what I thought was right…but he also said he wanted me to do another interview with him so he could further explain what happened. That interview never took place. I went back to the editing room, took a hard look at what I had done, and realized that the full story of what transpired was not substantiated enough—and I cut down the scene.

I returned to Columbia to screen the new cut for Sydney. He not only approved it but allowed me to show it to Dustin. Dustin liked the documentary but insisted we do a reshoot interview so he could further explain his displeasure with various aspects of the production. I explained to him that my film really wasn't about all of that, but I was happy to shoot whatever he wanted. None of the new interview material wound up in the finished documentary.

With both Sydney and Dustin liking my documentary, I was ready to wrap it. That's when Sydney called and asked me to watch his cut of *Tootsie* with his editorial staff. He was eager for someone to see it with fresh eyes. I loved it! It was everything I had hoped it would be; he hit it out of the park. After the screening, Sydney pulled me aside and asked me if I would watch it with Dustin the following day.

And so, it was the next day that I found myself at the urinals at Columbia, post-*Tootsie* screening, with an angry Dustin Hoffman. He hated the movie. We exited the restroom and as we walked toward the parking lot, the actor spied Sydney smoking a cigarette on his office balcony. We were maybe two hundred yards away when a shouting match broke out that was so loud, people emerged from their offices and cars. Dustin spewed volcanically about how he had been screwed over, spit flying. Sydney kept his cool for a while, and then started yelling back. *Damn, where was my camera when I needed it?*

Tootsie, after its release in December 1982, became an international hit, earning ten Academy Award nominations. The film I created, *The Making of Tootsie*, launched my career, leading me into directing series television. The documentary has since been shown in film classes across the country and was included as an extra on The Criterion Collection's special-edition DVD of *Tootsie*.

Rocky Lang *has produced, written and directed motion pictures, documentaries, television shows, movies-of-the-week, and miniseries. He recently executive produced* Girl Fight *for Lifetime Television and* Racing For Time *starring Charles Dutton, which received a Best Picture nomination by the Image Awards. Lang is currently developing* The Patty Hearst Story *at CBS. He has made five documentary films including the award-winning* The Making of Tootsie *and* Spinners, *which won Best Documentary at the Los Angeles Film and Script Festival in 2013. Directing assignments have included* Remington Steele, *as well as three features:* Nervous Ticks, Race For Glory, *and* All's Fair. *He produced* White Squall, *starring Jeff Bridges and directed by Ridley Scott, and the Emmy Award-winning* Titanic, *a four-hour miniseries for CBS. He is also the author of eight books, and coeditor of* Letters From Hollywood: Inside the Private World of Classic American Moviemaking.

MARIA WYE BERRY

Documentary Producer

"Things that might not happen if you work for an insurance company?
I was doing a documentary for The History Channel about Yahya
Ayyash, the guy who engineered the suicide vest in Palestine."

THE MAJORITY OF MY jobs involve filming product for the various cable networks. I wear a lot of different hats, from developing and pitching story ideas to overseeing shows from production through delivery. I was introduced to the business through my uncle, Chandran Rutnam, who had a film location services company in Sri Lanka back in the eighties. He was filming the movie *Tarzan*, with Bo Derek, and had brought his crew and cast through Kuala Lumpur, Malaysia, where I was living at the time. One of the producers was a well-known American industry veteran named Paul Mason. He entertained my family for hours with colorful Hollywood stories, regaling us with what it was like to work with big-name celebrities like John Travolta and Eric Estrada on the series *CHIPS* and *Welcome Back Kotter.* He talked about overblown budgets, fights, on-set romances, crazy parties, exotic locales, and all the inside info on what it takes to get a "picture," as he liked to call it, made. The idea that a person could actually make a living by playing make-believe with interesting, funny, and beautiful people *really* appealed to my eleven-year-old self. So, the next time Paul came by, I took him aside and asked how I could get involved. Paul gave me a funny smile and recommended I finish elementary school first. He then suggested that if I was still interested in pursuing a career in television, I go to film school in Los Angeles and call him once I'd earned my degree. He may or may not have been serious about the offer, but ten years later, degree in hand, I called. Paul Mason gave me my first job in television and a start in a career that's spanned over twenty years. I will forever be grateful.

◆◆◆

MANY PEOPLE HAVE THE preconceived notion that show business is all fun, but it can also be grueling, exhausting, and incredibly stressful. Staff and crew members take their jobs very seriously, whether dealing with animatronic cats, recreating WWII battle sequences on a shoestring budget, or designing Afghan villages in the hills of Santa Clarita. People take pride in their work and the results go out to the universe for all to see and critique. So while it looks like fun from the outside, there's a whole lot that goes into making the fun happen. Working in "the business" means you're exposed to hundreds of people with a variety of talents all under the banner of "entertainment." You literally work side by side and depend on everyone: from designers, engineers, technicians, caterers, and business people to writers, actors, and visionaries—all of you collaborating toward one goal. You spend a lot of hours with people in a condensed period of time and there is a feeling of "being in the trenches together." I have had long-lasting friendships with people I've only worked with for a few hyper-intense weeks. I'm not sure how many careers offer the kind of instant community that creates such bonds.

In twenty-four years of working in television, I can point to two very bad experiences, both of which came early in my career.

The first was being hired by the art department to place fish on a freezing cold, naked model who was doubling as a human sushi tray. The second was sitting in on an audition where a middle-aged male director asked each actress to remove her top so he could make sure they would "look good naked." (We weren't making a porno, it was a thriller with one love scene!!) I was in shock, and sat there feeling just as humiliated as the actresses. "Nudity Required" needed to be replaced by "Time's Up," but that wouldn't happen for two more decades.

Most of my jobs have been amazing. I really enjoyed being a production executive at Viacom, which exposed me to the freedom of big studio budgets and incredibly talented crews. My all-time favorite job (so far) was with Wild Eyes Productions—a documentary company I jumped into as VP of production with an old friend, David Keane. Together we produced hundreds of hours of doc TV and got to travel the world, meeting the most incredible people. It was an adventurous, adrenaline-pumping experience, and the company was small and it was ours. There wasn't a whole lot of oversight by the networks, for the most part, as long as we delivered quality programming. We had a lean, young team, and everyone was excited about the projects we worked on. Whether you were working the front desk or logging tapes, it was an inclusive environment. It was also a place of opportunity and learning—you might have been hired as a receptionist, but if you showed initiative, within months you'd be conducting an interview or playing an extra in a reenactment. Maybe it was the time or the place, but I've not had that kind of experience since.

Things that might not happen if you work for an insurance company? I was doing a documentary for The History Channel about Yahya Ayyash, the guy who engineered the suicide vest in Palestine. My cameraman Mark Morris and I traveled to Gaza to interview members of the Izz ad-Din al-Qassam Brigades, who used suicide bombers as a means of terror. It was a few days after the fall of Arafat's compound and things were tense. Among many memorable moments on this trip—interviewing members of the Palestinian Authority in their makeshift HQ while the electricity kept shutting down, evading Apache helicopters targeting people like the ones we also happened to be traveling with, sitting between a stack of guns and Mark in the back seat of a car, and having our driver look up to the sky and yell at the helicopters—"Come and get me Inshallah [If God wills it]"—and being escorted to a private room to share a delicious meal in a restaurant overlooking the Mediterranean Sea with one of Yahya Ayyash's cohorts. He was polite enough to put his gun on the table while we ate baked gray mullet.

Perhaps the most memorable moment was interviewing Mahmoud Al-Zahar. We met him in a beaten-down, half-shelled apartment building where we were led down a darkened hallway. Turning a corner, we saw benches on each side of a wall filled with people: women, children, and a couple of men waiting to be seen by a doctor, who was examining patients in a room lit with a single bulb. This doctor was Mahmoud Al-Zahar, also the cofounder of Hamas and a member of the Hamas leadership. During our interview, he often spoke in surgical terms as to how Israel was a cancer that needed to be cut out and removed. At one point I looked up at the doorway full of curious young faces watching us politely. I asked Al-Zahar how he could justify the suicide missions as martyrdom operations when many of the so-called martyrs were merely kids under the age of eighteen. He insisted that the use of the word "suicide" was incorrect. These were warriors doing Allah's work and would be greatly rewarded for their actions. He then waved his arm toward the kids in the doorway. "Each would do the same," he said. It's a sad irony that the same kids he was treating for various health ailments were also the ones he was so willing to send on suicide missions.

◆◆◆

THERE HAVE BEEN MANY meaningful moments in my career, but the interaction with talented and extraordinary people is probably what I value most, from the courageous subjects who have shared their stories and experiences to those in the industry who've shared their skill and knowledge. Paul Mason and David Keane were extraordinary mentors, helping set my course in the industry by taking risks, opening doors, and offering me opportunities I could never have gotten on my own. As a woman, having a mentor is especially important, and a role I hope to play for others as they come up in the biz.

To people who are just starting out—jump in whenever you get an opportunity. Don't be afraid to take risks or do something "beneath you." Making copies or doing runs serves a purpose and if you can make yourself an asset, people will want you to stick around. Make sure those same people who want you around to do the dirty work also see your potential and want to reward and support your ambitions. Otherwise, it's a waste of time. And lastly, when you see something wrong or feel taken advantage of, speak up, especially as a woman. The future is female after all!

Maria Wye Berry *is a producer, showrunner, and screenwriter, responsible for hundreds of hours of top-rated documentary and scripted television. Over twenty-plus years, she has traveled to some of the most exotic, beautiful, and dangerous locations around the world in her quest to tell important human stories. Her credits include:* The Green River Killer, Extreme Smuggling, Ancient Aliens, The X Prize, Mind Control, Targeted: Osama Bin Laden, Heroes Under Fire, True Story of Killing Pablo, True Story of Che Guevara, Inside Al Qaeda, Inside The Taliban, *and* Terrorism Close Calls.

SIX

THE PICTURE

WHEN A PRODUCTION TEAM *is assembled, two of the director's key supporting players are the cinematographer and the editor. They are the artists who help shape the look and tone of the entire film. Cinematographer* **Steven Fierberg**, *in his quest to create art and beauty, marvels at how* "we exist in a world of never really knowing if we're right, because not knowing is what keeps us growing." *Award-winning editor* **Steven Cohen** *chronicles his journey from film enthusiast to working professional and digital pioneer.*

In the animation field, visual design is supervised by the director, who generally comes from a drawing background and oversees the mountains of material created by storyboard artists and animators. We learn about the process firsthand from **Michael Polcino**, *director of* The Simpsons.

STEVEN FIERBERG

Cinematographer

"The greatest gift we give ourselves when we go into this field is that we keep our childlike sense of wonder and exploration."

I WORK CLOSELY WITH the director to create the visual landscape. We collaborate on how the film should look: its feel, texture, color, and composition. I begin by reading the script several times and making notes on my impressions. I record whatever visual ideas I might have. I search through images I may have saved— of paintings, photographs, fashion photos, or films I have seen, and collect these to present to the director. I then listen closely to whatever the director wants to communicate about his or her vision of the film. I present my images and ideas and we begin to move toward a unified vision.

I then shoot tests, in which I try to present an image that could actually belong in the film. I work with the production designer, makeup, hair, and wardrobe to put together the right elements. I will use lenses, cameras, lights, filters, and color choices to achieve this. Usually, when I get it right, there is no question. The director, production designer, producers, and everyone else watching the test will feel it is right.

Once the production starts, it is my job to maintain and even improve this "look." In terms of the camera position, lenses, and staging, I adjust my contribution to the director's needs and desires. Some directors will stage the actors, set the camera position and lens choice. In this situation, I may suggest an idea I have, if I think it can add to the scene; the director will decide if it is helpful or not. With other directors, I may assist in setting up the shot or even help with the staging. My goal is simply to help the director as much as I can.

After the shot is decided, I light the scene, usually without input from the director. The "feel," which is created by lighting and filtering, has now been entrusted to me to execute based on our decisions in preproduction. That way, the director can concentrate on staging and working with the actors.

I work with my gaffer and key grip to place and adjust lights, and the camera crew to refine framing, adjust the objects in the background and foreground, and use filters to adjust the "feel," diffusion, and depth of field. A primary concern is to also make sure the actors and actresses look their best.

When the film is edited and about to be finished, I go into a digital intermediate suite and adjust the color, brightness, and contrast of each shot, so that they blend together in the best possible way to tell the story. At all times, I am expected to be a master of both the artistic and technical aspects of filmmaking.

How did I get here? When I showed up as a freshman at Stanford University, I had a dream of becoming a filmmaker. I'd worked on 8mm films in high school. But I had no role models in the arts, so my aptitude for math and science led me to consider a "safer" choice—engineering. But my college advisor, the head of the engineering department, had other ideas. He pointed to these three guys down the hall who looked exactly how you'd expect engineers to look, with their pocket protectors, and he said, "Those guys are engineers. You're too interesting. You'll never be an engineer." It was a great lesson. Those guys loved engineering.

That's all they wanted to do. And even if I had more ability, they were going to be better than me, because they loved it.

My father owned a women's clothing store, a business. I would work there occasionally, and when it worked well, there was an endless flow of products coming in and out the door. That seemed very much like work to me, doing sort of the same thing each day. Filmmaking, like construction, is fundamentally different, since it is project-oriented. You do the one thing: build the house or make the film, and then stop until beginning the next one. I think that affects your adrenaline level, metabolism, sleep patterns, ability to connect with everyday activities such as eating with your family, and so on. I don't think it's a coincidence that my brother started as a contractor before going on to produce films. Our joy seems to be in this rhythm: totally concentrate on making one thing great, then relax until the next one. The greatest gift we give ourselves when we go into this field is that we keep our childlike sense of wonder and exploration. We exist in a world of never really knowing if we're right or doing the best thing. We just have to believe in our beliefs, and do something we think will work. Not knowing keeps us growing.

Friends and family outside the business never understand that I can't plan vacations; that I usually book a flight the day before, and that I work ridiculous hours. They may be amused or interested in the people I meet and the "celebrity" of it all, but the reality of never eating dinner at home, and the total commitment required, quickly relieves them of jealousy, and is replaced by either awe or outright pity. Another downside is that as much as I thought normal business was frightening, at least once you had a job you kept it for a while, perhaps indefinitely. In the film industry, since it is freelance for the production workers, you are "out on the street" several times a year, looking for a job. And, of course, you will frequently be turned down before getting your next one. After working twelve hours a day, six months in a row, the first two months of not working are a relief, and seem like a well-deserved vacation. After that, you can start to get nervous… So it requires a fortitude of spirit and self-confidence that I did not anticipate.

It is also an intensely social industry. One great thing is that when we work, we almost never have to wear a suit. The dark side: most parties are about networking to get the next job, so the "work" looks casual, and the "play" requires looking sharp. We dress up to party, dress down to work.

You depend on personal relationships for the first job, the next job, and the last job. Someone has to believe in you to hire you the first time. To hire you the second time, they will be calling or hearing from all the people you worked with the last time, who hopefully will recommend you. When looking for crew members, I routinely call the other cinematographers they've worked with to see if they will be a good choice for me. Almost every film is a new group of people who need recommendations to get the job. Then we all have to find the best way of working together. It can be more challenging than other jobs, because many of the best people are obsessive and can lose sight of communication skills in the intense focus to make the thing beautiful. On the other hand, because we are all sharing in the quest to make something beautiful, there is a passion that brings us extremely close. By the time you are into the film, you can become a beautiful, only partly dysfunctional, family.

It's only natural that working together in such an intense environment can engender "side relationships," which can ultimately prove harmful when the shoot ends and people go back to their real lives. My personal solution to this is the "six-week rule." Years ago, I worked on a film called *Aspen Extreme*, which, surprisingly enough, was filmed in Aspen, far away from the crew's loved ones in LA. Some of these husbands, wives, girlfriends, and boyfriends came to visit their hardworking loved ones on the snowy slopes. Others did not find the time or opportunity. I will never forget the sixth weekend of that shoot. Everybody whose significant other had not visited hooked up with someone else on the crew. Monday morning, after a wild party weekend, the whole crew had "settled in" to new relationships.

The synchronicity was astounding; I think that our unconscious "love clock" rings an alarm at about six weeks, deciding that our husband/wife/girlfriend/boyfriend really doesn't love us that much if they haven't visited. It was great for me, because I went there single and met a wonderful woman who became my girlfriend for long after the film ended.

Since that experience, I have made it a rule to ensure that one of us is flying to see the other about once a month, at the longest.

One of my favorite working moments was on a television show called *Kingpin*. We shot mostly on a stage, and the look meant that the stage was filled with "atmospheric smoke." We were about to roll camera when the second assistant cameraperson said: "I think we need a little more smoke." It made me so happy that she cared enough about the image to suggest such a fine touch improvement. "How lucky can I be," I thought, "to be surrounded and supported by such people?"

To this day, I am grateful and astonished to be able to work with people who passionately seek to create something beautiful.

For me, the life-changing epiphany came early on, as I was directing an AFI student film about the death of my grandmother. We were filming the scene where she finally recognizes her son, who had been visiting her in the hospital for a few days. As

I witnessed the actors totally committing to my story, I realized that their performances were taking the material to a much deeper level. I was emotionally overwhelmed. I *saw* why filmmaking was the art I needed to do. It would be my outlet for telling the truth about the world as I experienced it.

In general, I don't feel the business is harder than it used to be. What *is* harder is that so many jobs are out of town, or out of the country. That is a huge stress on family and personal relationships. The hours seem longer (I'm not sure this is actually true), but most of the six-day weeks are gone. What is much better is that anyone can now make a film without getting "permission." It has become like writing a novel or painting a canvas. The ability to shoot with a digital camera and minimal crew is a game-changing opportunity for beginning filmmakers. You don't have to convince someone else to give you thousands of dollars. Your vision, desire, and determination will get your film done.

My advice to people who aspire to this life? Go to a shrink who can help you come to your senses. Pay them a lot. If that doesn't work, tie one end of a rope to your leg, the other to a really heavy stone. Get on a boat and throw the rock overboard. That will be much more humane than drowning slowly over many years.

If none of those choices appeal to you, watch as many movies as you can, study the history of art and structure of storytelling, take a lot of photographs, make *your own* short films, read about and study the films you like the best, and be ready to commit your heart and soul—your passion—to being an artist. And go to a film school that will provide not just good training, but other students who are likely to go into the world you want to join. They will become your partners and comrades for the rest of your life, a "film mafia" in which you all help each other grow and succeed.

If I could live my life over, would I do this again? I kinda live my life over every time I start another film. I also restart my life every time I finish shooting and return to my family. If I could change how things happened, I think I would go about my priorities better, and take a different path—go to a great film or art school rather than work my way up—but would probably go into the same damn field. I love it. My life is an example of doing what you *want* to do, not what you *can* do.

Steven Fierberg, *ASC, is an award-winning cinematographer whose work spans both the big and small screens, including lensing the first twenty-five episodes of Doug Ellin's hit HBO series* Entourage, *as well as the Warner Bros. feature of* Entourage. *His most recent work includes Showtime's Golden Globe Award-winner* The Affair *and Amazon's series* Good Girls Revolt. *Fierberg has served on the board of the ASC and the screening committee of the Academy of Motion Picture Arts and Sciences (AMPAS). Between projects, he teaches Camera & Visual Storytelling at the Maine Photographic Workshops as well as classes at AFI and USC.*

STEVEN COHEN

Motion Picture Editor

*"Routine is your enemy. The challenge of the new,
of not knowing how to do something, is your friend.
When you are too sure, you are probably wrong."*

THE EDITOR'S JOB IS to take the thousands of shots that are created by the director, actors, and crew and shape them into a coherent whole that reveals character and tells a story with rhythm and feeling. Easy to say, hard to do. My work begins with a script, sometimes an early draft, sometimes nearly final. Either way, I try to steep myself in those words, to understand each scene and character and the relationships between them. I need to understand the writer and director, their intentions, and the ideas that move them.

Once production begins, I start my days by looking at the material that was shot the day before. I work on one scene at a time, reviewing everything and then pulling the best pieces. From that material I'll build a rough first cut, which I'll then polish: trimming, refining, and shaping until the scene flows smoothly and every story beat is realized. We do not typically shoot in scene order, so the story is built up in pieces, and I tie adjacent scenes together as soon as I can. Eventually a full film emerges—that's my first cut. My assistant and I will watch it, then go back and refine some more. We'll add temporary music, sound effects, and visual effects, trying to shape something that's as compelling as possible. When that's done, we've got what's called an editor's cut.

Up until that point, I'm typically working in relative isolation with a lot of autonomy. I'm trying to make the film work for me. But after I've got an editor's cut, I begin working with a director and, after that, with producers. The quality of that time is dependent on the nature of the relationships I have with those people. Filmmaking is a collaborative art. We work together, and how we do so shapes the film we make and the experiences we have making it. We often seem like a family, and not always the most functional family. But when the chemistry works, when we're all pulling in the same direction, then any tension or disagreements (and they can be heated) will ultimately help us tell the story in the best way possible.

I got into the entertainment business out of college. I came of age during the sixties and was very much influenced by the political turmoil of that period: the threat of nuclear annihilation, the Civil Rights and Women's movements, political assassinations, the riots, the draft and the Vietnam War. Filmmaking seemed like the most vital and exciting way to be part of that time. We weren't yet bored by an omnipresent media. It was still possible to believe that film could change the world, and the films of that period seemed to be doing just that.

I don't want to imply that I knew exactly what I wanted to do or where I was going. Some people are given that gift, but most of us fumble around, looking for a path. I was fortunate enough to be admitted to Yale University on a scholarship. I went in thinking I'd be a biologist and ended up majoring in Fine Art with an emphasis in Photography. And crucially, I made a student film, something that wasn't easy to do in those days.

I'd grown up in the New York area, and after graduation, I went back to the city. My mother's sister had become a union script supervisor, and she introduced me to some of the people she knew in the New York film community. With those introductions, I was able to land a job as a bicycle messenger, working for a small company that edited national commercials. So I went from the hallowed halls of higher learning to the smoggy streets of Manhattan, dodging cars and carrying film cans. Tedious as it was, I tried to make it a learning experience, getting everybody I met to show me what they were doing. I discovered that some people had no idea why they did what they did and could resent being asked. But I persisted and learned a great deal in a short time. Soon, I left the street and became an assistant editor.

I always loved the craft of film, the physicality of it, the merging of the mechanical and the artistic. In those days, we used Moviolas, the most beautifully simple editing machine I know of—a noisy cross between a sewing machine and a potter's wheel. You fed the film into it with your hands and used your arm and shoulder as a brake, so you felt the cut points in a very physical way. Simplicity meant that much of the mechanism was exposed, and if you didn't know what you were doing, you could easily tear the film. But if you were good, if you knew the machine, and your reflexes were trained, that rarely happened. We also had something new, a flatbed editing system from a German company called KEM. The KEM was as complicated and refined as the Moviola was simple and raw, with all kinds of beautiful servos and electronics. I was fascinated by that machine, too.

The guy I was working for, who'd made a reputation for himself in the New York commercial world, decided to move to California and offered to take me along. I agreed, and managed to find a small apartment, a beat-up old Volkswagen for $750, and an amazing mechanic who took pity on me and kept it running. LA was like a small town in those days. Traffic was rarely an issue, there was lots of open space, and I loved the smell of the ocean—on the days when the smog didn't overpower it. (I remember thinking that NYC smelled like a toilet and LA smelled like a garage.)

It wasn't long before I got laid off, which afforded me a swift, hard lesson in how important a nest egg is in this line of work. I then found a job working for a documentary company making films about writers and artists, and eventually ended up in the apprentice pool at Paramount, also known as Film Shipping. This would be my second stint as a messenger, but since I had been assisting for quite a while at that point, it felt like a major step backward. But I'd been able to get into the Editors Guild, and this job paid pretty well and kept me in health insurance. It also had another crucial advantage. When the editing teams on the lot were overloaded, the apprentices in the shipping room were sent to help them. So I was able to learn from a new and diverse group of people. I discovered that everybody had a different way of doing things, and I wanted to learn it all. Eventually, the head of postproduction noticed me and offered me a very big break—a first assistant position on a feature.

The motion picture business is unlike any other. It's illogical, ephemeral, high-pressured, idiosyncratic, and often downright crazy. Film is a commercial art. There are lots of extremely creative people doing innovative and deeply felt work. But no matter how artistic the product, it has to be something people are willing to pay for. That tension, the artistic versus the commercial, shapes the business. It is a world full of eccentric, larger-than-life personalities, arguments that get out of hand, pranks that get played, and crackpot things done for a laugh or for a stronger opening weekend. So much seems to be at stake in the making of a film, and the pressure in the editing room can be so intense that a release, any kind of release, is an essential tonic.

◆◆◆

FILMMAKERS ARE MIGRANT WORKERS. We operate in small teams that are assembled for a project, and then disperse to look for other jobs. Production and postproduction work in parallel but different universes. Production moves into a location like a military unit; they establish a base camp, film a scene, and are often gone in a day. Postproduction stays in one place for six or nine months at a time. We work indoors; they work outdoors. They hang out with fifty or more coworkers; our team is much smaller. Too often there's a sense of rivalry between the two camps. It's an inevitable result of a lack of communication, and it's something I try to avoid on every show. The more we communicate, the more we know each other, the better the experience and the better the film. We may not see the script in the same way, but we all need to support a unified vision of the movie.

After many years of working as an assistant, I eventually got the call that changed my life. The editor I'd been assisting was unavailable, and I'd made a good impression on the producer we'd been working for. He needed someone to edit a TV movie. I didn't know if I was ready, but I instantly agreed to do the job. Other assignments followed, and I began to develop a group of producers and directors who wanted me. Eventually I won an Emmy for a show called *LBJ: The Early Years*, and that led to feature films. Over the years, I've been fortunate to work on many projects that have stood the test of time. If you are lucky, you learn and grow on every show. Routine is your enemy. The challenge of the new, of not knowing how to do something, is your friend. When you are too sure, you are probably wrong.

Editors inevitably deal with being overwhelmed by too much choice, and younger editors can sometimes freeze when facing so many options. But even if you aren't sure what to do, it's generally important to take a first step, to put two shots together and see what happens. Every cut creates a synthesis, something unexpected or new. From that first cut, a second reveals itself, and before you know it, a scene begins to take shape. Every editor discovers unique ways to find the heart of a scene: organizing and memorizing, sifting and selecting, cutting and recutting, and hoping that in the end, a story will be revealed.

I was fortunate to come of age as digital technology was just taking off. At a time when many people had yet to see their first personal computer, I bought a used Commodore 64 and taught myself to program it. As much as I loved the analog editing tools I cut my teeth on, I soon came to believe that computers had a huge role to play in the editing room. Several companies were developing nascent systems, and I sought out assignments where I could experiment with them, went to trade shows, and started introducing myself to people. I was something of an amateur inventor as a kid, and I had lots of ideas about how hard drives, mice, and keyboards could be used for editing. I eventually began working with the people at Avid Technology, consulting with the engineers, and helping to design their system. As my career blossomed, I used prototypes and beta versions on most of the films I cut. My goal was to do something new, pushing the technology further on every project.

But as much as I enjoyed the technology, my first love has always been storytelling, and I strongly believe that the tools, whatever they are, have to serve the story and not the other way around. Working with Avid, my intent was to create something so organic, so fluid, so intuitive, that the technology would seem to disappear. That's true of a potter's wheel, a carpenter's hammer, a painter's brush—or a Moviola. Each one creates a deep connection between artist and material, and I wanted the same to be true of the digital systems I was helping to design.

The technology was changing rapidly and the people using it were changing, too. I felt a responsibility to my friends and mentors to help them make the transition. I began to participate in user group meetings, showing off the new tools, and I put together what I thought would be a one-page tip sheet to hand out. That short list soon grew to one hundred pages. With the help of friends, I photocopied it, stapled it together, and gave it away. It finally became a self-published book, which was widely read in the professional editing community. Years later, I wrote a second book, *Avid Agility*, which is available on Amazon. I also helped create the editing department at the American Film Institute, the first MFA program in motion picture editing, and I later helped found my union's magazine.

We all thought that the rate of change would abate; that things would settle down. And for a while, that seemed to be true. But then came the revolution in file-based digital cameras and our world turned upside down again. So we're still learning, still growing, still trying to use new tools to do something very traditional—telling stories that move and transport an audience.

What advice do I have for people just entering the business? Be prepared for a bumpy, frustrating, indirect road. Save your money so you can weather the down times. Don't give up—as the *I Ching* says, "Perseverance furthers." Success means story sense, technical chops, and people skills in equal measure. Try to work with people you like, because they'll probably like you. Work on projects that inspire you, even if that means working below your skill level. Try to eat right, exercise, and see daylight every day. Embrace the craziness of the business, but stay focused on the art. Most importantly, do the work you love.

Steven Cohen, *ACE, is an award-winning editor, writer, and technology pioneer. His feature credits include* 15 Minutes, Blood and Wine, Rambling Rose, Lost in Yonkers, Angie, *and* No Man's Land. *He received an Emmy for* LBJ: The Early Years *and an ACE Eddie Award for* Don King: Only in America. *He has worked with Avid, helping develop a wide range of software features, and cut the first digitally edited studio feature film* (Lost in Yonkers). *He was the first chairman of the editing department at the American Film Institute, the first publisher of the Editors Guild Magazine, and currently serves on the board of the Avid Customer Association. The author of two books, he received ACE's prestigious Robert Wise Award for his writing. He recently finished his fourth season on Amazon's* Bosch.

MICHAEL POLCINO

Animation Director

"When I tell people that I direct The Simpsons, *I am often met
with some version of the joke, 'Is Homer hard to work with?'
'Do you tell Bart what to do?' Those people are not hilarious."*

WHEN I GRADUATED HIGH school in San Diego, I decided
to follow my lifelong dream of becoming an animator.
I started working on my animation portfolio, which I knew
nothing about doing. I had a few odd graphic design jobs where
I had drawn some cartoons and also compiled a series of flip-
books. Hollywood needed to see these flip-books.

In those days, the guy running the show at Disney was
named Donald Duckwall (his real name). I donned a tie, the
most embarrassing bell-bottom corduroy suit you can imagine,
hopped in my eight-hundred-dollar 1966 Mustang, and headed to
Hollywood (which is actually in Burbank—they never tell you that
part). The Mustang was sporting a bad radiator puncture, which
meant that I needed to keep twenty gallons of water in the back
seat. Every fifteen to twenty miles it would start smoking. I would
pull over on the freeway, pop the hood, pour water on top of the
radiator to cool it, then carefully twist off the cap and pour in the
new water. Needless to say, it took all day to get to Disney Studios.

I arrived just before the offices were closing at around
6:00 p.m. I didn't think to actually make an appointment, so I was

lucky they even let me in the lobby. Anyway, this receptionist lady took my portfolio to show Donald (I assume that's what happened, because she said she did). She came back thirty minutes later and told me condescendingly that I should go to Cal Arts, a well-respected art school in Valencia, California, that is quite expensive. As it turned out, Cal Arts wasn't accepting flip-books either, so I went into the ad biz.

Flash-forward to 1987. I decided to open an animation school in San Diego, then take the classes. I hired former Cal Arts graduates and Disney animators to come down and teach on the weekends. I made no cash, but I started to learn the basic tools needed to do this stuff. I quit my day job and wholeheartedly leapt into developing myself. I still had the dream, but my fear of Los Angeles dictated that I suck it up and try to fit animation into my life down south. I actually thought that I could somehow create a movement to bring the animation industry down there. Clearly, I was delusional.

After a few years of struggle, *The Simpsons* came into the world. My younger brother Dominic was hired out of the animation program at UCLA and suggested I take a shot at the animation test they used for hiring. I took it and *voila*, I got the job. Then, just as I had completed my first season as an animator, I received a call from my director. He said that they would not be hiring me back. I was completely devastated. I had thrown everything into the ring for this career. After about a month of stress and insomnia, I went as deep as I could. I started taking life-drawing classes at the animation union, then was hired by the *Simpsons* Comic Books and publicity department. I was going to learn to draw these characters perfectly if it killed me. I put everything I could into getting back to the show and if not that, onto another animated show. After a lot of soul-searching and work, I submitted another test and was rehired.

Flash-forward—after years drawing and then timing *The Simpsons*, I became an assistant director—the guy who the director has do the hard scenes and sometimes fix little things. Then, I somehow got the director nod from the supervising director at the time, Jim Reardon (future writer of *WALL-E* and *Zootopia*).

As a director of *The Simpsons*, we start with a script and a voice tape. Sometimes the tape is 95-percent complete with the voice-over actors, and sometimes big parts are still temp voices (this happens often when we are going to record a celebrity guest later). I take the script and start visualizing it and make my notes, then I have a meeting with the storyboard artists to give them ideas on how to play certain scenes and jokes. The storyboard artist comes up with specific shots/cuts to help support the comedy and feel of the show. In the earlier days, I would often take one of the acts and storyboard it myself, but the newer schedule has made that harder for me to do. After a couple of weeks, the storyboard artist brings in the rough boards and we go over them until we are both happy with the overall staging and acting. A final storyboard looks a bit like a comic book, with a drawing for any important acting bits and the dialogue written beneath the drawings.

While all this is happening, the design department is simultaneously coming up with designs for any new backgrounds, characters and props that will be needed for the new episode. Sometimes they are easy things, like a basketball or a pickup truck, and sometimes they are a bit more difficult, like creating a *Simpsons*-universe depiction of the Grand Canyon or the Sistine Chapel.

The next step is to edit the rough storyboard and new designs, and time it into a presentation with some sound effects and the voices. This is called an animatic, which we then take over to Fox Studios, where all the writers and the showrunner will screen it, then give notes, ideas, and usually a small rewrite.

This is when we really start to do our magic. Now that we have a tight storyboard, the scenes will get spread out to a team of animators who will draw rough, but on-model (meaning accurate to what the designs look like) drawings fleshing out all the major movement needed for the show. This process takes at least fifty thousand drawings. The background artists will create the proper-perspective artwork to match the animation. Then it goes to a person called a timer. The timer takes exposure sheets, which have all the voices written in vertically so that we can sync up drawing with sound. The timer takes all the "key" drawings and writes down the pose number where we want the overseas studio (in Korea) to put the drawing, and then we have a code to tell them how many drawings we want "in between" the next drawing. After this tedium, we will often pass the scenes back to an FX artist who will add any shadows, fire, water, or explosions. Finally, we send it all to Korea where they draw clean drawings, do the in-betweens, then color it in the computer. Right after we send all the scenes to Korea, we go over every single character and prop and assign a color to it.

When the show comes back two months later, we screen it again, the writers do another little rewrite, fix all the mistakes and record any new lines. Then they lock the picture and our composer (usually Alf Clausen) writes all the orchestrations (they still use a full orchestra for every episode). And then, a couple of days later, it is on the air.

When I tell people that I direct *The Simpsons*, I am often met with some version of the joke, "Is Homer hard to work with?" "Do you tell Bart what to do?" Those people are not hilarious. And of course, smarter people often suggest that it must be so much fun at the studio. Well, it is fun. It is also a tremendous amount of work. The deadlines seem to get shorter and shorter, while the expectations for the show get huge. Last season I directed an episode where they went to the Grand Canyon. This meant that every background needed to be a new design. Whenever the background artists need to draw new locations, it is incredibly time-consuming. We even tried to be accurate with the types of trees that appear at the different altitudes.

There are roughly ten episode directors, and we all take our responsibility as director very seriously. No one wants to be the guy who destroyed the legacy of the show. I am always trying to up my game in this respect. I want each of my shows to be better filmically and comically. You can never blame the script for not bringing it. Now, it is on you, the director.

Having worked on the same show for over twenty-five years is incredibly odd in Hollywood. We've been around so long that people have had their kids start working here…kids who didn't previously exist. We have seen each other's families grow, divorce, and pass away. Some have gone crazy, gone to jail (including a former Film Roman CEO), or just gotten fired for having ten thousand pieces of porn on their computer…that kind of thing.

Many of our brood have also go on to other very successful lives. Brad Bird, of course, who directed *The Incredibles* and *Mission Impossible: Ghost Protocol*. Rich Moore directed *Wreck-It Ralph* and *Zootopia*. Dan Povenmire and Jeff "Swampy" Marsh created *Phineas and Ferb*. Eric Stefani toured with his band No Doubt and retired off "Don't Speak" while in his thirties.

◆◆◆

PEOPLE WHO WORK IN animation are a breed unto themselves. I'll always remember how it seemed like all the successful directors drove the crappiest cars. A lot of us spent much of our childhoods drawing, out of the sun, reading comic books. The great thing about working with grown adult nerds is that it is a safe place to be creative and sometimes silly. I never feel like I have to be the coolest guy in the room, even when I am, which I usually am, because I am usually the only guy in the room.

My advice to those starting out in this or any business is to become completely immersed in what you want to do. There will always be time to delve into other things in your future, but first make sure that you got this. When you get to a certain point, you are a "made" guy. To get to that point, people around you will want you to work harder than they do. They want you to care more than they do. And they want you on time, no matter what. Get there on time, stay late, get your shit done right, then go and get drunk. You deserve it.

Michael Polcino *has been a director on* The Simpsons *since 1998. He has directed pilots for Disney and was animation director on* Family Guy *for its third season. He has produced films for MTV on the Liquid Television Series and has written for animation (*Adventures of Felix the Cat*) and for short films (*Last Straight Man *and* Dogfiend*). Last Straight Man *was featured in the Hollywood Film Festival. He has also written several spec screenplays and is hard at work on a memoir about his twenty-seven years on* The Simpsons.

SEVEN
THE SOUND

DURING THE SILENT FILM era of the mid-1890s–1920s, a pianist, theater organist or small orchestra might play music to enhance the moving images. By 1927, however, the advent of "talkies" heralded the beginning of composers, sound recorders, mixers, and sound editors becoming integral parts of the entertainment whole.

In this chapter, series television composer **Dan Foliart** and cutting-edge entrepreneur **Dylan Berry** share their musical journeys, as well as how they help hone the final product. **Kenn Fuller** and **Matt Knudsen** take us through the challenges of recording dialogue on set. And finally, sound effects editor **Steve Mann** discusses the many finishing touches added after the director and the picture editor complete their cut.

DAN FOLIART

TV/Film Composer

"There may be a tendency to skip the rudiments of writing good music and be romanced by the technology. Don't give in to that."

My job is to make the comedy more amusing, the drama more compelling, and the action more riveting, enhancing the story without bringing attention to what I'm adding to the mix. I also write the opening and closing music that sets the tone for a television series and write songs when needed.

My first professional job was during college. A college friend of my father, G. D. Spradlin, decided to leave a lucrative career in the oil business to pursue acting in his mid-forties. He was inspired to write, direct, and produce an independent feature, *The Only Way Home* and had heard that I was majoring in music at Amherst College. He gave me a script and along with Tom Shapiro, I wrote the song score to the movie and introduced him to Uke Hart, who composed the underscore.

Being able to create music for a living has been a joy. I guess if you are able to find a career path that allows you to do something that inspires you, without the confines of a "typical job," then you've found the secret to life. My father was a lawyer. That would never have inspired me in the same fashion. I suppose I never really thought about my career versus the real world, because I was always driven by self-motivation and education to continually better my craft. In that sense, it was a real-world job, because I felt that preparation was essential to succeeding.

I'm not sure that my father truly understood the intricacies of what I did, as he called me a songwriter through the whole of my career. My friends were amazed to see my name on the screen every week. I don't think that many people outside of the profession truly understand what a composer does.

The music is the last step. I wasn't on the stage week to week, so much of the camaraderie of the day-to-day working community on a show was not as apparent in my life. That said, being part of a weekly series made you feel like you were extended family. It was heartbreaking when a show came to an end, and you realized that you might not be working with many of these people again. I was fortunate to be able to have essentially a thirty-five-year run without a lapse in employment.

Probably the most fulfilling show for me was *Paradise* (renamed *Guns of Paradise*), an underrated Western starring Lee Horsley (who would go on to do *Django Unchained* and *The Hateful 8*). I was able to work with a large orchestra while writing Americana music. Working with the producers of *Roseanne* and *Home Improvement* were certainly two of the high points. I was fortunate to have a long relationship in the Spelling Organization, particularly with Brenda Hampton on *7th Heaven* and *The Secret Life of the American Teenager*. What made all of the above so rewarding was that the producers I worked for essentially let me do my job without any degree of micromanaging. I wrote the music, delivered it, and it went into the show. I didn't even have to write alternate cues. I had about a 99-percent success rate in composing a piece and having it put into the show at the exact point that I had conceived it. The worst experiences were on two shows where the production team (my champions) were removed from their positions, so I, too, lost my job.

When Howard Pearl and I first wrote the theme song for *Roseanne*, we presented creator Matt Williams with, of all things, a dance-oriented piece. It couldn't have been more inappropriate. Fortunately Matt was a charitable and patient soul. He spoke to us in terms that were sometimes very specific (e.g., more Muddy Waters and less Al Jarreau) and other times ethereal (e.g., more blue and less yellow). To set the tone right, we took the musicians into Sound City Studio—a documentary has been done about that place. It was the most rocked-out studio that anyone could imagine. I'm not sure that it had been dusted since Dylan and the Band had been there years before. Make no mistake, it had the vibe. I didn't shave, wore a torn-up shirt, took my most funked-out guitar, and started strumming out the opening bars with the greatest musicians in town. I could see the booth was rocking out and when I walked in, Matt said; "Now that's more like it."

In another situation on *Home Improvement*, I took recurring characters, the K&B Boys, into the studio. In this case it was O'Henry in Burbank. These guys had varying degrees of musicianship, but perhaps the most outlandish thing I did was have an oil drum hauled into the studio. To execute the part that I had composed, the actor had to utilize a circular saw and move it over the top of the metallic top of the drum. Sparks started flying, the studio manager (and maybe the fire marshal) was summoned and as I recall, we were escorted out of the studio—even though we were paying a high hourly rate. Go figure...

One experience I'll never forget was having an actor tell me that initially, he wasn't sure he'd delivered the performance he wanted, but after I added my element of underscore, it became the satisfying work he had always intended.

When I first started my thirty-five-year run in 1978, there were only sixty or so composers working in the business. Now there are thousands. Even so, there's still plenty of room for anyone with a creative genius for scoring. The important thing is to focus on exactly what it is you want to do. I see too many people trying to do too many things. I had a little of that myself. I was trying to perform, write songs, study acting and so on, but it wasn't until I keyed in on film scoring that I was able to truly start down the path. The business is so competitive that there isn't time to have a less than clear direction on what the prize is. Learn the craft of scoring for a picture. Do due diligence in educating yourself in traditional disciplines while also taking full use of the countless tools at your disposal. Ennio Morricone told me, "Study the three B's: Bach, Beethoven, and Brahms." There may be a tendency to skip the rudiments of writing good music and be romanced by the technology. Don't give in to that.

I mentioned the word "champion" earlier. You must have a champion or champions. I've had a handful of these over the course of my career. These are people who truly believe in you and what you can bring to a project. Also remember that perhaps the key ingredient is the personal connection. Producers like to be around people they feel comfortable spending time with. People skills are as integral to a successful career as having mastered the technique of scoring.

Dan Foliart's *music has been indelibly etched into the landscape of network television. The fifty-plus series he has composed for include such favorites as* Roseanne, Home Improvement, Soul Man, Carol & Co., The Secret Life of the American Teenager, 7th Heaven, Happy Days, Laverne and Shirley, Angie, Bosom Buddies, Joanie Loves Chachi, *and cable's first series,* Brothers. *His music can also be heard on* Beverly Hills 90210, 9 to 5, Guns of Paradise, Island Son, Burke's Law, Malibu Shores, *and* 8 Simple Rules. *Along with Emmy nominations, Foliart has garnered thirty-four ASCAP Film and Television Awards. During his tenure at Paramount, he composed the music for* Marblehead Manor *and* The Royal Family *and is presently collaborating with those shows' writer-producer Rob Dames on a new musical,* Back in the Game.

DYLAN BERRY

Music Producer

"I literally wake up and create my own reality...imagine walking into your office and saying, you know, I think we should blow those walls out, make a bowling alley, charge the folks downstairs to use it, and work from the café today."

MY FIRST ENTERTAINMENT GIG was in my teens playing drums in a band. That led me to LA where I got a gig in TV in the art department as a means of paying the bills until "my music career took off." I was an on-set grunt, then moved up to set dresser, set decorator, prop master, art director...after seven years, I got pulled into a TV series as a composer by my girlfriend (later to be wife), which led to me scoring hundreds of TV shows, network theme packages, and more.

In an attempt to duplicate myself as a composer and scale my biz, I built some of the first crowd-sourced technology, allowing me to harness composers from all over the world to create custom music at scale. This enabled me to provide music in droves to Hollywood media productions. To reach more clients, I partnered and embedded in the leading post-production and editorial houses in Hollywood who have a steady flow of media producers rolling through. As an internal ally, I was considered a "made man" by association and ushered into many valuable relationships.

My company, SmashHaus, was a threat to the big dogs in the music space as a nimble, faster and more custom solution for catalog music. We did our thing. In 2015, I began hosting a weekly radio show called *Bompop Radio* (later *Bompop TV*), an entertainment-based talk show that explores the roots and realities of "The Dream Factory" life here in Hollywood. It put me in the room with a Who's Who in the biz, from superstar talent to industry influencers.

In short. I have made my living being creative in many formats through sheer determination, relationship building, and a love for what I do. I still am not quite sure how to explain it all, but in the end, it is the creative industry of making my ideas a tangible product.

◆◆◆

I LEARNED TO WORK extremely hard at a very young age (four-teen). My father owned a marine construction company in Seattle that built ferry terminals, dams, and other amazing water-based feats of construction. It dawned on me one windy, frozen morning while I was covered in oil with my knuckles bleeding: If this was my life at sixteen, seventeen, eighteen, what would it be like at thirty, forty? I think the sentiment was "ahhhh, hell no. I may as well give music a try."

Having been a drummer since the age of ten, I started a band. We had a little local Seattle buzz cooking at the tail end of the grunge thing, but I was unhappy with the micromanagement of the lead dude, so I started sniffing around for a new mission. I ended up sitting in with a band called Trulio Disgracious at Phoenix Above Ground in Seattle at age twenty (I snuck in). Trulio Disgracious included members of my favorite bands, Fishbone, Red Hot Chili Peppers, Funkadelic, Spearhead, Circle Jerks, Busta Rhymes, Weapon Of Choice, and more.

Living in a grunge-filled music community, I was blown away by this greasy funk-rock/ska hybrid coming out of LA and was a huge Fishbone fan. I went to the show, and on a dare from my big brother, Sam (the reason I started playing drums at all), I asked the lead singer of Fishbone if I could "sit in" on a couple songs. It was a ballsy move considering the level of talent on that stage. Angelo took one look at my silly country-grunge Seattle-drenched arse and said, "Well, goddamn…I mean, why the f— not?" He grabbed me by the hoodie and laughed as he pulled my little white ass on stage next to about twelve of the most badass (and most intimidating) live musicians I had ever seen. It was exhilarating to say the least. After the show, I ended up in the muck backstage and rumor had it that Eddie Rickets (the percussionist) was feeling sick and bailed the tour. Norwood from Fishbone was standing there and, of course, I offered up my services (to the chuckle of the cats around me, most of whom I idolized). Norwood politely and sarcastically said, "Well, if you happen to be in the area, we play Portland next week."

I went home, sold all my shit in a garage sale the next day, copped $450, jumped in my truck bucket, and was in Portland by sound check, then did the same in Santa Cruz. I just kept showing up and what were they going to do? Send a dude with heart packing? Ha. They put up with me. Long story short, tour ends, Norwood says, "If you are ever in LA, come by the studio." The next week, I showed up. I will never forget rolling up to the door of the Nuttsactor 5, Fishbone's studio on Highland and Franklin (where Hollywood and Highland is now), and Dirty Walt (Fishbone) answering the door. He said, "Whaaaaat the f— are yoooou doing here?" I explained that Norwood had invited me (knowing full well he really didn't want to). Walt said,

"Weeeeeell…you may as well come in, then." Twenty-two years later, I'm still in Hollywood.

I literally wake up and create my own reality. Even the work I do is my own version of what is being asked of me creatively. Imagine walking into your office and saying, you know, I think we should blow those walls out, make a bowling alley, charge the folks downstairs to use it, and work from the café today. It is this kind of freedom and creative approach to everything that keeps me excited about what I do. I still don't understand how I make a living. The business for me is juggling chainsaws while chopping wood as all the chips land in a few buckets we call a living. This month, I handled the voice casting for an animated TV series, composed music, and creatively directed talent for a Korean and Vietnamese Direct TV commercial. I got my retainer client, an indie artist, to #8 on the Billboard Dance Charts via the radio and promo team I put together. A song I produced had over one million streams on Spotify; I licensed twelve songs to a fitness video they play in workout facilities; I licensed a song I wrote to a major motion picture trailer; I finished recording and directing a voiceover artist doing an audiobook, and I composed a theme song for a TV series. Collectively, I worked about eighty hours this week. It's a sacrifice, but I would not trade it for the world. I have not worked a day in this biz that I regret.

The entertainment community is like one big semi-dysfunctional migratory family. In what other business can you meet eighty new people and work by their side for three months, twenty hours a day, cementing lifetime bonds, then poof, they are gone, then poof, there they are again? It's a lot of fun. We're all here because we want to be. No one is forced to work in entertainment, and it is far too competitive to just happen upon it. Everyone I have worked for fought to get those jobs and got them because they had the skill, talent, and unique disposition to maintain them. This kind of dedication creates an adhesive bond between industry people that is unspoken and strong.

In this biz, you put your heart and soul into your contribution, you set it sail and wave goodbye. But when you see the energy come back to you, it does so in very interesting ways. A few years ago, a fellow I vaguely knew from sophomore year in high school (long before I knew I'd be a lifer in the biz) came up to me and said that the pep talk I gave him—"Band is cool, tell the haters to f— off"—had inspired him to become a professional musician. It was mind-boggling to me. Apparently I said: "Marching Band could be your thing, done your way, so what if the caps with feathers look stupid? You get to travel and make noise with other creative people and that is art in motion. Be it and don't apologize."

His reminder still resonates as I struggle to take my own advice and not apologize for the wacky things we all have to offer. It's not our place to judge the value of creative contributions. Our job is to be part of the mix and every scar I get in the process is a notch on my belt. Every loss, every win.

There have been so many meaningful moments in my career: the first time I saw my name in lights on the big screen at a theatre; the first time I heard my music on the radio; the first time I heard my voice on TV; the first time I won an award; the first time I saw lyrics I wrote tattooed on someone's body; the time I heard my song sung in a stadium for one hundred thousand people; and the biggest—being told that my music or creative work affected or changed somebody's life. It doesn't get much better than that.

One hundred percent of the media industry is relationship- and exposure-based. Build on one or both of the two, and you might have a career. Show up, work hard, be a good person, provide more value to those you work with than they do to you in the early stages and you will make yourself an asset. Assets are indisputable and they continue to work. Also, *everyone* has something to contribute, from craft service to the CEO. Remember that. They all came here for a reason. They have talent and ambition. That, mixed with a little luck, can turn your PA into the next Tarantino.

Dylan Berry *is Noiz Society Founder / Music Producer / Owner—SmashHaus / Listed in the top 1 percent "most prolific" on IMDB / Aria Nominated / YouTube Silver Award Winner—1.5 billion hits / Hollywood Music in Media Award winning composer / Recording Academy member / Creator advocate.*

KENN FULLER

Production Sound Mixer

*"I met both of my wives on set. One common lament is that with
our hours, it's hard to meet people outside of work. A corollary
is that it's hard to have a life outside of work."*

MY OFFICIAL TITLE IS production sound mixer. I'm responsible for the hiring and administration of the production
sound crew, i.e. the three or more people tasked with recording
the actual dialogue spoken by the actors on set during the filming
of a show.

I started pretty much right out of high school. A friend was
involved in sound, working mainly on low-budget horror films,
and I would help him out. Carrying cases of gear, holding a boom,
just kind of apprenticing. As he became more successful and
more work followed, I got more involved. Around 1979, I became
a union member, which opened up more job possibilities. He was
hired onto the crew of the television show *The Waltons* about that
time and I went with him. It was my first full-time gig and the
start of a thirty-eight-year career in sound.

People on the outside have a tough time wrapping their heads
around our work schedules. Sixty-hour weeks are the pattern and
seventy- to eighty-hour weeks are more common. Travel away
from home for months at a time is common. We work in extreme
environments, rain or shine. But we are also privy to amazing

locations and interesting people. When we shoot a location, we have an "all access pass" to that sight, getting a real behind-the-scenes peek. Be it a fancy restaurant, high-end hotel, castle in Europe, or even a dive bar on skid row, we get to see things outsiders rarely do.

People who see only the glamour of our business are often disabused of this once they visit us on set. It's generally a boring place to hang out. Once you've gotten over the initial impression of being on a studio lot, seen the beautiful sets, and sampled craft service, it's basically hours of waiting broken up by minutes of filming.

It is true that the long hours, distant travel, and "keep shooting no matter what" ethos can create a brothers-in-arms feeling. We all have very specific skill sets and need to work both as a team and as uniquely qualified individuals to create an environment where the performers can do their thing. At the end of the day, they are the reason we are all there. A film set is an organic entity. Each crew and cast member needs to know the ebb and flow of production, their place in it, and how to move in and around each other to maximize all of our talents and responsibilities.

After thirty-eight years you'd think the pressure would be nonexistent. But in truth, it's always there to some extent and it should be. Television production is expensive and delays are rarely tolerated. You are expected to be professional, prepared, and efficient day in and day out, in all kinds of environments. If not, you don't last long. The show I'm currently on costs $3–$5 million per episode, and we do twenty-two per season. Most of the crew, and especially the department heads, are paid pretty well for our expertise. And that expertise is expected all day, every day. Everybody is replaceable.

When you do land on a successful series, it's the closest thing to job security you'll have in this biz. My father was a teacher.

He had the same job for forty-five years at the same school he graduated from. Forty-five years at the same place! He could never understand how every six months or so I'd be looking for a new job. Continuing to be employed is always a concern, but after thirty-eight years, I've learned to manage.

I met both of my wives on set. One common lament is that with our hours, it's hard to meet people outside of work. A corollary is that it's hard to have a life outside of work. Hobbies and interests are difficult to develop when you are working five to six days a week, sixty to eighty hours. Also, if your significant other has no experience in production, it's difficult for them to relate to the stresses, both physical and mental.

My most memorable show was *The West Wing*. Being present among that talented group of writers was special. Difficult show for a sound guy, but so rewarding. I joined during its second season, coming in to replace a sound team that wasn't delivering what the producers wanted. I didn't ask specifically what that meant—I didn't really care. I was going to go in and do what I've always done in my own style. Just another job, right? Well, no. It was a well-oiled production with a pace unlike anything I'd seen before. It was like jumping onto a moving train going a hundred miles an hour. Most of the cast and crew had been together for months, so not only did I have to learn the unique system, I had to meet everybody, fit in, and not slow the train down. I don't think I had time to hit the bathroom until lunch. It was exhilarating, exhausting, and more than a little overwhelming. The "walk-and-talks" can be a sound nightmare. Options are limited and, by this point in the show, the style was pretty much set. It was incumbent upon me to learn it and figure out how to deliver broadcast-quality audio at a very fast pace. Fortunately, because this was a hit show, I was given every resource I asked for. If I needed more manpower or gear, no problem. The producers, studio, and network were very supportive.

The cast was another matter. Radio mics are the norm in television, especially with a show like this. Not every actor likes wearing them. I was constantly questioned by a couple of the regulars as to whether they were really necessary. It gets old after a while but it's one of the games you need to play. It actually got funny with Martin Sheen. I'd hear him bellowing my name from the other side of the soundstage almost every day, looking for me to ask whether or not a radio mic was really necessary for the scene. After I said good morning, and yes, we needed to mic him, he'd say okay and then we'd talk sports for the rest of our time together. He is a very charming, generous, warm-hearted man, and one of my favorites of all time.

Working on *The West Wing* pushed me outside of my comfort zone, and pulling it off gave me an abundance of confidence. It made me a better sound mixer. Nothing since has tested me quite the way that show did. On top of the production demands, we had a very high-octane cast and big-time producers. As you can imagine, egos needed to be served. There was definitely a pecking order and you needed to know where you fit in. For the most part, everybody was pleasant and professional.

My worst show is a harder call. I've been in places where I was miserable because I was far from home, but the show was interesting. I've been on shows where one cast member made everybody miserable. I'll leave it at that.

There have been quite a few meaningful moments along the way. Getting five Emmy nominations was very cool. The Academy throws a great party. I did a show for ABC years ago where I was given an opportunity to direct. That was a great experience. And of course meeting my wife (on set) and mother of my amazing daughter was the highlight.

◆◆◆

I LOVE WRITERS. ALWAYS get along with them. Usually network execs don't hang with the sound guys much. Actors and directors are another thing. As a sound guy, I have a pretty intimate relationship with actors. Putting mics on their bodies every day needs to be done with discretion. I'm also one of the few people to give notes to actors. Writers, directors, camera operators, and script supervisors all need to communicate within their scopes of expertise. So too, the sound mixers. Generally, my notes are limited to "a little more volume please" or "can you shut the door after your line?" Things like that. Directors are similar. I need to have a positive working dialogue with them. Mostly I can pull that off. Occasionally, I'll run across a director that has no regard for audio, but that is rare.

◆◆◆

WITH EXPERIENCE, I'VE LEARNED to navigate the pitfalls of working in Hollywood. What is less satisfying nowadays is the depersonalization of the business. When I started, shows were produced by companies whose sole business was production. The executives knew who you were. There were company picnics. Now I work for Marvel Studios, which is owned by ABC, which is owned by Disney. I'm an asset to them, not an artist.

It's a tough way to make a living. Many sacrifices have to be made to be successful. The only way to thrive is to truly love what you are doing.

Kenn Fuller *has spent the last thirty-eight-plus years recording sound for all of the major networks, and some minor ones as well. Because of that, he will be survived by his lovely wife, Bonnie, and incredibly talented daughter, Caitlin.*

MATT KNUDSEN

Boom Operator

*"I'm not sure it's ever really been easy to create and sustain
a career in show business. In any freelance life, every day
you have to get up and chop wood."*

THE BOOM OPERATOR IS a member of the sound department
and records the live dialogue and action on set—the person
you see holding the microphone above the actors' heads while
they're performing.

Before I got into the industry, I was a merchant marine. As
a teenager, I dropped out of college and got my first job on a
ship that was sailing to Africa. I loved every second of it and was
grateful for the opportunity to see the world, but being a sailor
wasn't my prime directive. My dream was to be an actor and
comedian. I knew if I wanted to make that happen I'd have to live
in Los Angeles or New York. After almost five years, I hung up my
seabag and moved to LA.

I didn't have any family or friends in the business, so I got
in by working for free as a production assistant. Being a PA was
a great place to start. You're literally on the bottom rung and
working for zero money, so nobody expects much from you. If
you show up on time, get the lunch orders right, and empty a
trash can with a good attitude, you're already miles ahead of the
game. While I was working on an independent short, I met a first

assistant director named John, who wasn't really a first AD. He was a boom operator who'd only agreed to AD the short as a favor to his friend, the director. He had years of experience on set and knew how to keep things focused and running on time.

Over the course of the shoot, I got to know John and gave him a card with my pager number on it. A few months later, he was booming a feature and needed a "cable" guy. In the sound department on studio features and episodic television, they always have a cable person or, as it's sometimes known, a "third." There's the sound mixer, the boom operator, and the utility sound technician or third. The third not only operates the second boom if there is a large gap between the actors on camera but is also responsible for maintaining the equipment and timecards and keeping the expendables in stock. The cable person also gets the lights and bell system run to the sound mixers cart so they can put us "on a bell" and lock up the set before the camera slates. If you see the red flashing light on the outside of a soundstage, the person controlling that switch is actually the sound mixer.

After being a third on a number of projects, I began to boom on smaller shows to learn the craft and get more experience. Eventually, I joined IATSE Local 695 and am currently a vested pensioner. While I was working on sets full-time, I still took acting classes and performed stand-up and improv comedy at night and on weekends.

When I was shipping out, I used to work twelve to sixteen hours a day, seven days a week for months, so the hours on set were not that shocking. In fact, I probably worked fewer hours as a PA than as a sailor. I've always been grateful to have avoided a traditional nine-to-five job. I'm not knocking people who have them, I just know it's not for me. In show business, there is no security and you never know what the next day will bring, but I wouldn't have it any other way.

I think people definitely get tighter on sets than they do in any other business for a few reasons. In most industries, you're not spending sixty-plus hours a week within fifty feet of your seventy coworkers. A good crew is like a family and when you have good chemistry, birthdays get celebrated, deaths get memorialized, Super Bowl pools get created, and the whole environment is a pleasure.

You're all working on the same project, with your own specific set of responsibilities, but you're forced to collaborate. As a boom guy, I would have to work with the wardrobe department if I was going to radio mic an actor and we needed to make an adjustment to her costume. If I had a giant boom shadow on set, I'd have to work with the grips and electricians to fix the problem. If an actor clanked his plate over the dialogue, I'd tell the AD to ask him to try not doing it on the next take. I could go on, but you get the picture. A good set is only as strong as its weakest link.

One of my favorite jobs was an independent movie that shot in Southern Illinois. Within an hour of wrapping, you could find almost the entire cast and crew showered up and hanging out in the hotel bar. During our days off we'd take road trips, shoot off fireworks—the producers even rented a couple of pontoon boats one weekend and we spent the entire day floating in the local lake. It was like summer camp for adults.

One of my worst experiences on set was during the advent of digital recording. When I first started, the camera was usually loaded with 35mm film. You could only roll for so long before you had to cut and reload. With digital you could do much longer takes of ten to twenty minutes. As a boom guy with your arms raised about your head and trying to hit cues, it was very taxing and frustrating. I was on one of the first shows that used digital, and I remember walking off the soundstage in a huff after a particularly exhausting take. As digital became the standard, sound mixers started radio mic-ing all the actors.

◆◆◆

ONE OF THE MOST memorable scenes I ever boomed was on a series called *American Family*. The stars were Edward James Olmos (you get to call him Eddie if he likes you) and Sônia Braga, aka Jess and Berta Gonzales. In the scene, Jess had just received a phone call from Berta's doctor informing him that she had an inoperable brain tumor and was going to die. Berta didn't know about her diagnosis and Jess had to tell her. It was the most authentic and heart-wrenching acting I had ever seen. Even though I knew everything they were saying was carefully scripted, I felt like I was eavesdropping on a private conversation in a couple's bedroom. It choked me up. When we finally cut, there were a couple of minutes of total silence on set. Usually after you cut, the crew will explode into various conversations, but this time as I looked around, everyone was wiping tears from their eyes.

During the last few years of my sound career, I worked on three seasons of *7th Heaven*. It was a long-running series (eleven seasons) and some of the crew had been around since the pilot. It was a very close-knit group. Between seasons eight and nine, I was forced to make a decision: whether to pursue acting full-time or continue with my sound career. Trying to do both had become unsustainable. It was a tough decision, but I followed my heart and said goodbye to the show. Three months later, out of total coincidence, I auditioned for *7th Heaven* and was cast in a one-day role. I showed up on set and everyone thought I was just there for a visit. When we got to my scene, the assistant director called for a rehearsal and I stepped out onto the set. That was the first time the crew realized I was actually there to act. When I finished the scene, the AD announced my name, "Ladies and gentlemen, Matt Knudsen," and the entire crew burst into applause. They were all in my corner and supporting my decision to hang up the boom pole. It was an amazing moment, and I still get goose bumps whenever I think about it.

At the end of the day, we're all just making entertainment and not saving the world. I don't make too big a deal out of it and I rarely talk shop. When I do share stories, I like to make them sound intriguing yet ridiculous, e.g.: "Did I ever tell you about the time that Papa John, the daughter of Michael Landon, and I spent a weekend together at the Lakewood Mall?" "I hate to brag, but Scott Bakula is impressed with the way I drive a Corvette." "So there I was in the White House meeting President Obama…." All true stories.

I'm not sure it's ever been easy to create and sustain a career in show business. In any freelance life, every day you have to get up and chop wood. I've been in LA for almost twenty years and I feel like I'm a part of the community, but I still have bouts of anxiety and uncertainty about the future. You're either working or you're unemployed. No vacations; no sick days. You're only as legit as your last job and the number one question people always want to know is, "What have you been working on?" There is no clear road map for success and everyone has a different story about how they got to where they are. The only true north is your instinct.

As in any industry, you have one reputation and it's your full-time job to protect it. You have to create your reputation steadily, over time, with hard work and integrity: by showing up with the right attitude, staying till the work is done, and exceeding people's expectations of you. One of my favorite quotes of all time is from Maya Angelou: "People will forget what you said, people will forget what you did, but people will never forget how you made them feel."

After a long career in sound, **Matt Knudsen** *put down his boom to become a full-time stand-up comic and actor. He's appeared on* Conan, The Late Late Show, Last Call, ASX Live, Comics Unleashed, *at dozens of festivals, and at the White House for President and Mrs. Obama. As an actor, he's seen in the film* Gangster Squad *and the shows* Crazy Ex-Girlfriend, Key & Peele, Workaholics, The League, Big Love, Boston Legal, *and* Malcolm in the Middle, *to name a few. He has also been a part of high-profile commercial campaigns for Apple, IBM, GE, Volkswagen, DirecTV, Pepsi, and more. His critically acclaimed albums* The Comedy Stylings of Matt Knudsen *and* American *are top downloads on iTunes and heard regularly on SiriusXM and Pandora radio.*

STEVE MANN

Sound Effects Editor and Designer

*"A lot of people are very surprised that the sound effects aren't done
at the time of shooting. Or that everything you hear in the film
is a sound effect, not just explosions and car crashes."*

M Y OVERALL MISSION IS to breathe "life" into a film project.
I do this by putting in the sounds that are required to
accommodate the attitude of a particular shot or scene. All of the
studios have a vast sound library, which I access to accomplish
this. I love using organic sounds to create sound effects, because
they have a bigger dynamic range than inanimate objects. Many
times I go out and record if a library doesn't satisfy me on a
specific sound I am looking for. I also stack tracks to thicken
a sound to make it larger than life. In many cases, this action
is necessary, particularly since the appearance of 5.1 surround
sound. All of those speakers have to be saying something at
some point.

I started out as a composer. Back in the mid-seventies, I was
living in Chicago and writing music for Fisher-Price Toys, Sears,
and Quaker Oats. A friend of mine was the staff director for
Coronet Films, a company that made educational movies for
schools. For one of his projects, he told me he wanted me to edit
the sound effects. I informed him that I didn't know anything
about sound effects. He assured me that since I already had an

ear for music, I would have an ear for sounds. Since he seemed to have so much faith in my abilities, I thought I'd give it a shot.

As it turned out, I did have a knack for sounds. It was amazing how many different choices I could come up with to make the action work.

I then set out to look for other projects. Chicago isn't a feature film town, so I managed to find jobs on industrial films. I developed a real bug for the sound effects business, but I eventually got bored working on industrials. So, I decided to gather my guts and move to Hollywood to see if I could get into the big time. It took a couple of years, but after working on several non-union films, I met a few union editors who had become fans of my effects work. They introduced me to Sound Deluxe, which at that time was the largest sound house in town. I was lucky enough to get hired on *Glory* (starring Matthew Broderick and Denzel Washington, directed by Ed Zwick). I had to run down to the Editors Guild and join up. From then on, my career went steadily upward. I never again had to use a résumé.

Working in the film industry is a world apart from the normal stream. I woke up every morning saying, "I get to go to work today." I actually looked forward to having to work overtime or weekends. It was the creativity of my job that kept me going and kept me young, as well. Every show I had worked on had a different kind of spin to it, so I never got bored. I never had so much fun.

Most people outside the film industry are fascinated by what I do. They say I'm the luckiest guy in the world, which I am. Most of them ask if I know any movie stars. You can't help but meet them, occasionally, but usually I'm far too busy to get involved with all of that. Also, a lot of people are very surprised that the sound effects aren't done at the time of shooting. Or that *everything* you hear in the film is a sound effect, not just explosions and car crashes. They never realized that things like traffic, footsteps, cloth movement, birds, wind, and more were cut in after the film was edited.

I've had so many "best" jobs...I think *Space Cowboys* would be among them, or maybe *The Fast And The Furious*, or maybe *Letters From Iwo Jima*, or *LA Confidential*, or *A Time To Kill*, or *Glory*. I can tell you the worst film I worked on—*Bubble Boy*. Not that it wasn't professionally made, it just wasn't very sensitive to the plight of people who suffer that terrible disease. There are probably other movies that weren't so good, but I can't think of them offhand.

I was working on a miniseries in the mid-eighties called *On Wings Of Eagles*. I will never forget it, simply because of the deadline that lay before me. Now deadlines at my end of the business are commonplace, because it's the last thing to be done on a show, but this particular deadline was unprecedented. The miniseries was to be aired in Canada before being aired in the US. We had a two-week dubbing schedule before airtime. Very doable. The first half of the show seemed to go pretty smoothly. All the tracks for FX, dialogue, ADR, etc. were sent to the dubbing stage in a timely manner and every reel was being mixed, one after the other. The deadline was getting closer but there was nothing to panic about...until the second part of the show. Mixing problems reared their ugly heads, with reels starting to back up on the dubbing stage. We now had two days before airtime in Canada. There was no problem getting through the first airing day, but the second airing day was beginning to look like a dead-air situation. We dubbed the show all the way up to the airing time. You want to talk about a tight deadline? We were using a satellite to send the dubbed reels to the TV station in Canada *as* the show was being aired. While the viewing audience was watching Reel #1, Reel #7 was still being mixed. We barely made it—and the audience never knew the paint was still wet.

The most meaningful moment in my career was when I was hired to do the sound effects for *Robin Hood: Prince Of Thieves*. I remember watching TV one night and seeing a teaser/trailer for that movie. It was the *perfect* movie for me. Still six months away from its release date, I tried to figure out how I could get on that team, but I had no idea how to make it happen. On and off, I would ask people who to contact. Nobody knew. Then one day, I went to visit a friend at a sound house in Burbank and saw a sign on the wall: "*Robin Hood: Prince Of Thieves*, Sound Editorial" with an arrow. What were the odds? I went directly to the supervisor's office and told him I was the best he ever saw, and that if he hired me to cut the sound effects on this movie, he would never be sorry. He hired me immediately. After we finished the dub, he walked up to me and said, "You told me I wouldn't be sorry and you were right." I went on to work on a lot more projects for that supervisor.

I believe the only thing hard about the industry today is trying to get a gig. Runaway production has been going on for years, but now it's even worse. A lot of the post work is being done in other countries because they get a better rate. In addition, if the post *is* done over here, the budgets have gotten so ridiculously low that often times the supervisors are doing all the work. It's crazy.

My advice to someone breaking in today who wants to do this? Find another career. There's not enough work. That said, I can't think of another occupation I would rather have than creating sounds and editing them into a life form. I think it would be safe to say that I would do it all over again.

Steve Mann's *credits include* Glory, Home Alone, The Fast and the Furious, Space Cowboys, *and* Clear and Present Danger, *to name a few. Steve has won the Golden Reel Award, with a total of eighteen nominations. He has contributed to two Academy Award wins, with six nominations.*

EIGHT

THE SUPPORT

ASK ANY PRODUCER OR *director. You can't make a quality product without a top-notch crew. They are the unsung heroes who work tirelessly to make the actors and other "heavy hitters" look their best. This team includes script supervisor* **Catherine Cobb**, *production designer* **Glenda Rovello**, *costume designer* **Katie Sparks**, *hairstylist* **Roxanne Baker-Sarver**, *makeup artist*, **Nadyne T. Hicks**, *and prop master* **Rob Zylowski**.

We also hear from animal trainer par excellence **Cathy Pittman**, *who recalls throwing dead barracudas at one of the the Red Hot Chili Peppers while he was surfing, and releasing flies on James Woods while he was sitting on the toilet. (Imagine what that ticket would go for on Stub Hub!)*

Lastly, **Christy Jacobs** *paints a vivid and sometimes disturbing picture of a script coordinator toiling in a pre–Time' s Up Writer's Room.*

CATHERINE COBB

Script Supervisor

"The work is competitive and inconsistent and the hours are long, but people are willing to put up with the challenges and sacrifices because they are passionate about filmmaking."

THE FRUSTRATING THING IS that no one outside the business really understands what I do. People hear the word "script" and assume I am a writer. Perhaps if they buy this book, they'll learn the truth…

Most films and TV shows do not shoot in chronological order. Scenes are grouped by location, which is the most efficient and cost-effective way to do it. But it opens the door for confusion. In a nutshell, the job of the script supervisor is to keep track of everything. We make detailed notes—e.g., type of shot, best takes, dialogue flubbed, etc. The notes help the editor know where all the footage is, what part of the script each piece covers and which takes the director may prefer. The notes also help us make sure nothing gets missed during filming. Detail, concentration, and organization are key.

We also oversee all visual continuity. This ranges from the direction the actor is looking, to what they are wearing, to which hand the prop is in. The most important factor is making sure the footage will cut together later.

The script supervisor follows the script closely while filming to make sure all the lines are said accurately. We cue and correct (gently!) the actors as needed. At the end of the day we report to the production office on how many scenes and pages have been shot and what is still left to do.

My journey in the entertainment business began during my senior year in college. I applied for an internship through the Academy of Television Arts and Sciences (best known for awarding the Emmys). I won the lottery when I was not only selected for the program but placed on the TV show *Home Improvement*. The production company hired me to work in the development department. I read a lot of scripts and got to participate in the launch of several new sitcoms. None of the new shows were as successful as *Home Improvement*, but it was a great learning experience to see them develop from the ground up.

I continued in the TV development area, working for Paul Reiser's production company, before taking a break from television altogether. After a detour into the legal field, I returned to the business as a script supervisor. I wanted to be in a position on set, more directly involved in the physical production of the project. The trade-off was that crew positions are freelance and much less stable than my studio/production company jobs had been.

Working in the entertainment industry tends to be not just a job but a lifestyle. It's work, hobby, and mission all rolled into one. The dedication and heart involved in entertainment is not often found in "real-world" jobs—at least to the same degree. The work is competitive and inconsistent and the hours are long (it's easy to lose track of what day it is), but people are willing to put up with the challenges and sacrifices because they are passionate about filmmaking. At times that passion leads people to take the process a bit too seriously. It's fairly common to hear the reminder: "We're not curing cancer here!"

I think that people outside the business are only envious because they assume it is more fun and glamorous than it is. I tell them about having to use a pitch-black Porta Potty at midnight on location in the middle of nowhere with no cell reception. And working ten straight nights, 6:00 a.m. to 6:00 p.m., with no days off. Not much glamour in that. Though there are many fun days on set, it's still work.

The community, "family" aspect of show business is one of the pluses. Because you are working over twelve hours a day together, and often find yourselves in challenging circumstances, you do tend to form a bond with people. TV shows, especially, create a strong community, since they can last for several years. Filmmaking is also a very collaborative workplace, where all departments have to cooperate and work well together. This can lead to conflict, but generally the result is strong teamwork. I've worked on several projects with particularly enjoyable crews. It makes the long hours more bearable.

Although many friends seem to be impressed with my ability to live in a constant state of uncertainty, I do occasionally grow weary of looking at my bank account and wondering how I will pay my rent this month. Unless you're on a long-running show, you never really know where the next job is coming from. And the minute you book a vacation, you're guaranteed to get a call for work. It really is not like any other business.

I would say my best job was on *Bones*. I was not the primary script supervisor, but I came in fairly often during seasons eleven and twelve as a day-player. It was a great cast and crew and a smoothly run show. I had memorable experiences watching scenes with raccoons, lumberjacks, car crashes, cowboys, and radioactive party panthers.

One of my worst jobs was really just weather-related. It was a horror film that involved shooting for seven straight days in the snow. I've never been so cold and tired in my life. The other "worst" was not intentionally a horror film, but inexperienced and demanding bosses made for a horrible time. The crew was fantastic, though. There's usually some saving grace, even on the bad ones! And the good news is that even when they are bad, you know the project will end.

The most ridiculous experience I had was shooting a scene in which the director noticed that the actor's microphone pack was showing. She was furious that I had not noticed it. I tried to explain that that was not my job. Even though the sound mixer took responsibility for it, the director wanted to hold me responsible. I told her a mic pack is not related to my job of continuity. Her response was that it is continuity because sometimes it was showing and sometimes it was not. I really had no response to that absurdity.

I've worked on the beach, on a boat, in the snow, in the desert, in a barn, on a ranch, in a vintage train car—my "office" is always unique. I've had the pleasure of working with some talented actors who were class acts—Betty White, Tom Skerritt, John Stamos, Katee Sackhoff, and Reed Diamond, to name a few. I'm always appreciative when I receive positive feedback from an editor, director, or producer. Script supervisors tend to be in the background, and our work often goes unnoticed. It's nice to feel I am making a contribution.

The fact that everything has gone digital has actually made things harder, at least for script supervisors and editors. Directors keep bringing out more cameras and rolling and rolling without cutting. There is less time given to rehearsal and less planning and care taken with scenes. Directors like to roll on the rehearsal and see what happens, which is often frustrating to actors. Script supervisors are trying to take notes on three or more cameras at a time, and editors are sifting through thirty-minute takes. Digital may be cheaper, but it's not necessarily better.

For aspiring script supervisors, I would recommend two books—*Script Supervising and Film Continuity* by Pat Miller and *Beyond Continuity: Script Supervision for the Modern Filmmaker* by Mary Cybulski. I'd also try to get on set, perhaps as a production assistant, to see how the job operates and if it's really for you. There are a few teachers who offer classes in script supervising. There is no apprenticeship program, so being well trained is important.

I'd also have some additional skills that you can rely on for income when times are slow. Ideally, you should be in a good financial situation before you try to start working freelance. Be prepared for down times and instability. Networking is key, so make connections wherever you can.

The only thing I've ever wanted to do is work in television. There are times I wished I wanted to be an accountant. It would make life easier.

Catherine Cobb *works in film, TV, web series, and commercials, and is a proud member of IATSE Local 871. Recent projects include a pilot for YouTube Red, an independent feature starring Jeremy Sisto and Katee Sackhoff, as well as a regular gig as Second Unit Script Supervisor on the final season of the FOX series* Bones. *Catherine is also a certified Braille transcriber and volunteers with families affected by disabilities.*

GLENDA ROVELLO

Production Designer

"In architecture, there are three design principles: firmness, commodity, and delight. I have always kept these in mind when designing sets."

I WENT TO GRADUATE school for architecture. In the back of my mind, I always thought about working in an art department for either features or television. After spending about a year and a half working in architectural offices, I became even more interested in entertainment and how my skills would/could be used. I had a friend who worked at Paramount at that time (on the business side) and he was able to make an introduction to a production designer of a popular late-night talk show.

When I met that designer for lunch near Paramount, there were two producers at the restaurant who happened to join us. They asked me many questions, which I supposed I answered to some degree of competency. When I returned home from the lunch, there was a message on my answering machine from another production designer, Bruce Ryan. He had been contacted by one of the producers and the other production designer from lunch. Bruce introduced himself as "the ticket to my success in Hollywood." I worked for him for the next thirteen years on a wide range of projects such as variety shows, talk shows, and sitcoms. During the summers, I was also able to work on a few feature films. I worked for the amazing production designers Catherine

Hardwicke and Jeannine Oppewall. I became a production designer myself in the second season of *Will & Grace*, which was a huge leap and a total joy for me.

The production designer is the head of the Art Department. After reading the script, I imagine how the actors will move through a space, which takes the form of a plan. Then the set will begin to become dimensional in my mind. I really enjoy working with materials such as plaster, wallpaper, and/or veneers. Cameras now can show remarkable detail, so very little is lost. In architecture, there are three design principles: firmness, commodity, and delight. I have always kept these in mind when designing sets. It is important that the design choices serve the story. Whether it is the movement through the space for the actors or cameras, or the envelope that is helping the narration of the story, I want the materials and building details to look as real as possible.

I do not have many rules regarding managing the department, but the main rule is: production should NEVER be waiting on the Art Department. We produce the drawings as quickly and thoroughly as possible. Earlier is so important for episodic television. If construction can begin early and the building labor doesn't require overtime, then we can afford so much more in details.

Friends and family are usually very surprised by how intricate and elaborate the sets are. Almost on a weekly basis I, too, am so happily impressed by the different crafts. On *Disjointed*, we had two scenic artists creating amazing original artwork for the sets in the form of chalkboard murals, and in one room, a large painted mural that was a riff on Washington Crossing the Delaware. In our mural, it was Cathy Bates on a paddleboard crossing Santa Monica Bay.

I know other production designers from their work on television, and when invited I jump at any opportunity to visit their stages and see the sets up close...great field trips. In terms of the other departments, it seems that at the beginning of every season I meet someone new that I have not worked with before. Mostly, I'm happily surprised by how many people on the crew I know and already have worked with. I have been very lucky to have had two shows with long runs: eight seasons and six seasons.

Other lucky experiences? Sitting next to Prince before he went on stage. Taping out a stage for Madonna so she could see how much space she had to dance. Getting to watch her rehearse "Vogue." In the same week, creating a debris field you might see after a hurricane and building a fantasy forest for another scene.

We often do extensive research to accurately recreate places. Currently, I am about to print a rug for an Oval Office set, which will look very much like the rug being used by the current president. I also had to build a historically accurate piece of the Manzanar internment camp.

My advice to someone breaking in today: have good technical skills, know how to draw, know how a building goes together, know that there are many solutions to a problem, not just one. Design is qualitative. Be your best critic and editor. Love to read and imagine. Keep rereading the script—you may find something new each time. You are a storyteller.

Glenda Rovello *has had a lifelong interest in visual storytelling. She received a graduate degree in Architecture from the University of Texas at Austin. Among her credits are* Will & Grace, 2 Broke Girls, Good Luck Charlie, *and* Man With a Plan. *She has eleven Emmy Award nominations with four wins, and twelve nominations for the Art Directors Guild Excellence in Production Design Award with four wins.*

KATIE SPARKS

Costume Designer

"My job is to interpret who these characters are so the audience can instantly grasp and connect to them in a visual shorthand."

I STUDIED FASHION AND business in college and was on track to become a fashion buyer. I realized from a short stint at Neiman Marcus in Houston that my boss, the buyer, spent most of her time in a closet-sized office, working with numbers. Disillusioned, I began drifting from job to job, not knowing what to do with myself.

A call from a college friend changed my trajectory. My friend was working as an assistant editor on a film called *Irreconcilable Differences* with Nancy Meyers and Charles Shyer, who had written, directed, and produced the film. Nancy and Charles had been interviewing nannies with discouraging results, and my friend remembered how much I liked children. Without much thought, I flew down from the Bay Area and met this couple and their daughter, who was three at the time. Then I went home, packed up my apartment, and moved to Los Angeles to become the Meyers/Shyer's nanny. I enjoyed the job and through osmosis, learned a lot about the film business. I also saw firsthand how difficult it was to balance a home life with this kind of work.

I left after a year and a half to pursue a career as a fashion stylist in print work. I worked for a couple of years as an assistant when I got the call to costume design my first film, a Roger

Corman low-budget feature. With no knowledge of his legacy or my good fortune, my goal was simply to earn more money and get back to becoming a fashion stylist. Then, after the film ended, I got an offer to do another film. I caught the bug and that was it. I knew I wanted to work as a costume designer.

Whether I am designing costumes that are to be sketched and then built from my designs, or buying clothing from stores, my job is to interpret who these characters are so the audience can instantly grasp and connect to them in a visual shorthand. This involves collaborating with the executive producers/writers, director, actors, production designer, prop master, hair and makeup artists. Television is a very fast storytelling medium, so the costumes must do their part to engage the audience.

I begin by reading the script several times. For the first round, I let the script wash over me and get a sense of the story. During my second pass, I begin to make notes. They could be as simple as "Is this a stunt?" to "How many background artists will be cast for the homecoming dance?" to "What are the color palettes in the character's home?"

Next I meet with the executive producers/writers and occasionally the directors, but in television, the producers/writers often have a stronger voice in creating the look, especially for a pilot. I ask the writers about each character. Where did they grow up, go to school, where do they live, what kind of car do they drive, what kind of books or movies do they read or see? The conversations quickly go into "pitch mode," where ideas spew out like firecrackers, one idea better than the next. This is where I get a better sense of how the writers see their characters and where the characters begin to come to life.

Next, I hire my crew, starting with the costume supervisor. This position is extremely important in making my job go smoothly. The supervisor helps hire and manage my crew, assists me in fittings with the actors, and helps me create a budget, determining the story days in the script and assembling a costume breakdown for each character. If our budget seems too big for the production manager (which it often is), I go over the costume breakdown with my supervisor and try to consolidate story days in order to save money. Writers often do not know how many story days are in the script until my department begins to break it down and pleads with them to compress story days.

If I have the luxury of designing costumes, I begin to sketch different looks, gather fabric swatches, and show these designs to the writers/producers. I have learned not to begin envisioning a concrete look for the actor. In the early years of my career, I might imagine a tall lanky actress for the lead, only to discover a short, busty actress cast for the role. I would then need to recalibrate before beginning my creative process.

Next, I wait for actors to be cast and "locked" (meaning their deals are signed and sealed) before I contact them. This is where the frustration and flying by the seat of your pants comes in. With many executive producers/writers, their goal is to aim high, so, for example, they might say to me, for the role of "Mary" we are offering Meryl Streep the part. At this phase, the writers' glassy eyes and frenzied speech exude both confidence and a bit of delusion. "Meryl loves the script but we're just waiting for her people to get back to us." This is my cue to know that, much as I wish she would, Meryl is not signing on. It's time to call the casting director and try to get clues as to who else might be in the running for the role. This often becomes "Beat the Clock." Last-minute casting combined with an early morning call—time is never on my side.

This is where I go into "blind shopping" mode. I send my crew to costume houses for clothing that we can rent. I have a costumer on the computer purchasing anything that can be delivered in less than twenty-four hours. I "pull" clothing for the actors from "Studio Services" in selected department stores. (This is a specific department that is set up for designers and costumers who need a vast selection of clothing with a quick turnaround time.) I pull just enough to keep my relationship with Studio Services honest. This is often a tricky balance—having enough choices for an actor yet not being charged a horrendous restocking fee for the over-pull of clothing needed to do a fitting early the next morning.

I don't know if it is the luck of the Irish or if I really do well under pressure, but I have always managed to make something work in fittings that begin before 6:00 a.m., where I have never met the actors. I'm like the maître d' of the production, introducing myself and making the actors feel comfortable as they try on clothing until we find a "look" that we can both be excited about. I have my assistant pin the clothing that needs alterations and take photos of the costumes for each scene to show to the producer for approval. I schlep the next rack of clothing to the actor's trailer for each fitting, frequently needing six or seven costume changes. The alterations are quickly given to the seamstress, who takes the clothing to her machine like a Tasmanian devil, knowing that precision and speed are essential. Then I flit back to the costume trailer, pull another rack of clothing for the next actor's trailer, and repeat. Following me throughout this frantic pursuit is the assistant director, nervously asking how long these fittings will take. After the executive producer/writer approves the costumes, I head to the hair and makeup trailer to inform the actors. I also collaborate with the hair and makeup artists to complete the final look.

◆◆◆

I DO THINK WORKING in this business is different from working in the real world because we are only as good as our last project. I feel like I had to be uber-responsible to become successful. An extreme example of this coincided with the 1994 earthquake in Los Angeles. I was working on a television show, and we had a very early call time Monday morning. When the earthquake happened, I assessed the damage, handed my dog to my neighbor and said, "I have to go. I am in the film business, I cannot be late for work." As I drove through a pitch-black city and rolled onto Universal's lot, the guard at the gate looked at me and said, "Honey, go home and be with your family. Everything is closed today."

The best job I had was *Arrested Development*. The level of creativity and spontaneous adventure, combined with a funny crew and talented actors, made the set ripe for tremendous fun. It was also the hardest job I have ever had because of the lack of prep time. One day, we were scheduled to have a production meeting at 1:00 p.m. to go over the next script, which would begin shooting the next day. The meeting kept getting pushed later and later with no script in sight to begin prepping. Finally the production meeting began at 6:00 p.m. There was a funny bit in the script where Tony Hale, "Buster," stands against the wallpaper in the dining room and blends in wearing a shirt of the same design. As I read it, my mind went blank. I couldn't even remember what the wallpaper looked like. When Mitch Hurwitz asked how I would make this shirt, I deflected by saying, "I have my magic!" I remember my assistant scribbling on my notepaper: "How the hell are we going to make this? And have it ready for the first scene up tomorrow?" I scribbled back, "No worries, I have an idea," which of course I didn't. After the meeting, I went to the set decorator and begged for any piece of wallpaper. There was no time to have a "Buster" shirt silkscreened, and it was getting close to 8:00 p.m. by the time I left the lot to buy some fabric paint. Back home at 8:30 p.m. with paints in hand and only one shirt from "Buster's" closet, I began hand-drawing the wallpaper design on the shirt. As the night progressed, I lost any objectivity. All I kept thinking was "this damn shirt better be dry by 6:00 a.m.!"

Standing on set, looking at Tony Hale wearing his wallpaper shirt, and Mitch glancing at him with a hearty laugh, I knew my magic had worked.

I was nominated for best comedy by the Costume Designer's Guild for my work on *Arrested Development*. Let's just say the costume designers aren't the easiest crowd to please, so even though I did not win, I felt respected by my peers.

The worst job was *Shopping Mall Massacre*, the Roger Corman production. It was all-night shooting at a shopping mall in the valley. I was green and didn't know to ask for an assistant or, more importantly, that there was such a thing as "studio cleaners." After working a twelve- to fourteen-hour day, I would go home to do the cast laundry, setting my alarm to ensure that I woke up to switch the clothes from the washer to the dryer and crossing my fingers that no one else in my building was using the facilities. Later, I discovered that studio cleaners pick up and deliver clothes to be cleaned, ironed, or dry-cleaned overnight.

◆◆◆

THE BUSINESS IS HARDER today because there are more people competing for jobs. My salary went *down* as I got more experience, which was discouraging. I knew my male colleagues were often paid more than the females. The producers' attitude was "take it or leave it," and I knew there would be a line a mile long waiting to replace me if I left.

My advice to someone breaking in would be to assist the best designers you can in order to understand how to work with a crew and deal with the pressures of the business. Leave your ego at home. Remember that costume designing is a collaborative, creative endeavor. Be polite, don't complain about the long hours, and write handwritten thank-you notes to the designer, production managers, producers, and actors you work with. And never, ever be late.

Katie Sparks *has been fascinated with the visual shorthand costumes bring to an audience while providing physical and emotional support to the actors. Katie received a nomination from the Costume Designer's Guild Excellence in costume design for* Arrested Development. *Katie studied fashion and business from Stephens College in Colombia, Missouri. Most recently she received a graduate degree in clinical psychology from Antioch University, Los Angeles.*

CATHY PITTMAN

Animal Trainer

"The most important part of my job is to protect my animals. I would never ask them to do more than I would do, and I always have to make sure that when we walk on set nothing will scare or harm them"

I TRAIN AND SUPPLY animals for the entertainment business—anything from maggots to elephants. As far as the union I'm in, we were put in Teamsters Local 399 because the drivers of horses were teamsters and that's where we stayed.

I have always been an animal lover. I think you're just born that way. As a small child, I wanted to pet any dog—if it bit me, so be it. I just had to hug it and make it my friend. Early on, I wanted to be both a horse vet and a small animal vet. Every spare minute was spent working or playing with animals. Instead of babysitting, I would pet-sit, train, or exercise the neighborhood menagerie. I studied pre-vet medicine in college. I brought along three dogs, a cat, a cockatoo, and two horses. I met the love of my life while castrating baby pigs in a swine husbandry class. We lived on a thoroughbred farm that we managed in a converted two-horse stall…loved it. Then I changed gears. Gregg and I got married, and I went to work for an animal company that provided animals for the entertainment industry and soon we started our own company. I was able to figure out a way to make a living, and be with the animals I love. Today I still work every day with my husband of thirty-two years and with now our son who is also a trainer, so it doesn't get much better than that.

The animal world is unique. I don't call it a job. It's a 24/7 lifestyle. You don't just show up on set and go home and be done for the day. You have to care for your animals and make sure all their needs are met before your own, just like having kids. I wind up doing a lot of explaining about what my job is, even to people in the business. "No, we don't just send down the tiger to set! Trainers will be bringing it and working with the tiger." Yes, I have been asked that. People who love animals and are true animal people have often said that they are jealous of what we do and tell us we have the best job in the world—as if we didn't already know.

I love going from one project to the next, especially when you are on a job that is hard and tedious. You can see the light at the end of the tunnel. A lot of times the animals are just day players and you have to jump in and get with the program. Your animals have to trust you because you are putting them into an unfamiliar situation.

I have to say the best series I have been on was *Sabrina the Teenage Witch*. I supplied everything from a cockroach running on a treadmill to an elephant showing up in the kitchen. You name it, we had it on the show and it was probably wearing a costume! It was really fun to have all the animals we love as part of our team, training them to do fun and crazy things. We also had a wonderful team to work with the black cat, Salem, a series regular. I have worked on many movies, TV shows, and commercials over the years, but I felt the strongest bond on *Sabrina*. It starts from the top with the producers, and on that show, they were so positive and approachable that it continued down through the ranks. We were a family and a lot of us remain friends.

Another great show I worked on was a series for Italy called *Lucky Luke*. It was shot in Santa Fe, and for months it was riding horses in awesome settings and iconic Western towns. My horse, Jolly Jumper, the talking sidekick to Lucky Luke, performs fun stunts like dancing on stage in a saloon.

Unique work experiences? Who else gets to say that my husband is out in the ocean, throwing dead barracudas at one of the members of the Red Hot Chili Peppers while he is surfing? (Sidenote: We did not kill the fish. We bought them from a fish market.) Who else gets to release flies on James Woods while he's sitting on the toilet? Then there's my basset hound, George, who had to grab a fake latex penis that was attached to Josh Gad in front of forty twenty-year-old extras telling him to "pick it up, pull on it, good boy..."

The most important part of my job is to protect my animals. I would never ask them to do more than I would do, and I always have to make sure that when we walk on set nothing will scare or harm them. I was on a movie from start to finish because my dog was the star. There was a scene where the dog had to bite a plastic kiddie pool to let all the water out. The special effects guy said that he was going to put squibs in the water so it would allow the water to come out faster and have a more impactful look. He claimed that you wouldn't even hear it because it was under water on the inside of this blow-up pool. I said I was not going to allow the dog to be near it until I first saw a test and stood right were my dog would be. We were a month away from the shot. I asked every day to see a test and every day he was too busy. The day that the shot was to happen, they said they were ready for the dog, but I told them that I would not bring my dog in the building until I saw a test. After a lot of grumbling, everyone gathered around to see the demo. It was the biggest explosion, coupled with everyone's screams. After I stopped rolling my video camera, I said, "I rest my case" and walked out.

We wound up shooting the scene using the method I had first suggested, with little hoses spraying water after the dog bites it. It worked great and the dog's ears and face were left intact.

◆◆◆

THE HUSTLE FOR WORK is always hard, but it's even harder now with the use of CGI animals, combined with the crazy humaniacs' cries to stop exploiting animals in entertainment. We might as well be watching cartoons if we're never allowed to see the bond between man and beast. My animals don't even understand what "exploitation" means, nor do they care. All they know is that they are going to spend the day with Mom.

My advice to someone breaking in today would be to follow your dreams. If you change gears, that's okay too, and if you really want to get into the animal biz, look up the EATM Program at Moorpark College. And if you can get yourself onscreen along with your animals, it's considered a Screen Actor's Guild role. You get residuals!!!

Cathy Pittman *has spent thirty-plus years as an animal expert. She runs her own company, Performing Animal Troupe, which services commercials, television, film, and live performances.*

ROB ZYLOWSKI

Property Master

"My worst job? So many blur together. I worked for years in nonunion reality television and hidden camera shows. Train wreck television."

I WORK ON SET with actors and directors, providing them with whatever props are required in the script and beyond. I came to LA in 1998 with hopes of acting, playing music, and cartooning, and dabbled in all of that for a while. I still do the cartooning. I had been a carpenter and deckhand at a theater in New York before moving out here. When I first got to town, needing a job and not knowing how to get into any aspect of the "business," I worked in women's retail. I then found my way into theaters around LA, doing everything behind the scenes: carpentry, lighting, sound, and stage-managing. These were skills I could translate and transfer to film and television. I figured if I couldn't be acting, working behind the scenes was way closer to the action than women's retail. I've been a lead man, set dresser, art director, production designer, prop master, and props person. It pays the bills. I've been stuck here ever since.

Once I established myself, I never had to do much searching for work. I've been lucky enough to have bosses who continue to hire me, and I haven't had to use a résumé in well over a decade.

Some of my oldest friendships in LA have been forged on jobs. Close quarters for long hours can definitely bring people together. I've never been to war but I do understand the concept of "being in the trenches" with somebody. You get to know people and develop shorthand with each other because you know how the business works. Friendship is not the only thing that blossoms in these situations. "Showmances" are a real thing. I've dallied in a few myself. I think it's only natural. Sometimes it's hard to explain how your workday goes to someone who's never experienced it. On the other hand, it can be really refreshing to spend time with someone who is far removed from the industry.

One of my best jobs was working on a low-budget horror movie in Virginia for a month. It was all with buddies of mine. We lived in a cabin in the woods and the entire production was built with a bunch of sweethearts. The project was not great but it didn't matter. The experience was a delight. I've only had one other job like that, well, maybe two—rare situations where egos are kept in check and everyone just enjoys being around each other, regardless of rank and status and call sheet listing.

As far as my worst job goes, so many blur together. I worked for years on non-union reality and hidden camera shows. Train wreck television. I once worked on a hidden camera show for the Playboy channel. I saw a lot of boobs. And dildos. Dildos come in many colors. Boobs, too, I suppose. I worked in Vegas for two months, which was a nightmare. The crew hated each other. The hours were grueling. I haven't been back to Vegas since. I also worked on a tween sitcom that was equally horrific. It may sound like I'm exaggerating, but I would have nightmares about the job every night, and then they would come true the next day. I'm in a more civilized and comfortable situation now.

To be honest, I've been doing this job so long, not really loving it, that it's hard to find meaning other than a means to an end. But let me try. Going back to the cartooning, I did do cartoon backdrops for a network television show for three seasons. That gave me some validation for the cartoon work I've done most of my life. That would have to be my proudest moment and, in turn, probably the most meaningful.

Being a creative person, I often take issue with the writing, and the networks, and the actors and directors. It's hard to remember your position and suck up the things around you sometimes. It can be an "ours is not to question why, ours is just to do or die" existence. One job had me hating pretty much everybody. The actors were spoiled. The creators and the producers of the show were conniving, garbage people, and the network was horrendous, too. That job made me leave the business for nearly two years. But then I ran out of money. It was good for the soul, though.

In some ways, the business is easier for me now just because I understand it better. Being in a union made things a bit easier in some regards. But big business is always going to try and get the most for the least amount of money. That can be frustrating. "It is what it is" is a shitty way to look at it, but sometimes that's all there is.

My advice to someone breaking in today would be to knock on every door. Talk to as many people as you can. I didn't know how any of it worked when I got to town and I still kind of don't. I made all my connections through friends and word of mouth. I think the best advice is to be a good person. Be kind, but not a pushover. Trust your gut and try to focus on what you want to be doing.

If I could live my life over, I would put more focus on my art and my arts, I suppose. (Currently I also do a podcast.) I would make an effort to learn more skills and apply more discipline. I didn't really know what I wanted, and what I thought I wanted shifted over time, which I guess is what time does. They say it's never too late, but I'm old and have kind of lost that "I don't know any better" mentality, which nurtures a more adventurous spirit. Sometimes I feel like I know too much and nothing at all at the same time.

But I've still got some fight in me. I still draw. The podcast feeds the performer bug, and I like a cocktail from time to time as well. Sorry if it got a little bleak there, but that's my story.

Rob Zylowski *has worked as a property master, set dresser, and in the art department of TV shows and movies such as* Disjointed, Wipeout, Stay Cool, *and* The Challenge. *You can also see him as the pizza delivery man in* The Princess Diaries.

NADYNE T. HICKS

Makeup Artist

*"This industry has taught me how to grow up and how to love me.
I have learned that I am valuable and that even though the
attention is primarily on 'stars,' I'm a star as well."*

I'M THE BUFFER BETWEEN the actors and the production. The makeup/hair trailer is the first place the actors enter in the morning and it sets the tone for the day. If the trailer has negative energy and madness swirling inside, it can affect the actor's mindset. I listen and gauge the mood of the talent, knowing that I can make things better or worse based on how I interact with them. The job is about much more than applying makeup.

How did I get here? At nine years old, I enjoyed braiding the neighborhood children's hair on my Camden, New Jersey porch. By senior year of high school, we moved to Los Angeles and I asked my mom if I could attend cosmetology school at night. She said I needed to go to college. So I went to Santa Monica College and when I transferred to San Diego State my junior year, I pondered what I was doing majoring in math. I had a conversation with my mother and opted to drop out and attend cosmetology school. I wanted to be a makeup artist in the entertainment industry and thought I needed a cosmetology license.

After I received my license, I worked in a hair salon for three years because that was the amount of time it took for me to lock into various production companies and begin earning a consistent income. I also attended makeup school during my three years at the salon. A week after I graduated makeup school, I landed a job on Michael Jackson's "Black Or White" video. I only worked one day but it was exciting—and my first paycheck as a professional makeup artist. It was amazing to watch Michael in action. I knew my entertainment industry journey had begun.

Makeup artists arrive before the talent, so our work schedules vary depending on the production. The day can begin at 4:12 a.m. and it doesn't end until we wrap, which could be 8:00 p.m. or whenever the last shot is complete. With these kinds of hours, dinner or after-work dates are nil, and much thought goes into how to attend your child's school events. On the upside, because I work on comedies, there's lots of laughter on set and between scenes. With Tracee Ellis Ross, Anthony Anderson, and Jenifer Lewis on *Black-ish,* we hold our bellies a lot.

The creative side of the business does keep you connected to your childhood dream, and being in the presence of other creative people is invigorating—provided you are working with grounded people. If not, it can feel like hell to work around crazy energy, among people who resort to acting like children. The bottom line for me, though, was that I had to grow up completely in order to sustain a career in entertainment. Since there are no guarantees as to the success of a show, we often find ourselves in the position of looking for work, which involves time, commitment, and a definite amount of skill. Most series have a four- or five-month hiatus and although the break is much needed, life goes on and bills continue to roll in.

The most challenging part of my job has always been the pressure of not knowing when I would receive another check after my show wrapped. But once I truly realized that the universe has me and I'm always taken care of, I stopped worrying, the pressure rolled away and I have never been without. Now that I'm used to it, I don't trip when we wrap. I can look back over twenty-five years and see that all is good. But at the beginning of my career, I panicked a lot. I'm grateful for this lesson of trust.

Some of the things people say when they hear that I am an entertainment makeup artist is, "that must be amazing," or "you are so lucky." They ask questions like: "who's the biggest star you've worked with?" I smile because family members and people close to me know the truth. My job consumes the majority of my time, and they don't see me for weeks on end. This isn't magical or fascinating to them. It's a challenge for people to get to know me outside of work because my time is limited. I'm sure that envy and jealousy are part of it for some people, but I don't hang around folks who give me that vibe.

I do feel that community is stronger than it is in other businesses, especially in my position, which is an intimate job. I get to know people closely and they get to know me. We develop a safe place to vent, cry, laugh, and share that lasts for seven months. We may not talk much during hiatus, but the love remains. We see each other on social media. I believe it's balanced after spending so much time together.

Here's an example of the close family I have developed on *Black-ish*. When Yara Shahidi (who plays Zoey) went to speak at Georgetown University in Washington, DC, she and her mother spent the day with my son, a freshman who attends American University. It was a way for my extended family to check on my blood. This filled me with joy and it put a smile on his face to spend time with familiar folks.

The closeness that develops over the long hours and time spent together on shoots can and does lead to "side relationships."

I saw this happen on a location film. We were out of state and it was one of my first jobs. I was shocked because I just didn't know. There were married people sleeping with other married people, and when we returned home it was as if it never happened. That job taught me that I didn't want to work in movies. I missed my family too much, and I wasn't down for having short-term intimate relationships and going home like it didn't happen. I knew that I desired in-town jobs, preferably in television.

The job I'm most proud of was *The Tuskegee Airman,* the story of the great African-American fighter pilots who had to overcome racist opposition in WWII. It was my second film and I learned so much about those black men who served our country. It was also a pleasure to work with so many talented black actors. Another job I totally enjoyed was *Malcolm and Eddie* (Malcolm Jamal-Warner and Eddie Griffin), because it was a multi-camera sitcom. I worked two days a week and we taped in front of a live audience. It was such a well-oiled machine that we got the job done in eight-hour days and my deal guaranteed pay for twelve. It was magical. Not to mention the laughter and fun I had with my work family.

A really special moment for me was when I worked on *Moesha* and Maya Angelou had a role where she recited "Phenomenal Woman." I think I remember hugging her, but I was in such awe, I didn't take a picture with her. Just soaking up some of her energy was good enough for me. It's a day I will always remember.

There have been some extremely funny behind-the-scenes moments on *Black-ish.* One year on Tracee's birthday, we piled into the makeup trailer to surprise her and sing "Happy Birthday" when she walked in. At one point, she and Anthony started twerking to the Stevie Wonder version. We all laughed so hard, but later Tracee said, "Why does Anthony twerk better than me?"

I fell out laughing because he *had* moved his booty pretty good there (talk about "*behind*-the-scenes"). If only you could have been a fly on the wall to see and feel the comedy.

◆◆◆

I'M NOT SURE IF the business is harder than it used to be, but it definitely has changed. There are so many cable channels and Internet productions, which means new contracts with different budgets. I find it interesting that the price of living is rising, but not our pay. As makeup artists, we used to make extra pay when the show had photo shoots. Now, productions schedule shoots while we are filming during the week. I'm not the happiest about this but change is constant so I go with the flow.

I'm currently mentoring a young woman who wants to be a makeup artist. I tell her everything about the job so she's under no illusions about what she's getting herself into. She has also come to set with me and has seen how I have no time for life. As a result of our interaction, she's revised her makeup career goals because she desires balance. I encouraged her to give herself a certain amount of time, say five to ten years, and invest in property or something that can give her multiple streams of income without thinning herself. I'm happy to provide a reality check and grateful that she's taking it in.

If I could go back and change anything, I would still do this for a living, but not as long. I had a moment in my career where I was depressed and had to do something new and different, so in 2008, I returned to college and completed my BA in English at UCLA. I decided that I wanted to write. Even though I wished I had transitioned sooner, I learned that it wasn't too late to pursue my passion. I wrote a novel, *Through Eyes That See*, published in 2011, and I have also written a few first draft film scripts. It feels good to be creating with words and telling stories that are meaningful to me, and I am truly grateful to have this experience.

This industry has taught me how to grow up and how to love *me*. I have learned that I am valuable and that even though the attention is primarily on "stars," I'm a star as well. In an odd way, this crazy business has helped me see my worth.

In addition to working full-time as a makeup artist, **Nadyne T. Hicks** *earned a BA in English from UCLA at age forty-three. When she's not doing makeup, she's writing, and if she's not writing, she's practicing yoga. She resides in Los Angeles with her family.*

ROXANNE BAKER-SARVER

Hairstylist

"There are the occasional crazy actor stories...certain actors who won't use a bathroom and demand that someone empty their urine-filled containers from their dressing rooms..."

I AM A DEPARTMENT head hairstylist in the television and print business. My job consists of getting actors ready for the roles they are about to play, whether the desired look is glamour, everyday casual, or even dramatic: e.g., beat up or disheveled. Hair and makeup are usually the first stop in an actor's workday, which means we get the brutal early calls.

I have been a hairdresser for over thirty years. I started out in a few Beverly Hills salons, and then, in around 1987, I was working in a salon in West Hollywood when one of the guys I was working with asked if I'd help him out on a show he was doing. This sounded really glamorous to me, so I said: "Yes, of course!" The show was a sitcom called *Who's The Boss*. After that first day of work, they asked me back a few times, and then gave me a permanent position for the last two years of the show. I've been working steadily on some classic sitcoms in the television business ever since.

People outside this business have no idea what my day consists of, no matter how many times I explain the hours or my schedule or how unglamorous it all is. They just don't get it. "What do you mean you have to work on Tuesday? Don't they know it's Passover?" or "What on earth could you be doing till eleven at night?" No matter what, at the end of the day, most people are envious and think what I do is pretty cool—and so do I. I work with friends, so when we're not hustling to get people ready and out on stage, we're usually talking, laughing, eating, or playing on our iPads, so in that sense it's really not so much of a grown-up job.

There are the occasional crazy actor stories: people locking themselves in their dressing rooms for hours, holding up a production; certain actors who won't use a bathroom and demand that someone empty urine-filled containers from their dressing rooms; being told an actress won't come into my trailer if there are fluorescent lights on. To this day, I laugh at the absurdity of it all.

When you've been in this business as long as I have, you've met a lot of people and sort of build this family that you work with for sometimes years on end. You can start a new show and there is usually a bunch of people that you haven't seen in years but you know from another project. Eventually, you can't walk through a studio lot without stopping constantly to say "hi," or quickly catching up with another crew or cast member from a show gone by. It's a very cool club to be a member of. I actually met my husband and father of my beautiful daughter on the job. He worked in the production office and I was on stage, so we really didn't work together very often, but after live tapings of our show, most of the cast and crew would go out for drinks and we really got to know each other there. We kept it quiet at first because we didn't want to be "that couple," but eventually everyone knew (kind of like high school). Then, in the middle of our last season on the show, he proposed, *on camera, of course.* Almost nineteen years later, we are no longer a couple but very much a family coparenting our amazing child.

I've honestly been really lucky in my TV career. I've worked on mostly long-running series, and somehow when one ends, another has been there to fill the space. There have been many great shows with great crews, but *Home Improvement* had a feeling of camaraderie and family that has been difficult to find again. Yet to this day, nearly twenty years later, I have been fortunate to continue working closely with Tim Allen thanks to his loyalty and, I guess, our work chemistry. My worst job was on a low-budget HBO show that almost killed me. Between the hours, the conditions, and the diva actresses, I almost quit in the middle, which I have never done.

The most rewarding part of my job is having an executive producer thank me for doing stellar work and helping make her vision for the character come to life. Having an actor plead with me to come with him to his next project also feels pretty good. I know we're not curing cancer, but that kind of validation helps remind us why we chose this career.

The only conflicts I have occur when a writer or producer doesn't realize what they're asking of me or my department, and I have to explain why this can't be done properly in the allotted time or budget. Sometimes you get a production office team that is not helpful, or resents you because the "star" has insisted on hiring you. (They *hate* that.) I once had a director literally shove me out of his path. That was fun.

◆◆◆

THE BUSINESS IS so different than it was when I started in the eighties. The rules have changed and so has the game. Most productions try to pay you as little as they can get away with for as much work as they can legally get out of you. The "above the line/below the line" divide is alive and well in Hollywood.

My advice to anyone wanting to do what I do is to be patient, professional, and go above and beyond to build yourself a good reputation, because that is all you have to get your next job. Also, you really have to love what you do, because it takes years to make it to a place where this pays off financially: meaning pension, health insurance, and other vested benefits. But when you get there, it's really wonderful what you can build for yourself as far as security.

Roxanne Baker-Sarver's *long and successful career as a hairstylist has encompassed the series* Who's the Boss, Saved by The Bell, The Nanny, Home Improvement, Titus, Grounded for Life, According to Jim, Wizards of Waverly Place, *and* Last Man Standing.

CHRISTY JACOBS

Script Coordinator

*"When it was announced in the writers' room that I would get to write
my first freelance episode, one of the consulting producers said,
'Are we giving our dogs scripts now?' I was sitting right there."*

I'M BASICALLY A MUSE for the writers. I sit at the computer and
inspire them with my brilliant personality and winning smile.
Ha ha. In comedy, the script coordinator is basically the "head"
writers' assistant. We spend most of our time behind a computer
in the writers' room, taking notes while the writers scrutinize
what we type (and how accurately we do it) on a large TV/
computer screen. We also proof, format, and distribute the scripts
to the cast and crew, handle clearances, and hang with the writers,
hoping some of their brilliance will rub off on us and maybe, just
maybe, someday the showrunner will assign us a freelance script.
All writers' assistants are writers in training, honing their craft,
and praying to be promoted to staff one day.

I didn't have a career before the entertainment business.
I graduated from UCLA and a few months later landed my first
job as a PA on a Saturday morning ABC show called *Fudge*. The
job came through a friend from UCLA with whom I'd worked
as a lifeguard. In this biz, it's all about connections and, since
I knew someone, I fortunately breezed on in. I don't have much to
compare it to, except what I've seen from my family and friends

who work in the corporate world. We don't punch a time clock or wear suits, but we also dedicate our lives to our jobs. Instead of a forty-hour week, our weeks are sixty-plus. But it's understood and most people don't complain about it.

I feel like I grew up really fast in my twenties, working straight out of college in an industry that required all my time and dedication. I didn't have the slacker party time that some kids have in their twenties. But then again, if going to work in jeans and laughing with a bunch of hilarious writers all day long means not growing up, then I guess I never had to. From the outside world, I'm sure it looks like fantasyland!

I think family and friends are seduced by the glamour of Hollywood. I remember when I worked on *The Drew Carey Show*, people would say to me, "I don't watch that show. You know what show you should work on? *Friends*! I love that show! Do you know Joey?" As if I could just choose my jobs at random based on the popularity of the show and what my friends liked. I always wanted to respond, "You know which insurance company you should work for? Farmers! I love their discount bundles! Can you hook me up?"

When I first started out, going from job to job was easy. Once you were "in," you were part of a network of people who recommended you. I enjoyed the "fresh start" that each new show provided: meeting new people, working at a different studio. It was a lot of fun. Of course, I did move around as a child, going to three different high schools, so maybe my upbringing prepared me for a job in show biz.

There were good and bad aspects to all my jobs. The best experience of my career was working on *8 Simple Rules* prior to John Ritter's death. It was where I received my "big break" and was promoted to staff writer in season two. I loved the show.

There was a magic about it that you don't always find, and I felt that when I first watched the pilot. Even though we worked long hours, as with most TV shows, I loved going to work every day. As a script coordinator, the writers were very supportive of me, encouraging me to pitch in the room and asking for my feedback on their scripts. This is rare in comedy rooms. The writers' assistant is often seen but not heard.

My worst job would have to be *The Librarians*. This was my first show back in TV as a script coordinator after taking some time off, and everything had changed with the invention of the smartphone. I was on call twenty-four hours a day, seven days a week for five months. The show shot on location in Portland, but the writers were based in LA. Because of this, the show lacked personal relationships and camaraderie—the two things I loved most about working in TV. All communication was done through emails, which made me feel disconnected from the creative aspect as well. And even though I could often work from home, the anxiety I felt, never knowing when I was going to get a script to put out, was enough to drive a person insane. It took me a month to recover from that show. I still hear the Gmail alert sounds in my dreams.

◆◆◆

IT'S TOUGH BEING A woman television comedy writer or even writers' assistant. Some of the things I heard in rooms were very challenging to my self-esteem. I was sitting at the table as a writers' assistant on *The Drew Carey Show* when our EP actually said, "Pretty women aren't funny." I was shocked that he would say that, given that two other female writers were also in the room. So was I pretty or funny? And did I have to choose? Another *Drew Carey* experience—when it was announced in the writers' room that I would get to write my first freelance episode, one of the consulting producers said, "Are we giving our dogs scripts now?" I was sitting right there. Little did I know at the time that this writer was very fond of dogs, and gave his entire fortune to a canine foundation when he died, so I guess this was a compliment?

The highlight of my career was getting to write the Christmas episode of *8 Simple Rules*. After the table read, John Ritter called out to me, "Christy, this is really funny!" This was the first episode I'd written that went to table without being totally rewritten by other writers. It was really mine. I'll never forget it. Finally, I felt like a legitimate comedy writer.

After John Ritter died, *8 Simple Rules* went off the rails in a lot of ways. I was a staff writer at the time, and at the end of the season, the EP called me into his office to talk about my option for the next season. "I thought you did a great job," he said, "so I'm picking up your option. I loved your story pitches and next season I'm going to give you your own episodes."

"Great!" I thought. I was so relieved. He then went on. "I just need you to do one thing for me—make friends with Bonnie. You don't have to ask her to go shoe shopping right away, but be nice to her."

I had no idea what he meant. I didn't even know there was a problem with Bonnie. At least he didn't ask me to sleep with him! The next week, after the show wrapped (and before this EP resigned after an infamous letter to the network), my agent called to tell me my option wasn't picked up. I guess I should've invited Bonnie to go shoe shopping…

Then there was *Desperate Housewives*. I was so excited to work on the show because I'd been a fan for years. It was season five when I joined the crew. My spirits were quickly dashed when the EP refused to learn my name and instead shouted "sweetie!" at me while I worked at the computer. Even though I loved everyone else on the show, my writing career was taking off, so I left after four months.

◆◆◆

THE BUSINESS IS A lot harder than it used to be. I was fortunate early on in my career, because I landed on many hit shows that ran for multiple seasons. Then I took a break to join the real world: got a master's degree, wrote a book, traveled, met people outside of Hollywood (shocking, but they do exist), and became a life coach. When my heart called me back to TV, I was in for a rude awakening. In my absence, a slew of fresh, young writers' assistants had entered the biz. It used to be difficult to find writers' assistants with any experience and now they were *everywhere*. And with the new trend toward short seasons, producing as few as ten episodes, you could no longer survive on just one show. You needed two or three a year.

But the biggest surprise of all? The pay was exactly the same as it was in 1995.

You have to be passionate to make it in this business. If you're just breaking in because it seems cool and you want to make a bunch of money and meet TV stars, find something else. I mean that in the kindest way. It's what I'd tell my kids (if I had any). The business can be brutal and if you're thin-skinned, afraid of rejection, can't handle being out of work for long periods of time, aren't prepared to struggle and starve for your dream, it's not worth it. That being said, if you can't imagine yourself doing anything else—go for it! You'll need to dig deep and remember that dream many times along your path, so keep it somewhere safe.

It certainly has not been easy for me, and I haven't risen to the level of success I always thought I'd achieve. But even after all these years of hard work and sacrifice, I have to say this business is still my first love, and screenwriting is my passion. Every time I've felt uninspired, unable to write, and wanting to quit, something pulls me back in—an unknown force that screams, "Oh, hell no, you're not giving up!" In the end, it's a calling that I can't ignore, an eternal itch that needs to be scratched. It'd be so much easier to invest in a backscratcher.

And off to therapy I go…

Christy Jacobs *has worked as a TV writer, script coordinator, and writers' assistant for twenty years. Her credits include* The Librarians, Desperate Housewives, 8 Simple Rules, The Drew Carey Show, *and* Home Improvement. *Christy took some time away from the business to obtain a master's degree in Psychology and publish her memoir,* He Swept Me Off My Feet...and Dropped Me on My Head. *She returned to TV to work on ABC's* The Middle.

NINE

THE STRUGGLE

EVERY CREATIVE PERSON IN *Hollywood must negotiate the challenge of working in an inherently collaborative medium. When the teamwork truly comes together, we all make each other better. In less than ideal situations, of which there are many, we see our unique visions casually watered down or mangled beyond repair. If the road to hell is paved with good intentions, the path to artistic fulfillment is littered with heartbreak, failure, and a generous dose of existential doubt.*

In this chapter, **Roberto Loiederman** *likens his Hollywood experience to "a surreal, grotesque amusement park," where soap opera becomes indistinguishable from war-torn Vietnam.* **Elliot Shoenman** *sees his green-lit movie go up in smoke when the star sells out the director, his own best friend.* **Roy Teicher** *detects a parallel between the arc of his career and that of the famously elusive drug lord, El Chapo.* **Lloyd Garver** *watches his fortune change overnight, all because of a salad. And* **Bruce Ferber**, *your editor, examines the ever-tenuous status of the writer's voice.*

BEFORE ME TODAY

By Roberto Loiederman

"What had my life been worth, after all? Some of it had been spent delivering ammo to a vile war zone, and getting paid a bonus to do it. Some of it had been spent writing scenarios intended to lull people into a stupor so they'd buy whatever the sponsor was selling."

FIFTY YEARS AGO I worked as a deck hand on ammo ships that went to a war zone. We carried thousands of tons of all kinds of ammunition, from small arms to big bombs to napalm. The joke aboard was that if a disaster happened—a fire or explosion—the ship wouldn't go down.

Uh-uh. She'd go straight up.

As we crossed the Pacific, I read *The Egyptian Book of the Dead*, an ancient treatise on how to prepare for death. I told myself that I read it in order to get into a war mood. On the day we spotted the green coastline of Vietnam, I put a quote from that book on the messroom blackboard:

"Death is before me today, as the odor of lotus-flowers, as when one sitteth on the shore of drunkenness."

A couple of hours later, I went back to the messroom and found that someone had erased most of the quote. It now read:

"…before me today… drunkenness."

Since then, I've been rewritten many times, but never as well.

Yes, I have been rewritten many times. A TV episode I wrote once was so heavily edited that the aired episode had one line intact from my original script. Another time, an executive producer wrote on the manila envelope that held one of my scripts: "CAUTION! Toxic material!"

Years ago, I was a staff writer on *Days of Our Lives*. After a season on that show, I was fired. I convinced myself it was because I was older than the other writers. Yeah, that was it: ageism.

After that, my agent kept calling *General Hospital* and managed to set up a meeting with the executive producer. On the day I went to meet with her, my agent phoned me. He said, "Call me as soon as they offer you something."

I went to the *General Hospital* studio at the arranged time. It was in a part of LA that had been pleasant eighty years ago but now had pickup trucks and cars—their guts disassembled—sitting on lawns.

A neighborhood of graffiti, barred windows, and scruffy kids on tricycles. The studio had stubbornly remained in that area, inside a locked compound. I drove in, parked, went into the building, and then sat in the waiting room.

I waited an hour. Then another half hour. Finally, the producer came out. Without even looking at me, she said: "Please tell your agent to stop pestering us. We're not going to hire you." She turned quickly and left. That was it. The meeting was over. It had lasted ten seconds. Maybe less.

I left the building, got in my car, and drove just outside the lot, parking on the street. Wow! For a month I'd watched *General Hospital* day after day until my eyes bled. I got to know the characters. Learned who they were. Learned their backstories.

While I'd watched a month's worth of episodes, I jotted down notes. Ideas about where to take the characters, what kind of short and long storylines could be developed. I had my notes with me when I'd gone to the meeting but never got the chance to use them.

So now, in my car, I looked at my notes. Blah-blah and blah-blah have an affair. Blah-blah and blah-blah strengthen their relationship. Blah-blah and blah-blah have a problem with a child. Blah-blah gets a life-threatening illness. Blah-blah finds religion. Blah-blah opens up a night club. Blah-blah-blah-blah.

It was all painfully unoriginal. I was grateful not to have gotten the chance to embarrass myself even more, if that was possible. I crumpled my notes into paper balls and threw them on top of my tuxedo, laid flat across the back seat of the car.

I'd brought my tux because I had no idea how long the meeting would last and I had a black-tie affair later that day. I changed clothes in the car and quickly became an object of amused spectatorship: little kids stopped playing to watch me struggle putting on my tux pants, which had shrunk since the last time I'd worn them.

The gala was something called "The Environmental Media Awards Show," invented and bankrolled by Ted Turner, who decided it would be a good idea to reward TV shows and movies that showed sensitivity toward the earth and all living things.

The Days of Our Lives writing staff was being honored because we had done a storyline in which a young, pretty female doctor— Is there any other kind in soap operas?—campaigned against a factory whose waste polluted the air and poisoned a local river.

The truth is, no one on that staff cared a mouse dropping about the environment. It was an exercise in stupid soap tricks— we did it in order to make a new character instantly sympathetic, but Ted Turner liked the storyline and thought the show deserved an award.

For reasons I still don't understand, I decided to go to the event, even though I'd already been fired from the show. I would be sitting with ex-colleagues who'd give me that phony-sympathy look you use with someone who's been booted from a job you still have. A rational person wouldn't have gone. But my showbiz career was circling the drain and I wasn't feeling rational.

I arrived early at what had once been the MGM lot and walked around in my too-small tux, staring at soundstages.

During the 1980s, the decade before my stint on *Days of Our Lives*, I'd worked on that lot. My then writing partner and I did a version of *Pirates of the Caribbean* years before someone else wrote the megahit that became a feature-film franchise. There were days, while working on the *Pirates* script, that my head was deep into sailing ships, and derring-do, and the New Orleans of hundreds of years ago.

Soundstages look very much like the warehouses on the docks that are used for storing cargo. So while I was on the MGM lot, waiting for the environmental gala to begin, my mind drifted back not only to my years on that lot in the 1980s but also to my own seafaring years in the 1960s, to ships I'd worked on as a deck hand, to exotic ports in the Far East.

For me, wartime Vietnam had been a surreal, grotesque amusement park. Disneyland for the weird. The large Styrofoam pads that had been used to cushion the big bombs during our trip across the Pacific ended up in the hands of scrawny Vietnamese children who used them to surf the contaminated shore.

The ammo ports my ships went to—Cam Ranh, Nha Trang, Qui Nhon—were suffused with the overwhelming smells of frying fish oil…garbage…kerosene…urine…cheap perfume… tropical rain…lush vegetation.

I hung out at the Press Club in Da Nang with Dana Stone, a combat photographer who gave me a tour which included "Graham Greene's favorite opium den": opium addicts lying in racks, surrounded by a cloud of yellow smoke. Two years later, Dana disappeared in Cambodia, one more of the missing.

My mind drifted from Vietnam in the 1960s…to New Orleans in 1700…to Culver City in the 1980s. A jumble of images: soundstages, cargo warehouses, pirates, sailing ships, ammo for a useless war, soap operas…things I had done and places I'd been overlapped—fueled, I suppose, by that dreadful meeting I'd had a couple of hours earlier.

Suddenly I lost my bearings. I felt my life telescoping: years and places compressed into a blurry present. I had no idea where I was or what year it was.

Yo-ho-ho, it's a pirate's life for me.

Tell your agent to stop pestering us.

She ain't goin' down. Uh-uh. She's goin' straight up.

I was disoriented…hyperventilating. Where the hell was I? When was I? Then I went deeper into the rabbit hole.

What had my life been worth, after all? Some of it had been spent delivering ammo to a vile war zone, and getting paid a bonus to do it. Some of it had been spent writing scenarios intended to lull people into a stupor so they'd buy whatever the sponsor was selling.

It wasn't my scripts that needed rewriting, it was my life. Was it too late for that?

After a few minutes, I came back to my right mind, to the right time and place, and, in the end, I didn't go to the awards show. I just couldn't.

I staggered back to the parking lot. After some wrong turns, I found my car. I slid inside and sat there, sweating. I threw off my jacket and cummerbund, loosened my pants. Took a few deep breaths.

The only image that came to mind was that long-ago messroom blackboard.

…before me today…drunkenness.

The memory of that perfect rewrite burned brightly and helped guide me, like a lighthouse, through a dark night at sea.

Roberto Loiederman *has been a journalist, merchant seaman, and TV scriptwriter for* Dynasty, Knots Landing, Days of Our Lives, *and other shows; has had more than one hundred articles and stories published in* The Los Angeles Times, Washington Post, Baltimore Sun, Penthouse, *and many other publications. His essay,* "Roadblock," *published in* Fifth Wednesday Journal, *was named a Notable Essay in The Best American Essays 2016. He is coauthor of* The Eagle Mutiny, *a nonfiction account of the only mutiny on an American ship in modern times. Info at* eaglemutiny.com.

TO UNCLE MAXIE, WHO ALWAYS BELIEVED

By Elliot Shoenman

"In Hollywood, being blamed for a flop is a significantly bigger offense than trying to neuter a man NRA-style."

WHEN I BEGAN WRITING in 1971, I ran into the usual brick wall. Nobody was interested in what I submitted. As the days passed and the rejections mounted, I started to doubt my ability. I kept thinking about what my mother's brother Maxie had said when he heard what I was doing: "Stop pissing in the wind and get a normal job." I didn't tend to listen to Uncle Maxie's advice, primarily because he was a slumlord who, in his youth, had been friends with Bugsy Siegel. But I started to think that in this case, maybe he was right. Then, the phone rang. It was Joe Bologna.

I had mailed a screenplay to Joe and his wife, Renée Taylor, who were the toast of New York after their show *Lovers and Other Strangers* became a Broadway hit. Joe said they were impressed with my script and wanted to hire me to write for *Calucci's Department,* a show they had just sold to CBS. I was beyond thrilled.

Joe and Renée had an office in the furrier's district of New York and the setup was unusual, to say the least. The two of them sat behind face-to-face desks in what had been the showroom, a twenty-by-twenty area surrounded by mirrors. Their secretary, Vickie, was stationed in the back of the room in a floor-to-ceiling safe with its steel door kept ajar. When a visitor would arrive, he would be told to check in with Vickie. The person would then enter the safe and be announced back into the main room. On occasion, Joe and Renée would say they were too busy to meet and the person would have to walk back past them as he left. When Joe and Renée wanted to have a private meeting, they would close the safe door with Vickie inside. To the best of my knowledge, they always remembered to let her back out.

Calucci was well received, but airing opposite *Sanford & Son*, it quickly went down in flames. During that period, I became friendly with an up-and-coming comedy writer named Norman Steinberg. Norman helped me get an agent at William Morris and recommended me to Alan King, who hired me to write an episode of a summer replacement show, *The Corner Bar*. Then, I got a giant break, which was a direct result of Norman's giant break. Norman had happened to be at the counter of a coffee shop when Mel Brooks came in and sat in the next seat. They struck up a conversation, Mel took a liking to him, and, out of nowhere, offered Norman a job cowriting Mel's next film, *Blazing Saddles*. Work was to begin immediately, which presented a problem for Norman. He was scheduled to leave for Los Angeles to work on a variety show starring John Denver and Lily Tomlin. The solution: he asked me if I would go to California and take his place.

"Is that okay with the people running the show?" I asked.

"Yes. I talked to the head writer and he said, 'Send the kid out.'"

I threw some underwear into a suitcase and headed for the airport.

After a few days in Los Angeles, I had a meeting with my West Coast William Morris representative, Sylvia Hirsch. She was an old-timer who said I should take advantage of my time in "TV land," so she set up a meeting for me with Alan Levitt, one of the writers on Norman Lear's *Maude*. The next day, I went to his office at CBS Fairfax and pitched my heart out. Nothing. But I kept after it and, on my last scheduled day in town, sold an idea for an episode. I locked myself away in a motel room, wrote the script, Alan Levitt decided to leave the show, and I was offered a staff position.

Suddenly I was in the big leagues. There were three legendary writers on *Maude* and four across the hall on *All In The Family*. I was twenty-seven; the next youngest guy was fifty-two. I learned as much as I could, as fast as I could, but sometimes my lack of experience in the craft, and in life, was a liability. Early on, unable to come up with a button (the last joke of the scene, also known as the "blow"), I used a line I had heard years earlier on *The Honeymooners*. It was recognized instantly by one of the writers, who was its originator. Lucky to have survived that near miss, I later found myself in the thick of a discussion where the staff was weighing whether or not we should write an episode in which Maude gets a hysterectomy. The other writers were all in favor of it and when asked what I thought, I agreed wholeheartedly, proclaiming it an absolutely great idea that we should embrace without hesitation. Then I went home and looked up what a hysterectomy was.

Halfway into the season, I got a call from a William Morris film agent named Ron Mardigian. He said that Bea Arthur's husband, Gene Saks, was looking for a young writer to collaborate with on a screenplay. I was swamped, trying to keep up with the intense *Maude* schedule, but…Gene Saks was one of the hottest directors on Broadway and also a high-end film director, having done *The Odd Couple* and a number of other successful comedies.

He was currently editing a big-budget musical and this new script would be his next project. I met with Gene and just like that, the whirlwind got windier. We started working on Saturdays and Sundays to flesh out his idea. I was now up to my ass seven days a week. But I was in rarified air and on top of the world. Along the way, incidentally, Uncle Maxie called to see if I could get him an autographed photo of Bea Arthur. When I told her the irony of Maxie's naysaying backstory, she laughed and proceeded to autograph the picture: "To Uncle Maxie, who always believed."

Gene and I worked at his home in Brentwood and, being there every weekend, I got to spend quite a bit of time with Bea. Around noon, she would make lunch for us and when we finished a day's work, the three of us would have cocktails together. A couple of times, I had a little too much to drink and they didn't want me to drive home. So, I slept over. The next morning, we would have breakfast together. This was all great, but it also put me in an odd position: I became the unofficial link between the star of the show and the show itself. As soon as I walked in the door, she would ask me about the next week's script. And when I got to work on Monday morning, they would ask me about how Bea was on the weekend, what kind of mood she was in, etc. I walked the tightrope as best I could, trying not to reveal more than I should and not get on anyone's bad side.

Meanwhile, Gene and I were blasting through our screenplay. It was called *Not A Hair Out Of Place* and was based on Bea's grumpy and eccentric uncle who was an old-time waiter. By the end of the *Maude* season, Gene and I had finished the script.

I was quite full of myself—on a hit show and cowriting a film that was likely to get made. I tried to be humble around my friends, but I doubt I succeeded. In my defense, it was indeed heady stuff. Then it got even better. Bea and Gene had gone to acting school with Walter Matthau and they remained close. Matthau was a major movie star at that point and he would be perfect as our main character, Harry. Gene invited Matthau to the house for a meeting. Before we could talk about the script, we had to wait for Walter to watch the second half of a football game he had bet on. Luckily, he won. We then told him about Harry and he was intrigued. He said his schedule was open and he would read the script immediately.

Matthau called Gene the next day and said he would do our movie. He had a deal at Universal and would set up a "sit-down" with the head of production, Jennings Lang, who he said was "a stand-up guy." I had no idea who Jennings Lang was, but was fascinated when Gene filled me in. In the fifties and sixties, Lang was a high-profile agent involved in developing, creating, and selling television series. He also represented actress Joan Bennett. On December 13, 1951, Bennett parked her Cadillac convertible in the lot behind Lang's office on Santa Monica Boulevard and Rexford Drive and she and Lang drove off in his car. Shortly thereafter, Bennett's husband, movie producer Walter Wanger, drove by and noticed his wife's car parked there. He became suspicious and waited nearby. A few hours later, Bennett and Lang drove up. Bennett got into her convertible and Lang leaned on the car, talking to her. At that moment, Wanger walked up, pulled out a gun and, in a jealous rage, shot Lang in the groin. Lang was rushed to a hospital and Wanger arrested. Lang somehow recovered. Wanger pleaded temporary insanity and served four months in prison. After he was released, he quickly returned to his career. His crime meant little, as long as he could deliver at the box office.

On the day of our scheduled meeting, Gene, Matthau, and I met at Gene's house in Sullivan Canyon, where he and Bea were now living. Matthau insisted on driving. Gene sat next to him and I was in the back seat. We pulled onto Sunset and Matthau started taking the curves at very high speeds. It was unnerving and Gene told him to slow down. We had given ourselves plenty of time and there was no reason to go that fast.

Matthau then explained that he had to get there early. "Last night a soft-throwing righty just brought up from the minors was pitching for Cleveland in Yankee Stadium. It was a no-brainer to bet on New York, with their left-handed power and the short porch. Unfortunately, logic didn't prevail. You see that case on the seat next to the kid?"

"Yeah."

"In that case is five thousand dollars. When we get to Universal, we're going to go into the commissary, you guys will have a cup of coffee, and I'll go to a booth in the back and meet my bookie."

"You bet five thousand dollars on an everyday ball game?"

"It was a sure thing, until it wasn't."

Matthau agreed to slow down—a little—and we arrived at Universal and went into the commissary. He pointed out where Gene and I should sit, then moved to a back booth and joined a man nursing a cigar stub. They engaged in an animated conversation for about ten minutes, then Matthau handed him the briefcase full of money and came back to get us.

"Ready?"

"Are we going to have to come back here to pick up the empty case?"

"Nah. I have a few of them."

◆◆◆

WE PROCEEDED TO JENNINGS Lang's office and were announced. But Matthau didn't wait for Lang to reply and headed inside.

We followed. Lang was sitting behind a large desk and we were invited to sit in three chairs directly in front of him. He had read the script and was very enthusiastic. In fact, he had already mapped out a production date. Matthau and Gene were thrilled and talked about details. I was also thrilled, but I couldn't help thinking about the story Gene had told me. My eyes drifted down Lang's body and I wondered, had he really recovered from the shooting? Or, was I sitting opposite a man with no balls? Compromised balls? Artificial balls? Is there such a thing as ball replacement? If there is, would the balls work like normal balls? Or, would they just be decorative? (*EDITOR'S NOTE*: According to contributor Rocky Lang, the infamous "testicle story" is Hollywood myth. His father was shot in the leg.)

While I was focused on Lang, Gene and Walter had apparently arranged a notes meeting to take place in a few weeks. I was made aware of this when they rose and said we were going. The three of us were excited as we left the office and moved to the parking lot. When we got into Matthau's car, he asked if we were in a hurry. Gene said, "What now?"

"I want to pull around to the back, where there's a gas pump. They fill me up for free. But sometimes it takes a while until I can get somebody's attention."

This was when gas was fifty-five cents a gallon. Assuming Walter Matthau's Mercedes needed twenty gallons, he would be saving approximately eleven dollars. After just losing $5,000. Gene was aghast. But we went with him to the pump and waited. On the way home, Matthau drove at a normal speed and hummed.

The next Wednesday, the film Gene had been editing came out. It was *Mame*, starring Lucille Ball and Bea Arthur. Time Magazine's review: "The movie spans about twenty years, and seems that long in running time… Miss Ball has been molded over the years into some sort of national monument, and she performs like one. Her grace, timing, and vigor have all vanished." Virtually every critic said that Lucille Ball was much too old to play the part and took notice of the soft focus used in her close-ups. Rex Reed joked that chicken fat must have been smeared over the lens. The movie was a giant bomb and Gene took a tremendous hit, even though he came onto the project after Lucille Ball was cast. I felt really badly for Gene, who was one of the nicest people I had ever met.

That Saturday, I was home vegetating. Between *Maude* and the screenplay, it had been a very intense and tiring year. But I was also in seventh heaven: working on a hit show, having a film about to go... Then, the phone rang. It was Walter Matthau. I was taken aback and had no idea how he had gotten my number.

"How you doing, kid?"

"Good."

"So, I want to talk to you."

"Okay."

"Does Gene have to direct?"

"What?

"Does he have to direct the project?"

"It's his project."

"It's your story, he made some suggestions and put his name on it, correct?"

"No. He initiated the whole thing and brought me on."

"It's very nice of you, saying that out of loyalty."

"It's what happened."

"Here's the bottom line: Gene is now as cold as my dead mother's tits. If he has to direct, I can't do the film."

I was totally stunned. This was Gene's friend? "You're saying...?"

"If you can get him off the picture, we can proceed. If not, I'm moving on."

"There's no way I can do that. I wouldn't do it."

"You're sure?"

"Positive."

"So be it. Nice talking to you and no hard feelings." Matthau told Gene he was pulling out due to a serious health issue. Then, he committed to do somebody else's film, about a grumpy and eccentric old-time horse trainer. Gene took it—both the *Mame* blowback and the Matthau snub—like the gentleman he was. And that's when I got my first dose of show business reality: in Hollywood, being blamed for a flop is a significantly bigger offense than trying to neuter a man NRA-style. I remained close to Gene and I refused to ever see another Matthau movie, except for *The Front Page*, *The Sunshine Boys,* and *I'm Not Rappaport*.

Elliot Shoenman *started his career as a writer on* Maude *and was executive producer and showrunner of* The Cosby Show *and* Home Improvement. *He is coauthor, with Marley Sims, of the play* Sunset Park *and wrote the plays* Moment In The Sun, Old Glories, AfterMath, *and* A Heap Of Livin'. *He is also author of the book* Nobody's Business.

EL CHAPO

By Roy Teicher

"It is on Mork & Mindy *that I come to learn why 'consultant' is a much-coveted gig. You work two nights a week and make three times as much as your dentist."*

THE SITCOM BUSINESS OF the early Eighties boasted its share of fine television shows—*Taxi*, *Cheers*, and *Buffalo Bill* among them. Often overlooked, however, is the extent to which the quality pendulum swung the other way, bombarding America's small screens with the stalest of comic merchandise. Yet despite the proliferation of subpar product, Americans still tuned in with apparent enthusiasm to *Three's Company*, *The Facts of Life*, and other shows of comparable weight. Viewing standards and expectations were further suppressed by a steady output of even lesser shows, on the order of *Blansky's Beauties*, *Brothers and Sisters*, *Who's Watching the Kids?*, *Makin' It*, *Working Stiffs*, and *The Brady Brides*.

During this period, Paramount Television was responsible for much of the C- and D-level fare. Sitcoms such as *Out of the Blue* (angel goes to work as high school teacher to earn wings), *Angie* (Italian Cinderella marries rich doctor) *Goodtime Girls* (WWII slapstick female gang comedy), and *Joanie Loves Chachi* ('nuff said) were brazenly produced without resistance or pause. With understandable resistance and pause, I confess that I was a staff writer on *all four shows*. It wasn't as if I had gone into the business because I wanted to write bad comedy. But it was Paramount who saw talent in a nineteen-year-old where a vocal retail industry had not.

As little as I knew, the discovery that soon came to dictate every decision I would make in the eighties was this: it takes the same ridiculous number of hours to produce a shitty show as a good one. And here's a discovery about shitty shows in particular, that was life-correcting as well: there are shitty shows that are staffed by smart, funny people whose talents, for whatever reason, only gel on the way to their cars. And…there are shitty shows staffed by Garry Marshall's tennis coach.

In the comedy business, the late Garry Marshall was revered for many stellar qualities, none more than his kindness. If you were nice and you seemed funny, Garry would try to help you out. And if you did a particularly masterful job dry-cleaning his pants, you could find yourself the new story editor on *Laverne and Shirley*.

To wit. It's 3:00 a.m., and a joke deemed "gold" (yes, gold on *Joanie Loves Chachi*) has to be trimmed because Al Molinaro is moving on the line. Garry's son's piano teacher pitches his first line of the season, something that lacks every possible component of what is needed to get us home. As insane as Garry's well-meaning good deed always seemed, it seems exponentially more insane at this hour. We're in the eighteenth inning of a ball game when the left fielder comes in to pitch. The problem here, and with all these shows, is that we go eighteen goddamn innings, three nights a week. Not a sustainable life. Is there one to be had in this business?

The epiphany comes the following year when I get hired as a consultant on *Mork & Mindy*. This show is an odd hybrid.

It has the patina of quality because of the star's singular gifts, but examined in harsher light, it too is a shitty show—especially when I arrive in season six. A good friend of mine is the showrunner on *Mork*. He is a truly sweet man who finds *everything* funny. I make him laugh with some regularity, though he fails to notice that I get no lines into the actual show. It is on *Mork & Mindy* that I come to learn why "consultant" is a much-coveted gig. You work two nights a week and make three times as much as your dentist. You are there to pitch jokes in which you have zero investment, and you also have some sway on the choice of cuisine being ordered for the late-night rewrite. The most significant upside—for the other five days of the week, your time is your own.

I observe with interest as the idea of working part-time for exorbitant sums takes hold in the eighties. The idea is perfected when the studios give birth to the (pretty much now defunct) concept of development deals. Writer-producers are hired to exclusive, multi-year, often multimillion-dollar, deals to bring show ideas to the networks. The logic, if hunted down, is that a single hit show brings hundreds of millions to the studios in syndication. That is the bet. To mitigate said bet, one would think the studios would limit these deals to proven hit-creators, or, at the very least, established showrunners. I am neither. But for reasons that are still being studied, I will be signed to development deal after development deal for the next seven years.

To best illustrate my existence during that time, I offer up the saga of the pilot, *Betty and Al*.

Conventional wisdom ordains that a pilot's chances are significantly enhanced when the network uncorks an idea and gifts it to you to develop further. In 1986, Paul Simon releases his hit song, "You Can Call Me Al." The senior VP of comedy development at ABC seizes upon the lyric: "If you'll be my bodyguard…I can call you Betty…You can call me Al." After what I can only hope was a brief gestation period, he calls the studio at which I'm under contract, and pitches: "We're interested in developing a show based on a character named Betty and her bodyguard, Al."

In less than a heartbeat, the studio is all-in and everyone agrees that I am the perfect man to helm the "Betty and Al" project. I am summoned to the studio head's office where I meet with him and his director of development, a former actress in her thirties. He is very, very enthusiastic about this idea. The substance of an idea, to him, never seems to matter. The fact that it isn't even really an idea matters less. What he is simply saying, what he is always saying, either overtly or implicitly is: "I love show business."

He is beyond euphoric. The network had picked *us*. He turns to his Number Two to get her take on *Betty and Al*. She says that Betty needs to be strong; she should be a risk-taker. The studio head couldn't agree more. Her two cents only confirm his savvy in having hired a woman to be his second-in-command.

Now I don't pretend to be able to make a persuasive case for the money I was making or the existence I led. But if you were listening to the high-priced input outlined above, relatively speaking, I worked the mines.

I agree to flesh out *Betty and Al* and am given a month to prepare a network pitch. As a rule, honchos have no idea how long any writing function takes. They miss wildly on both sides. They don't understand that you can spend two hours on a line—or that you don't need a month to pitch a pilot. There is an astonishing amount of downtime. During my long, fully compensated stretches, I pass the hours palling around with my assistant, Bo.

Bo is about six foot six, 250 pounds, and can kick a football 75 yards. I often bring my eight-year-old son down to work so we can go to the nearest park to watch Bo kick the crap out of a football. As far as my son is concerned, my livelihood seems to involve the public showcasing of undiscovered might. Considering how impossible it is to explain to anyone what I do for a living, his guess was as close as many.

A couple of days before the ABC meeting, I pitch the *Betty and Al* characters and pilot episode to the studio execs. The studio head thinks it is wonderful. Frankly, he is just thrilled to be in that chair. And that whatever I might have said, I didn't say: "I need you to flush the radiator and cut the rotors." Life is good, don't tell anyone. She, the Number Two, thinks I need to emphasize Betty's independence. I agree because she will be running a studio in two years.

The network pitch takes place on the top floor of ABC's Century City headquarters. I am accompanied by the aforementioned studio reps and we are to meet with the network's three comedy development higher-ups.

For the writer, the first five minutes of a network pitch are crucial. The studio execs are hobnobbing with the network execs; you're immediately out of the loop and you're also the only one in sweatpants. Soon, there is a moment that has to be avoided at all costs. You cannot afford a protracted pause between the end of their conversation and the instant they turn to you say: "Okay, what do you got for us?" This assures a flat-footed start out of the gate—a voltage drop in the room.

To guard against this, you have to resort to any number of go-to measures. You have to grab focus before it's too late. A dependable go-to for me is a crude impression of my father-in-law. In every pitch, there is always a TV prominently displayed in the office and a remote control or two on the coffee table that separates buyer and seller. I pick one of them up and observe that the buttons on my father-in-law's remote have long since worn out as a result of not just repetition, but the intensity of the pushing, fueled by his disgust with TV as well as the state of the nation.

My father-in-law, as I demonstrate, stands up and walks over to the TV to adjust the appropriate knob. And here it is—the crux of the impression—he would always, for reasons forever unclear, take one step too many or one step too few.

The resulting gymnastics of a man already prone to irritation was well received in this room. Now keep in mind, my father-in-law was a war hero, and I wrote for *The Ted Knight Show*.

Gall notwithstanding, a crisis has been averted and the pitch can proceed on more receptive terms.

A pitch such as this one is bound to go fairly well since it is the network's idea in the first place. The studio can sense a sale is near. You can tell they are confident because their laughing is continual, but thoroughly disconnected, like a symphony orchestra tuning up.

Soon, the network starts offering up a series of wayward and contradictory ideas and the studio embraces every last one. Within minutes, the pitch turns into a scattershot free-for-all of familiar phrases like "upping the stakes" and "investing in the character," none of which add up to anything identifiable. Thirty minutes into the meeting, the studio utters the inevitable words:

"I think we got something here."

And the network agrees. I leave the room unable to join in on the surrounding hoopla. I have little idea what the hell we have all agreed upon. This is soon reflected in the *Betty and Al* script I deliver a few weeks later. The script will not go to pilot and will die alone, having been abandoned by all concerned including myself.

Or so I thought.

A full year later, ABC calls the studio and says they want to redevelop *Betty and Al* as a vehicle for Andrew Dice Clay.

Now before we tour the ruins of that idea, a word about writing for talent. In this particular idiom, "talent" means actors—or thereabouts. Any project with talent attached, as they say, has a far greater chance of advancing. As a result, writers are constantly encouraged to meet with actors who are being peddled that season.

I'd taken several of these meetings over the years. They all fit a similar pattern as evidenced in one such encounter. First, the network sells the studio on the natural fit between you and disco queen Donna Summer. Next, you meet with Donna Summer, pitching her the same ideas you pitched to Johnny Bench. Then she suggests a show about a single-mother disco queen struggling to balance kids and career. With that, it's time to excuse myself so I can get to the field and see Bo kick. Defying the vision of an addled few, Donna Summer and I will go our separate ways.

A new draft of *Betty and Al* is commissioned, but by the time the first draft is completed, Andrew Dice Clay is already selling out Madison Square Garden; he has no use for *Betty and Al*.

Undeterred, ABC decides to order a pilot on a script written for Andrew Dice Clay without Andrew Dice Clay. Instead, we cast the star of *Cats* to play the part. He is not convincing as a bodyguard and the pilot is not convincing as television. The show stands zero chance. It dies a far more visible death than the script of the previous year. My development days surely seem numbered as the failures mount.

Yet I will continue to sign more deals, escaping from one studio to the next. I am Hollywood's El Chapo.

You know, that's not a bad idea for a pitch.

Roy Teicher *was a staff writer for* The Tonight Show, *syndicated humor columnist for the* Los Angeles Times, *and joke writer for President Clinton. He served as managing editor of the* Kansas City Kansan *and was press secretary on four US Senate campaigns. He was a 2009 Eugene O'Neill National Playwrights Conference semifinalist.*

NOT EVERYTHING ABOUT IT IS APPEALING

By Lloyd Garver

"On this show, the 'too many cooks' didn't just spoil the broth—they tried to drown each other in it."

IN THE SUMMER OF 1969, like *The Graduate*'s Benjamin Braddock, I was a little worried about my future. I had gotten my bachelor's degree in history from Berkeley the year before, and as the Cubs were folding and the Mets were in the midst of their miracle, I was about to get a master's degree from Northwestern's School of Speech. I couldn't kid myself anymore. It was time to get a job. I wasn't concerned about finding one. Kids in the sixties didn't worry about such things. What I was afraid of was that when I did get a job, I'd stop having fun. (That's exactly what we worried about then.) What I wanted was a career without having to be a grown-up, and I knew that didn't exist.

I was wrong. I would soon learn that not only can you be in show business without acting like an adult, it is a field that actually rewards immaturity—the perfect fit for me.

A high school friend, Steve Friedman, had moved from Chicago to Los Angeles, where he became a news writer for KNBC. All summer, he kept encouraging me to join him there, even offering his couch until I found work writing for TV.

I'll never forget Steve's exact words, because they were probably never spoken before or since: "Come out to Hollywood. It's so easy to get work here." So I did.

Steve's couch was even better than advertised. It opened into a bed. The building was near the famous Sunset Boulevard and had a swimming pool. I was in Hollywood! Steve introduced me to a guy in the building named Ken Hecht, a writer on the hit NBC game show *Hollywood Squares*. Ken was a very funny guy, we hit it off right away, and he said he might be able to help me get a job writing jokes for the show.

This sounded very appealing to me, because I was no stranger to jokes. They were my constant companion for as long as I could remember. When I was a kid, I got a lot of laughs except from one specific demographic: my teachers. When I was in the fifth grade at Daniel Boone Elementary School, I got expelled for goofing around and telling too many jokes in class. I've always felt that was an overreaction. If they didn't like my jokes, they didn't have to kick me out of school. They could have just heckled.

On *Hollywood Squares*, celebrities were asked questions, and then the contestants would agree or disagree with the celebrities' answers. The fun was that before giving a serious answer, the celebrity would have a joke response. So the writer's job was to find an interesting fact and craft it into a straight line that could lead to a joke. The prized jokes tended to be about famous people or sex, or both. If the show were on today, a typical question for a celebrity might be:

MC: "Scarlett Johansson was recently photographed in a low-cut gown with a good-looking guy on her arm. The caption read, 'Twins.' Are they identical?"

CELEBRITY: "No, I think the left one is slightly larger."

Then the celebrity would give the real answer—"Of course not. She and her twin brother are fraternal twins." After that, the contestant would agree or disagree.

Ken explained that much of the job involved reading newspapers and magazines (especially women's magazines) to find the right kinds of facts. I quickly bought copies of *Ladies Home Journal, Women's Wear Daily,* and my personal favorite, *Cosmopolitan.* After a few days, I gave my questions and jokes to Ken, who passed them on to Bill Armstrong, the show's producer. While waiting to hear back, I realized that I had already become an expert on everything from Elizabeth Taylor's shoe size to vaginal versus clitoral orgasms. So if Bill didn't like my jokes, I could always get a job in a shoe store or a gynecologist's office.

A few days later, on a Friday, Bill called to offer me the job. He congratulated me and said the starting pay would be $175 a week. My response? Let's just say that being grateful doesn't negate acting like an idiot. I told him that I knew they paid Ken $225 a week. He had been doing it for a while, so I didn't think I was entitled to the same salary. I thought $200 would be fair. Bill paused—for about a year and a half. Then he said he didn't have the authority to go that high, so he would have to ask the executive producers and get back to me on Monday.

When we hung up, I couldn't believe what I had done. Why not just take the deal? What difference did the twenty-five dollars make? I should have been happy to work for free to get my foot in the door. I just didn't know anything about business or The Business. It was probably the longest weekend of my life, not involving houseguests. Bill called Monday morning and said the guys okayed the deal, and I would get my $200 a week. A few months later, Bill told me that he didn't really have to ask his bosses for the extra twenty-five dollars. "I wanted you to sweat it out for the weekend. I couldn't believe you had the balls to turn down an offer after being in Hollywood for just a few weeks." Neither could I. I knew I was very lucky Bill didn't just say no. In addition, without Steve and Ken, I might have ended up in a career that didn't involve laughing every day at the office.

For a writer on *Hollywood Squares*, it was joke training by fire. If you didn't write thirty jokes a day, you'd get fired. Thirty is a lot of jokes. I learned how to structure a joke. I also learned how to look at things in different ways until I found an angle that would lead to something funny. Perhaps most importantly, I learned the discipline of a professional writer, and that I didn't have to be in a funny mood to write funny stuff. Just like every other working person, you did your job no matter how you felt.

After a few years in the game show game, I made my move to situation comedy. For the next thirty-odd years (some odder than others), I wrote and produced hundreds of television episodes. I got to write for one of the great humorists of our time, Bob Newhart. While I was writing and producing *Family Ties,* Michael J. Fox had the good sense to ignore my business advice when I suggested that he turn down *Back to the Future.* Oprah Winfrey devoted an entire show to something I wrote. I met Don Rickles's manager, Joe Scandore (someone Rickles always said was "connected to the boys"), and used every scrawny muscle in my body to avoid staring at the dent in Scandore's forehead. I wrote for Big Bird and for an alien from the Planet Melmac. While working on *Home Improvement,* I had the thrill of landing on and taking off from an aircraft carrier. Is there any other field that could have given me these kinds of amazing experiences? To top it off, I rarely came across the stereotypical Hollywood dog-eat-dog, stab-in-the-back political situation. Throughout most of my career, I was lucky enough to work for and with people who just didn't operate that way.

Unfortunately, it was all a setup. The many years of being around people who respected writers and the tons of laughs in the writers' rooms had lulled me into dropping my guard. Lady Hollywood was about to kick me in the nuts. The year of infamy was 2002. I was no longer "hot." I was 55 years old, which in show business years is 110. One day, "Greg" (not his real name) a writer friend of mine, called to offer me a job as coexecutive producer on a show he had just created and sold to ABC/Disney. I said yes before he got out the "ney" in Disney.

◆◆◆

A FEW DAYS LATER, Greg called to say there was a problem with an ABC executive whom I'll call Leslie. She had told Greg that she heard from someone that the people who ran the previous show I worked on (*Norm,* starring Norm McDonald) had not been happy with my work. So she wouldn't approve me for the job. I knew that what she had heard wasn't true, so I told Greg I would get things straightened out. I called Bruce Helford and Bruce Rasmussen who had run *Norm.* They offered to call Leslie on my behalf. Ten minutes later, they called back to give me the report. When they asked her who had told her that they weren't happy with me, she refused to say. Then they asked if her problem with me had to do with my age. She hesitated (no doubt aware of the possible lawsuit that she could bring about), then carefully offered, "Well, don't you think Lloyd is a little out of step?" Both Bruces said no and told her they thought I'd be great for the show. Leslie was satisfied and called Greg to tell him that she was signing off on me. Then she called me.

It was nice of her to call. She wanted to clear the air and hoped there would be no ill feelings so that we could move forward with the show. I said I wanted to do that, too. Then I did something that out-stupided my holding up *Hollywood Squares* for twenty-five dollars. Even after being in show business all this time, it still bothered me when things were unfair. So I told her I thought it was awful that she would bar me from a job based on some gossip instead of checking with the people I worked for. I said that it could have easily ended my career. "It's like when somebody hears third-hand that an actor was drinking too much at a party. By the end of the day, the town is convinced the actor is an alcoholic, and he'll never work again. You did the same thing with me." She was shocked. Network executives normally don't hear these kinds of things from people who depend on their approval. Leslie said she was sorry and reiterated that she hoped we could move on from this. I assured her we could, and that I just needed to get it off my chest. Still, I didn't have a great feeling when we hung up.

When the job started, I could tell right away that this was not going to be the friendly, collegial experience I was used to. This job was filled with closed doors, secrets, and factions plotting against each other. The factions existed because there were three sets of executive producers, with one of the sets having a subset of three executive producers unto itself. On this show, the "too many cooks" didn't just spoil the broth—they tried to drown each other in it.

One of the executive producers, "Sandy," had previously been both a studio and a network executive. Sandy was also a good friend of the head of Disney television, Steve McPherson, and, from the studio's point of view, could help "steer the ship." The Sandys of the world are not necessarily evil. (Sandy loved dogs. How bad a guy could he have been?) They just have an entirely different perspective. Sandys are interested in the "business," not the "show." They love to go to meetings, while writers would rather go to a colonoscopy. They know things like who is supposed sit in which chairs at a meeting and which restaurants are the "in" places to eat. Writers sit as close as possible to the thermostat and eat takeout food on Styrofoam plates. I shouldn't overgeneralize. I dealt with some excellent executives in my career. They were people who understood the process, cared about others, and made significant contributions to the show. And those executives could easily fit into a Toyota Camry and there would still be room for groceries.

One day, I was on the set watching a rehearsal. They were setting up for a dinner scene, so I mentioned to the director that we decided that one of the daughters on the show would be a vegetarian. I suggested that he give the other characters the chicken dinner and give her a giant salad. Sandy happened to be on the set. He went ballistic. "What do you mean she's a vegetarian? Who decided this?"

I explained that Greg and the rest of the writers had come up with the idea.

"Nobody cleared it with me," he said angrily.

Nobody cleared it with him because none of us ever really understood what his job was. No, I didn't say that. I said, "Why don't we just give everybody chicken, and you and Greg can work out the vegetarian thing later." And yes, I was aware of the absurdity of this conversation even as it was going on.

My suggestion of a salad detente did not mollify him. "I can't believe you tried to do this behind my back," Sandy replied à la Captain Queeg. Then he stormed off.

Week after week, work became stranger and stranger with the executive producers disagreeing with each other in all kinds of demonstrative ways, including the throwing of furniture. If there had been as much drama on the stage, the show would probably still be on the air. One day, Greg pulled me aside and explained it was certainly not his wish, but "they" were not going to pick up my option for the rest of the season. In show business talk, that means, "You're fired." I couldn't believe it. I was working really hard, I contributed a great deal to each episode, and the star of the show liked me and my writing. So why would they want to fire me?

"It's about the salad, isn't it?" I asked Greg, half-kidding. He didn't laugh. He said that was a real possibility, since Sandy often brought up the salad incident, which he bizarrely referred to as a "power play" on my part. Greg said it was also possible that Leslie was still mad at me for telling the truth on the phone. Or maybe Disney wanted someone else to have my job. He honestly didn't know. I asked him to intercede on my behalf, but he said he couldn't. He explained that he was worried about his own job and feared he might get fired. So I called Sandy, then Leslie, and then Steve McPherson, trying to, if not save my job, at least understand why I was being fired. Not surprisingly, they all said they weren't the one firing me and blamed each other. I tried to have a meeting with all three of them in the same room at the same time, but (surprise) they weren't interested.

Getting fired is horrible, even if you didn't like the job and didn't deserve to get canned. You still blame yourself and feel ashamed. I was pretty sure that after I got fired, my career was over. I felt terrible. So a few weeks later, I did the kind of thing that fired people in show business do: I went to Paris. For Christmas vacation, my family and I flew to the city of lights to get away from the city of lies.

One night after dinner, we went for a walk. We turned onto the Champs-Élysées, one of the most magical avenues in the world, filled with sights too spectacular to be real. Then we almost bumped into something that, unfortunately, was real.

It was Sandy. In Paris! There he was, standing in front of me in the midst of my attempted escape from, well, from him. Suddenly he burst out, "Lloyd! What are you doing here?" It didn't sound like he meant, "What a coincidence to see you here." It was more like, "I can't believe you're in Paris. You should be penniless and sleeping in a cardboard box in a Target parking lot." After a few moments, we forced smiles and went our separate ways. Because we were in magical Paris, I didn't let this little event spoil my trip. Just a few days of it.

After I had a little perspective, it became clear to me that despite the last show being a disaster, it was just a blip in an exciting, fulfilling, enjoyable career. Most of the time, I didn't just have a good job. I had a job that was fun. In all the years since *Hollywood Squares*, I've continued to be thankful that there is such a thing as comedy writing, and that I was able to become a part of this ridiculous profession. The joyful irony is, of course, that I got paid to do exactly what got me in so much trouble when I was a kid: making people laugh.

Lloyd Garver *wrote and produced television shows ranging from* Sesame Street *to* The Bob Newhart Show *to* Family Ties *to* Frasier. *He has written hundreds of essays, columns, and blog posts. Garver recently finished a new book, which is fortunate since it's due back at the library on Thursday.*

WELCOME TO HOLLAND

By Bruce Ferber

"When starting out, you take the best gig you're offered, which, in my case, did a grave disservice to the word 'best.'"

IN 1987, WRITER EMILY Perl Kingsley, the mother of a boy with Down Syndrome, published an essay that would serve as an inspiration to parents of children with disabilities. In it, Ms. Kingsley likens the anticipation of having a baby to planning a whirlwind vacation in Italy. The expectant couple looks forward to seeing the Coliseum, the David, the canals of Venice. But just as their plane is about to touch down, the stewardess announces a change in plans. They're landing in Holland and they must stay there. The couple has to buy new guidebooks and learn a new language. It's overwhelming at first, but they eventually discover that there's nothing wrong with Holland—it's just different. Rather than mourn not getting to Italy, they begin to appreciate the windmills, the tulips, the Rembrandts…

"Welcome to Holland" would become both a salient metaphor for my life and an absurd episode in my television writing career. In the real world, I would ultimately make peace with and embrace having being diverted from Italy, but the TV version would afford no such luxury. That plane was destined for a bumpy landing in a tulip-free wasteland with the charm and hospitality of Gitmo.

◆◆◆

In our youthful search for a career and purpose that are not mutually exclusive, some of us get the bold idea that we should become writers. Those of us who make this daunting choice are united by a tenet we may never verbalize, or even admit, perhaps because it sounds presumptuous: *I have a unique point of view.* This is the engine that keeps returning us to the dreaded blank page.

Each writer has a voice, yet the range and nuances of that voice take years to develop. It changes along the way. It can go mute for a while, or suddenly start to sound like another writer's voice. In Hollywood, it faces a particular existential threat. One can become wildly successful, yet have one's voice buried so deeply that when it finally resurfaces, it doesn't recall what it ever had to say. To wit, I became a writer and producer on more than a dozen sitcoms, getting paid handsomely to be, well...a mimic.

A staff writer's job is to replicate the voice of the series creator or executive producer. You pitch your own stories, add your own jokes, even write in some new characters, but all within the parameters of the creator's vision. (You wouldn't pitch an abortion episode of *Laverne and Shirley*, just as you wouldn't suggest a pie-throwing episode of *Silicon Valley*.) During the collaborative rewriting process, the goal is to make sure your ideas and lines get into the shows. Input is the reimagined configuration of your writer's voice.

I just came up with a joke no one else thought of! I have a gift!

This is how you make peace with having become a "gang" writer. Your singular talent now serves the greater good.

To paraphrase Jonathan Safran Foer, my path was extremely slow and incredibly bumpy. When starting out, you take the best gig you're offered, which, in my case, did a grave disservice to the word "best." One of my first jobs was on a train wreck called *Star of the Family*. It featured consummate actor Brian Dennehy as a fireman with a teenage daughter who wanted to be a country-western singer, and a son with an IQ of twelve. One day, I got up the nerve to ask Dennehy, "Why are you doing this crap?" He looked me in the eye and said, "I bought a boat."

Brian had a boat. I had a wife and a young child who had just been diagnosed with autism. I now had bigger things to worry about than the embarrassment of working on a shitty show.

Next stop, *Webster*, featuring the cute little black kid who wasn't Gary Coleman. Sublime in its unfunniness, the producers would send the writers out to the bleachers to laugh, prompting the studio audience to follow suit. The results were less than stellar until one night, when a member of the audience seemed to howl at every joke. His infectious guffaws got others going, pleasing the producers in the booth to no end. I came up with the idea of inviting the man to every taping and making him our unofficial audience cheerleader, which would spare us having to sit in the stands and fake it. I pointed out the laugher to a studio page, but barely into my spiel, I was informed that the man belonged to a tour group with severe mental disabilities. We didn't have the heart to tell the producers.

I managed to rise through the ranks on shows of unavoidably better quality, perhaps the most enjoyable being the underrated *Duet* for the fledgling Fox network. Eventually I was signed to a development deal at Paramount, where I was given the opportunity to reawaken my long dormant voice. I wrote or cowrote a number of pilots that seemed promising, but none of the scripts I sold got picked up. The unsurprising result—neither did the option on my deal. Now with a second child, I found myself back on the market and far from a hot commodity.

I landed on a new NBC series, *Nurses*, from Witt-Thomas Productions (*The Golden Girls*). It was a writing room full of talented people (Van Zandt and Milmore, Eric Gilliland, future superstar Brent Forrester, to name a few), none of whom could figure out what the show was supposed to be. Susan Harris, of *Golden Girls* fame, had written the pilot but left the series to a nervous, first-time showrunner who had no other life. The hours were brutal. I was expected to work on the Saturday of my son's birthday party. I refused.

One night around 3:00 a.m., as we endlessly rewrote a script without making it better, Billy Van Zandt whispered to me, "Bruce, I want you to go outside, get in your car, drive it through this wall, and run me over."

I replied, "Only if you can guarantee that I die in the process." Mercifully, I got "traded" to another Witt-Thomas series.

The following season's opener for me was unemployment. I started to take serious stock of my dwindling bank account and the possibility of selling my house. Luckily, a writing team I'd worked with, Pillot and Peaslee, offered me a freelance script on *Coach*, a show I liked and respected. My episode was well received and led to a full-time position, for which I was extremely grateful.

Coach proved to be a minefield of its own. The creator, Barry Kemp, had exited the series; Pillot and Peaslee left mid-season to pursue their own pilots; and star Craig T. Nelson had to put his faith in a new showrunner. It was a rocky marriage that yielded sixteen-hour workdays. I was rarely able to have dinner with my kids, much less provide backup for my wife, Jenise. When I turned forty that season, I hated my life and would have gladly exchanged my writer's voice (in perpetuity) for any semblance of sanity. Unfortunately, that wasn't in the cards.

Until the following season. My year in the *Coach* trenches had gotten me a new agent, multiple job offers, and a reputation on the upswing. I decided to take a position on the ABC hit, *Home*

Improvement. While the Tim Allen vehicle was a hot show, my real reason for signing on was that the creators seemed genuine and the new showrunner had a measured, practical approach to the job. The added bonus—they had families and actually wanted to spend time with them.

It was on *Home Improvement* that I learned how to delegate to other writers and communicate with actors, the studio, and the network. Then, after three seasons on the job, the showrunner decided to step down and the creators asked if I would take over. Once Tim gave his blessing, the studio and network christened me top gun.

If the brass ring is putting your own successful series on the air, the next best option is being asked to run someone else's bona fide hit. I would not only be responsible for the writing but also approving everything from casting, to wardrobe, to sets, to editing. And as far as the studio, network, and Tim Allen were concerned, the buck stopped with Bruce Ferber. How did I feel about my new promotion? I was scared out of my fucking mind.

Terrified or not, I knew this was my golden opportunity. In success, I would be generously compensated for steering the ship in the right direction. If I failed… *Nurses* redux?

I needed no further motivation. I was all in, thinking about the characters constantly and jotting down story ideas in the middle of the night to bring into the writing room. I developed close relationships with my writing staff and members of the cast and crew, because I wanted everybody to share my enthusiasm. I established a good rapport with Tim and met with him regularly to discuss where the show was headed. My wife and kids came to tapings and had dinner with me in the commissary.

Eventually, I not only became comfortable being the boss, I realized I was good at it. Even if the networks never clamored to hear my original voice, I could still take pride in having learned how to get the best out of people and execute a funny show, week in and week out.

I ran *Home Improvement* for seasons six through eight. There was talk of a ninth, but squabbles over new contracts ultimately resulted in Tim deciding to wrap things up. He had started a movie career with *The Santa Clause*, and as much as he loved *Home Improvement*, it was time to move on.

As for me? My reputation solidified as a go-to showrunner and the financial coffers healthy, it was once again time to flex the vocal cords...

Susanne Daniels, president of the then relatively new WB network (now the CW), liked family shows. She asked to meet and we hit it off immediately, sharing stories about the trials and tribulations of raising kids. When I told her I had an autistic son, she mentioned that she was close with people in a similar situation. Susanne asked if I thought I could write a half-hour comedy about a family with an autistic child. Truthfully, I wasn't sure, but I said "absolutely." How could I not? What could be better tailored for my voice?

In honor of Emily Perl Kingsley, I would call the show *Welcome to Holland*.

It was the best television writing experience I'd ever had. I got to draw not only from the Ferbers' exploits but also those of the families we'd met along the way. The WB team loved the pilot story I pitched and was equally effusive about the script. It came down to the wire, but CEO Jamie Kellner decided not to pick it up. While I was disappointed, some part of me didn't believe the story was over. Sure enough, a few weeks later, Susanne called to see if I'd like to run *Sabrina the Teenage Witch*, which was about to move from ABC to the WB. I wasn't interested in producing someone else's show, but said I'd take the job if, at the end of my contract, the network shot the *Welcome to Holland* pilot. My agent reminded me that even if they agreed, I would have to run *Sabrina* for two full years in order to make a single half-hour of television. It was worth it to me. This was the show I was destined to make. My voice would finally be heard.

My mission on *Sabrina* was to make it a fun two seasons for all involved. We would be transitioning our lead character from high school to college, so we got to create a different format and cast three new series regulars. The writers had a blast, and the casting sessions boded well for the scripts we were generating. Then came a hiccup. A big one.

Jenise was diagnosed with stage-three breast cancer. With our lives about to get turned upside down, I prepared to quit work and become a stay-at-home parent. The doctor recommended a different approach, suggesting that having a job to go to, especially one that involved comedy, would help me deal with the tough times at home.

It seemed like the right move. Jenise did well with her treatments, the kids lived their normal lives, and the show ran without a hitch. Then, somewhere in the middle of my second season, Susanne Daniels decided to leave the network. I was sad to see her go, but I knew her replacement and remained optimistic about *Welcome to Holland*. Shortly after her departure, the new president (fake name "Lance") called to ask if I'd like to turn *Holland* into a one-hour comedy-drama. I'd never done an hour-long pilot, but I knew the format would allow me to delve into the more emotional components of the story. I was excited that Lance thought enough of the show to expand it, and I looked forward to the challenge.

I delivered my new draft and got back notes that, while not especially negative, seemed dry and uninvested compared to the reactions under Susanne's regime. I did a rewrite, incorporating the network suggestions. A week or two later, my agent called. Lance decided he didn't want to make the pilot.

I was confused. Didn't I just spend two years making forty-four episodes for them so they would make one episode of mine? It was right there in the contract. I had heard many a Hollywood horror story, but all I could think of in the moment was: "This can't really be happening. I have to do something."

◆◆◆

I ASK TO HAVE a meeting with Lance and he agrees. A couple of days later, I enter the double-wide trailer that houses the WB offices. As with every network meeting, it will be delayed by twenty minutes because they need you to know that they are busier than you will ever be. As compensation, a perky young assistant will offer you a bottle of water.

Finally I'm waved in. Lance is smallish in stature, with a face that can project "welcoming" or "weasel-y" as the mood dictates. The half-hearted handshake confirms that we are in full weasel mode.

"Thanks for meeting with me," I say, hoping a little warmth will chip away at the negative vibe.

It doesn't. Lance informs me that he still doesn't want to make the show. I remind him that we have a contract. He has no choice.

"Fine," he says. "Then I'll bury it. I'll tell every agent in town that the show's going nowhere and you won't get good casting."

"You would really do that?"

He really would. I make a heartfelt appeal for him to read the script one more time before continuing down this path. Lance says okay and promises to get back to me. He never does.

I search for an appropriate response. Should I sue these people? When I confer with my agent and lawyer, the subtext is clear: it's Hollywood. Writers' contracts don't mean anything.

To me, *Welcome to Holland* meant *everything*. Not only had I put my heart and soul into it, my wife and kids were built into the fabric of a series that, if executed successfully, could actually benefit the special needs community. The fact that Jenise was again getting chemo treatments somehow made Lance's about-face even more egregious.

One day, as I was venting on the tennis court to my litigator friend, "Barry," he asked me to send him an email detailing the sequence of events. Turned out, he thought I had a case. I was reluctant to get into a lawsuit with giant legal fees. His response: "You don't have to sue them. You just have to *say* you're going to sue them."

Would I get blackballed? Did I give a shit if I ever worked again? In the end, I had to stand up for what was right.

Ten pages of allegations and two weeks later, Barry and I are called to the WB for the only network meeting of my career that would conserve water by starting on time. In the legal world, the clock is God.

We enter the same conference room where my creative meetings with Susanne had gone so well, and sit down at the table with the head of business affairs, the VP of current programming, and a slightly nauseous-looking Lance. He clearly hadn't counted on his off-the-cuff edict landing him here.

The business affairs exec asks Barry what we want. Barry says, "Bruce wants to make his show." The exec counters that with Lance disposed against it, that probably isn't a realistic option. What else would we accept?

Without hesitation, Barry replies, "What it says in the suit—ten million dollars."

Silence. I wait for someone to crack a smile. No one does. Finally, the exec speaks: "We'll get back to you."

I knew that on some level, we had them by the balls, yet as pleased as I was with Barry's meticulous work, I felt like shit. I hadn't become a writer to sue people.

The network came back with a modest settlement offer, which Barry quickly got them to double. This number would be their limit, he felt, unless we wanted to go to trial. I had a sick wife and a family that needed me at home. The last thing I wanted was to spend my days in court. We settled for the second offer, the amount of which I am legally prevented from disclosing. Not long after, it was announced that Lance had "stepped down" from his post.

◆◆◆

I CONTINUED TO PITCH pilots to the networks and sold a couple, but by then, I'd lost a lot of the fire. A few years later, I lost Jenise. As my kids and I worked through the pain and began digging our way out, I couldn't imagine writing another sitcom. Eventually, though, I realized that I needed to write something. I just didn't know what. Prose seemed like a decent place to start...

Elevating Overman, my first novel, was published in 2012. My second, *Cascade Falls*, was published in 2015 and won awards. At last I had found my voice, albeit in a way I never could have predicted. As gratifying as it felt, there would be an even greater victory ahead—watching the real-life inspiration for my abandoned TV pilot go on to graduate college, live independently, and become a mechanical engineer.

Welcome to Holland.

Bruce Ferber *is a multiple Emmy and Golden Globe nominee, whose television writing and producing credits include* Bosom Buddies, Growing Pains, Sabrina the Teenage Witch, Coach, *and* Home Improvement, *where he served as executive producer and showrunner. He turned to writing fiction with the 2012 publication of his debut novel,* Elevating Overman, *its audiobook voiced by Jason Alexander. His second novel,* Cascade Falls, *was published in 2015 by Rare Bird Books, and went on to win the Foreword Book of the Year Bronze Prize for General Fiction, and Gold Prize for Humor, Fiction. Ferber's essay, "Bright Lights, B-City,"* *appears in the anthology* Los Angeles in the 1970s.

ACKNOWLEDGMENTS

Heartfelt thanks to Tyson Cornell for green-lighting a project that gave so many talented people the chance to tell their stories. Big ups to Julia Callahan, Hailie Johnson, Juliet Brooks, Jessica Szuszka, and the entire Rare Bird team for getting us to the finish line. As for the finish line and beyond, Jian Huang, you are an organizational marvel, a social media whiz, a master publicist, a true partner and friend. I can't imagine having done this without you.

Thank you to all the contributors, many of whom had to take time out of their busy work schedules to think of something enlightening to say about their busy work schedules. Special thanks to Rob Scheidlinger, Robert Towne, Chris Green, and J. J. Abrams for their help re: "The Plight of Screenwriters" and "Beginnings."

I'd also like to acknowledge a few of the people who played a part in my Hollywood journey, some of whom are no longer with us.

Thank you, Jason Alexander, Tim Allen, Paul Bartel, Bob Bendetson, Ruth Bennett, Dan Berendsen, Carol Black, Beth Broderick, Jeff Cooper, Gary Cosay, Susanne Daniels, Carmen Finestra, Marshall Flaum, Jay Fukuto, Laurie Gelman, Howard Gewirtz, Rob Golenberg, Chris Harbert, Paula Hart, Barry Kemp,

David Lerner, Gary Loder, David McFadzean, Neal Marlens, Alan Padula, Chris Pearson, John Peaslee, Paul Perlove, Judd Pillot, Ian Praiser, John Rappaport, Patricia Richardson, Susan Seeger, Elliot Shoenman, Perry Simon, Marley Sims, John Symes, Chris Thompson and Matt Williams.

Eternal love for Jenise, who was there to pick me up in the down times, Aaron and Sarah, who had to suffer through them, and Lyn, who holds it all together now.